Collaboration

COLLABORATION

Japanese Agents and
Local Elites in Wartime China

Timothy Brook

Harvard University Press

Cambridge, Massachusetts

London, England · 2005

Library of Congress Cataloging-in-Publication Data

Brook, Timothy, 1951–
Collaboration : Japanese agents and local elites in wartime China / Timothy Brook
p. cm.
Includes bibliographical references and index.
ISBN 0-674-01563-0 (alk. paper)
1. Sino-Japanese Conflict, 1937–1945—Collaborationists—China
I. Title: Japanese agents and local elites in wartime China.   II. Title.

DS777.553.C64B76 2004
940.53′163′0951–dc22   2004051130

In memory of my father, Jack Brook,
whose life this war also changed

Contents

Acknowledgments ix

Abbreviations Used in the Text xi

1 Considering Collaboration 1

2 The Plan 32

3 Appearances / Jiading 62

4 Costs / Zhenjiang 90

5 Complicities / Nanjing 125

6 Rivalries / Shanghai 159

7 Resistance / Chongming 197

8 Assembling the Occupation State 221

Conclusion: Four Ways Truth Disappears with History 240

Notes 251

Sources 271

Index 283

Acknowledgments

Of the many friends who encouraged me to write this book, Diana Lary and Stephen MacKinnon deserve special notice. They invited me to discuss early findings from this project at a conference at the University of British Columbia in April 1998, then asked me to present my conclusions at a conference they organized in Ezra Vogel's honor at Harvard University in June 2002. The latter opportunity was decisive in confirming what it was that I wanted to say. I also must acknowledge Bob Tadashi Wakabayashi, who played a similar role when he invited me to present the first version of my study of collaboration in Nanjing at a conference he hosted at York University in March 1999.

I completed the writing while the guest of Zhang Longxi at the City University of Hong Kong in the fall of 2002. Feedback from his seminar at the Centre for Cross-Cultural Studies greatly helped me clarify the consequences of my arguments. Lisa Raphals played the role of the sympathetic reader who grasped what I was trying to say and pushed me to say it more clearly, and Li Tiangang listened his way through my arguments and allowed that what I had to say was worth hearing. Not all my Chinese colleagues have been as willing to accept collaboration as a major feature of their Anti-Japanese War or even as a topic deserving study.

The initial archival research that began this project was made possible by a generous grant from Daniel Bays and the Luce project on the history of Chinese Christianity. Ongoing support has been provided by the University of Toronto and the Social Sciences and Humanities Research Council of Canada. Earlier versions of Chapters 3 and 6 appeared in *The Scars of War*, edited by Diana Lary and Stephen MacKinnon (University of British Columbia Press, 2001), and *Shanghai under Japanese Occupation*, edited by

Christian Henriot and Wen-hsin Yeh (Cambridge University Press, 2004). Revised portions of both are reprinted with their publishers' permission.

I am grateful to Kathleen McDermott for encouraging me to publish with Harvard, to Elizabeth Gilbert for copyediting the final manuscript, to Trish McAlaster for preparing the maps, and to Kevin Lu for helping with all the other tasks involved in producing this book. My final thanks I reserve for three friends: Bin Wong, whose early reading of the manuscript encouraged me to trim the evidence and hone the argument; Jim Retallack, whose late reading pointed out to me the thoughts I needed to complete; and Fay Sims, for understanding how important this project was to me and steering me to the times and places to write it.

Abbreviations Used in the Text

CCAA	Central China Area Army (Naka Shina hōmengun)
IC	International Committee for the Nanking Safety Zone
PMC	Peace Maintenance Committee (Zhian weichihui)
NCAA	North China Area Army (Kita Shina hōmengun)
SGC	Self-Government Committee (Zizhi weiyuanhui)
SSA	Special Service Agency (Tokumu kikan)
SSD	Special Service Department (Tokumu bu)

A foreign power has invaded. Battle and devastation are spreading their stain ever more widely. The innocent are dying, and no one is immune from the touch of violence. You are someone whose position, ambition, or sense of public service prompts you to step forward and assert leadership in troubled times. There is an armed resistance somewhere, but the guerrillas are out of sight deep in the countryside, and impossible to distinguish from bandits in any case. Civilian agents of the invading army appear in your town, at your door, seeking your cooperation. What do you do?

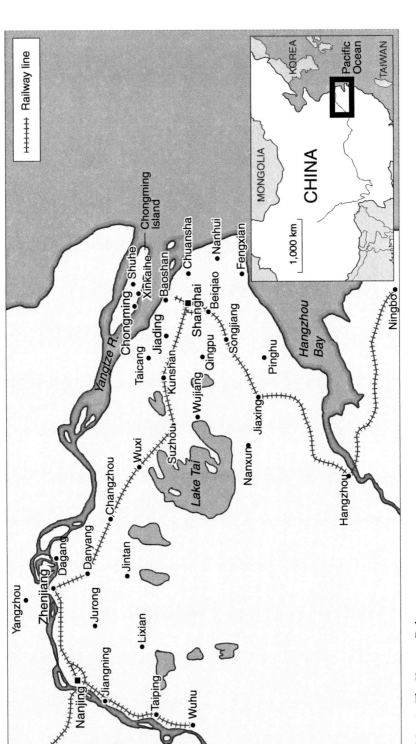

Map 1. The Yangtze Delta.

— 1 —

Considering Collaboration

On 30 October 1940, six days after meeting with Adolf Hitler in the railway station at Montoire, Philippe Pétain announced on French radio that "a *collaboration* has been envisioned between our two countries." Since then, "collaboration" has been the word by which we denigrate political cooperation with an occupying force. Pétain's choice of language to characterize the arrangement he made with Hitler—which he claimed would shield France from the greater threat of military occupation—was not of his own devising. The French army had signed an armistice with Germany four months earlier that committed French officials "to conform to the decisions of the German authorities and collaborate faithfully with them."[1] This first iteration was vague and innocent; Pétain's was not, and less and less could be. As war and occupation subordinated France's economy and polity to German control, collaboration unraveled into a tangle of compromises that few could anticipate at the outset of the war.

The purge of the winter of 1944–45 against those who had cooperated with the German occupiers, which consolidated the new postwar regimes across Europe, sealed the fate of the word. It also permitted it to expand, to refer to what Henrik Dethlefsen, writing of the term's charged history in Denmark (where the government stayed in power and accepted German supervision), has called "the necessary adaptation of the whole society" to existing political conditions. Dethlefsen has argued that this accommodation to power is "a type of social behaviour which is general and which occurs in all periods of history," and that it should not be inflated to the point of ignoring the peculiar dynamics of collaboration and reducing all who lived under occupation to the degraded status of "collaborators." Arguing against such usage, he suggests we restrict the word to what he terms its

1

political definition: "the continuing exercise of power under the pressure produced by the presence of an occupying power."[2] This is largely the definition I use in this book. Those who collaborate must exercise power to be said to have collaborated.

The study of collaboration has become a rich field of research and speculation in the ongoing history of the Second World War in Europe, but collaboration was hardly unique to Europe. Three years before Pétain's meeting with Hitler, collaborative arrangements were being worked out at the far end of the Eurasian continent, in the hinterland around Shanghai at the mouth of the Yangtze River, between Chinese and Japanese. Japan through the 1920s and 1930s had been steadily encroaching on the Chinese mainland, occupying the Northeast (Manchuria) in 1931 and then moving down into the Beijing region in July 1937, in both instances to international condemnation. Unable to bring the Chinese government to heel, Japan opened a second and far more violent front around Shanghai in August 1937. The Yangtze Delta—61,000 square kilometers (25,000 square miles) of densely populated alluvial land extending from Shanghai upriver to the national capital in Nanjing—became the battleground for what Japan would call the New Order in East Asia. After the initial military onslaught that fall and winter, the shock of invasion was transmuted into the daily reality of military occupation, and conquest shifted to collaboration. Collaboration would not begin at the top as it had in France, where a hastily reorganized regime came forward to deal with Hitler. It began, rather, at the bottom, in the county towns dotting the landscape across which the Japanese army rolled westward from Shanghai that winter toward Nanjing. There, at the local level of a new regime that would gradually be brought into being, minor elites came forward to enter into agreements with agents of the occupying Japanese army to "exercise power under the pressure produced by the presence of an occupying power."

It was a terrifying and devastating presence. Japanese soldiers treated Chinese soldiers and civilians with astonishing violence during their invasion of the winter of 1937. The disregard for the conventions of war has left an extraordinary archive of memories. These memories converge with particular force on a single memory, the capture of the national capital on 13 December. This atrocity quickly became known in the English-speaking world as the Rape of Nanjing (Nanking). That memory is still alive today and sits at the center of the popular conception of what Chinese call their Anti-Japanese War. But it is not the only story that can be told about those eight long years of occupation and armed resistance, which ended only when Japan surrendered to the United States in 1945. There were other ways of responding to the invasion, other ways of surviving the occupation. One of these, almost entirely unstudied, was to collaborate.

The history of local collaboration between Chinese and Japanese, which I reconstruct for the first year of the occupation, is not a story most Chinese wish to hear, or even to recognize as their own. Collective memory recalls this time instead as a period of Japanese atrocity and Chinese suffering and resistance. This is a compelling version of the story, and one which everything written about the period reinforces: the same heroes and villains, the same desperate plight for Chinese civilians, the same gross misconduct on the part of Japanese soldiers repeating itself, as it did in real life, over and over. To tell the story in any other way seems only to confirm Japan's wartime propaganda about the common cause that the yellow races should make against the colonialist white, and so to collude in the project that that propaganda did not dare name, Japan's right to colonize China. And yet many simply saw no alternative to going along with what the Japanese wanted, either because they regarded compliance as a more realistic survival strategy or, in a few cases, because they actually welcomed the conquerors as bringers of new solutions to China's problems and wanted to work with them. Contemporary Chinese consciousness has no way of making sense of such people, especially the minority that declared themselves willing to combine a Japanese allegiance with their Chinese identity.

Chinese historians of the war have had to acknowledge that a few people collaborated. One logic of explanation has been that the decision to collaborate must rest on purely personal connections tying certain Chinese to Japan. These connections are deemed sufficient to explain collaboration. Such connections are not hard to find. The first person to run Zhenjiang under the Japanese, Liu Zhaoqing (Chapter 4), graduated from a Japanese police academy. The head of the Nanjing Self-Government Committee, Tao Xisan (Chapter 5), had a degree in law from Hōsei University in Tokyo; most of his associates on that committee likewise had Japanese educations. The head of the first collaborationist regime in Shanghai, Su Xiwen (Chapter 6), studied political economy at Waseda University. Study in Japan meant that they had at least a common language with the occupier, which made them likelier than others to be the first people whom Japanese agents approached in their search for local contacts. Explaining collaboration on the basis of such ties creates a dead end, closing off the need to delve more deeply into the problem of what actually motivated these people. The problem is not thereby solved, for the simple reason that the exceptions outnumber the examples. Many Chinese who had personal ties with Japan chose to resist. Ma Chaojun, Nanjing's mayor in 1937, had studied aviation in Japan, yet he chose to flee west with the retreating Nationalist government rather than collaborate.

More saliently, most of the lesser elites whom we shall find working with the Japanese at the local level had no experience of traveling or studying in Japan—nor in China, for that matter. Unlike the powerful who congregated in Shanghai and Nanjing, minor county elites led lives that were purely local, pursuing what opportunities were at hand and dealing with problems that did not extend far beyond their horizons. Searching for prior connections to Japan leaves these people unnoticed, and thus becomes a way of diverting our attention from the wide spectrum of real conditions and motivations that induced some Chinese to go against type and accept Japanese rule, regardless of what their culture predicted, or demanded, they do.

Every culture tags collaboration as moral failure. What could otherwise be described simply as the political arrangement of dependency under the condition of military occupation is almost never permitted to remain simple or purely descriptive. It invariably shifts to the language of morality, which, in Teemu Ruskola's nice phrasing, gives voice to "normative systems that posit a pre-given moral subject and then elaborate guidelines for proper actions by that subject."[3] The moral subject the word "collaboration" brings into being is a national subject first and foremost. The grounding assumption of the word is that this moral subject must act to maintain and protect that nation and no other, regardless of whether another position—which might better be termed "ethical" than "moral" (in the sense of understanding not the norms that guide the moral subject, but the norms that construct him)—can post a higher claim. For those in the grip of a national identity, especially when the national cause is able to argue that it treads the path of justice, it is impossible to conceive of collaboration as a legitimate alternative to patriotism.

This inconceivability is not unique to Chinese who look back at the Second World War. Rebecca West passionately expressed the same patriotic certainty in *The Meaning of Treason,* a book she wrote cumulatively between the British treason trials of the late 1940s and the spy trials of the early 1960s. The notion that some Britons might choose to transfer their loyalty to Germany or the Soviet Union and advance those nations' interests over Britain's was, she declares flat out, "an ugly business, and it grew uglier in the handling."[4] In her view, citizenship is a contract of honor that protects the individual, and the duty to respect that obligation is beyond ambiguity. Her indictment of men who were put on trial for treason after the war such as William Joyce, Leonard Black, and John Amery, all of whom ended up in Germany working for the Nazis, draws some of its force from their distasteful personalities and odious political ideals. Black had a "long history behind him of inextricably confused idealistic effort and paid political adventure"; Amery "had no intelligence, only a vacancy around which there rolled a snowball of Fascist chatter."[5] Their weakness, venality, and anti-Semitism make it easy for her to declare patriotism the only morally defensible stance in the face of Hitlerian and Soviet politics. West does take pains to understand her subjects' moral formation in relation to the circumstances of their lives; indeed, she was able to build up far more informed portraits of her traitors than I have been able to assemble for my collaborators. She finds much there to help explain why the men who were put on trial worked for the German cause during the war. Yet none of it is sufficient in her eyes to justify the choice they made, given that most people in the same circumstances made a very different choice—and for her the natural one of defending their nation rather than supporting the nation attacking it.

For the historian rather than the polemicist, collaboration is a difficult word to use. Its almost inarguable moral force sensationalizes the acts of those who fall under its label and lends the topic an energy that only wartime occupation can excite. The capacity of the word to judge, even before we know upon what basis those judgments are being made, interferes with analysis, however. As soon as the word it uttered, it superimposes a moral map over the political landscape it ventures to describe and thus prevents the one from being surveyed except through the other. Historians must legitimately ask how the moral subject that collaboration presupposes was fashioned, not retrospectively judge that subject's acts. We cannot accept the superimposed landscape as historical reality, but nor can we pretend it does not exist. Our task is rather to look through the moral landscape to the political one underneath and figure out what was going on. I must confess that this separation of the moral and the political—which work at different discursive registers and yet often deploy the same language—has not been easy to sustain during the course of writing this book. I return to this question in the Conclusion.

Detaching the moral map from the political landscape can come as a surprise to those habituated to other conclusions. The looking-through that historians of Vichy France began to do in the 1970s, for instance, produced findings that went against many of the assumptions on which the French had relied since the war to insulate themselves against moral reproof. The new perspective excited a popular aversion to the Vichy regime when it exposed the degree to which French authorities had worked for German interests, most notably in assisting the Nazis' program to exterminate Jews in France. It also undermined the comfortable legacy of resistance to which French people felt entitled to lay claim by revealing that most did not work to resist the German occupation, and that many in fact abetted it. At one level, these findings confirmed the popular understanding that resistance had been the morally correct choice. In that sense, the attack on *résistancialisme*—the belief that all French had resisted—did not alter the value of loyalty as a transcendent virtue to an ideal of France that sustained the postwar generation. And yet the attack did put those who lived through the war on notice, unfairly or not, that they had failed to live up to the moral standards they had all along claimed as their heritage from the war. This unpleasant and unwelcome revelation could only come out once the generation that had benefited from the myth of resistance passed away. France is still preoccupied with sorting out the legacies of that war.[6]

Compared with the French, the Chinese are at a much earlier stage in coming to terms with their occupation. On the one hand, they continue to feel aggrieved that Japan has never clarified its responsibility for the Pacific War, nor has it been made to provide compensation for acts of aggression committed in China against Chinese. On the other, many Chinese are unprepared to look behind their collective memory of suffering and resistance to ask what most people in the occupied zone did during the war. The myth of resistance has been a powerful moral weapon in the arsenals that political elites on both sides of the Taiwan Strait have used to sustain their postwar dictatorships. Each party claims that it alone defeated the Japanese, and each stakes its moral legitimacy—its right to rule—on that claim. The consequences for thinking about the war do not end there, however. The misgovernment of China during the postwar decades has only deepened the sense of national humiliation that many Chinese have carried with them since the occupation, yet the sense of a Japanese debt unpaid has shielded Chinese from having to scrutinize the subsequent record of their own state. To dislodge the popular image of the war and shift some of the weight of blame from external invaders—to begin to take responsibility for what Chinese did to Chinese during the twentieth century—threatens to expose the interests of political elites, whether revolutionary or otherwise, lurking behind these beliefs.

For these reasons, the moral landscape of the Japanese occupation has remained unassailable in the Chinese historiography of the war. How then do we go about telling the story in a way that takes account of suppressed memories? In this book, my method is to go below the superstructure of ideology by which every state justifies its existence and look instead at what went on down at the most local level of the occupation state. It is plausible that collaboration there, in county towns on the Yangtze Delta, involved the considerations of national honor and personal integrity that haunted the politicians of the new regime; but most of the time, as we shall see, collaboration dealt with more mundane problems—supplying food, organizing transportation, arranging security—the sorts of matters that local elites and local officials have to solve under any political dispensation to ensure social reproduction and to maintain themselves in power. Adopting a perspective from below helps to turn collaboration into a problem to be investigated, not a moral failure to be tagged and condemned. This is not to say that moral considerations have no place in the study of collaboration, but it is to advise that we look more closely at the conditions within which individuals made choices.

Suspending established judgments on collaboration by going to the local level is not quite the innocent strategy I have implied. It changes the way the story gets told. General Matsui Iwane's lightning campaign from Shanghai to Nanjing in November–December 1937 is still a story of brutal invasion, but it can segue into a story of a postconquest restabilization in which some Japanese and some Chinese negotiated a working relationship under a new structure of authority. This approach yields a history in which the aggressor sometimes appears as a sympathetic civilian working to repair the damage the army has done by recruiting sympathetic locals to help with that work. It discovers the victim resurfacing as a pragmatist seeking accommodations that will allow him to reestablish his livelihood, shield his compatriots, and even build what the propagandists would soon be calling New China. At the beginning, when local conditions were fluid and no one knew how far the Japanese would go in their offensive, even whether they would stay or leave, a few gambled on the shift and threw their lot in with the invader. As the situation across the Yangtze Delta appeared to stabilize in Japan's favor in the spring of 1938, the incentives to cooperate with the new rulers increased. And so, for all manner of reasons as we shall see in the case studies, many worked out accommodations with the occupation state.

The complexity of this sort of accommodation can be illustrated by a letter I came across in the Shanghai Municipal Archives, which proved to be the richest trove of materials for my research. The letter was sent by a group of Shanghai residents to the collaborationist municipal government in January 1939 on a matter affecting the administration of their local area. The letter writers identified themselves as members of the Huangpu West Residents' Association. They knew well for whom the letter had to be written (the Japanese) even if it was addressed to a Chinese official, and so strove for appropriate rhetoric. "Looking at trends across the globe, we need to grasp the spirit of New China and engage in the work of collaboration," they declared. "Not only is Japan's culture quite advanced and its financial power great, but its people are sufficiently firm and sincere that they can serve as good neighbors and guides in the project of joining our vast territory with their fine culture." The letter writers do not blush or hold back as they launch themselves deeper into this act of political performance: "The committed and benevolent Japanese who are wholeheartedly participating in this project have a deep love of China. It is because of their participation that our two great East Asian peoples can walk a limitless path toward co-prosperity and mutual support."[7]

Our first reaction to such sycophantic rhetoric might be to condemn the authors as collaborators who have thoroughly compromised themselves with the occupation state. They do not even bother to euphemize Japan, as official texts during the occupation often did, as the "friend-country" (youbang). Jumping to the quick conclusion that they were sunk in hopeless collaboration is exactly the sort of judgment I suggest we suspend. We need not assume culpability or gullibility on anyone's part in this document, either the writers of the letter or the municipal official to whom they were writing. This was a transaction between two parties, not a testimonial from one to the other. Someone in the chain of communication may have believed every word written, but we have no evidence of that. Nor do we need to think that they believed what they wrote in order to write it. Look at this rhetoric instead as an exchange. Managing needs and interests within the new order might well mean parroting the hyperboles of Japanese propaganda in order to get what one needed. Guaranteeing that one's language was politically appropriate to the occasion for asking and giving favors was simply what one did to get things done in the new environment.

Whether the residents of Huangpu West actually thought such things is beside the point, which is that cooperation with the Japanese, or with the Chinese proxy administration, was the modus vivendi for those who stayed behind in occupied China. Occupation creates collaboration, but the need to collaborate in turn creates the appearance of collaborating. Those who chose the appearance over the reality may be hard to detect when we can only scan the surfaces of sources that are partial in both senses of the word. So too, those who appear to have chosen the reality of collaboration may have been engaging in a calculus of options and risks different from the simplicities that hindsight, and the nationalist narrative that thrives on it, hands to us. All of which suggests to me that there are more ambiguous stories to tell about the occupation than those we have accepted or assumed.

"The continuing exercise of power under the pressure produced by the presence of an occupying power," Henrik Dethlefson's definition, is of a word for which there is no precise counterpart in Chinese. Whether taken in this narrower political sense or permitted to expand out into the broader sense of simply going along with the occupier, which has come to dominate the popular pejorative use of the word, the Chinese language lacks a word that has been coded in the way "collaboration" has in European languages. When I translated the phrase in the Huangpu West residents' letter as declaring that they are ready to "engage in the work of collaboration," I narrowed their term into something less than what it says in Chinese. Their term is *hezuo*, a neutral expression meaning "to work together." It implies a relationship of equality between two parties acting in pursuit of a common goal and carries none of the negative tone we associate with "collaboration." Since "working together" is in fact what "collaboration" means, the literal fit with *hezuo* is perfect, except that it does not carry the pejorative nuance the English word does. "Cooperation" might better convey the sense of the word the letter writers used.

A fuller phrase, *qin Ri hezuo*, appears in the May 1939 declaration of principles of the Greater Shanghai Youth Corps, a paramilitary body organized by Japanese military officers: "feeling close to Japan and cooperating with it."[8] The collaborators and the Japanese also used *tixie*, or "mutual support." This term appears as the fourth principle of the Great People's Association, an official pro-Japanese mobilizational organization: the full phrase is *Zhong-Ri tixie*, or "mutual support between China and Japan." The same document also uses *xieli*, or "assistance," when it announces that the association's mission is "the work of assistance and mutual support" *(xieli tixie zhi gongzuo).* When Katō Kōzan, who was sent as a pacification agent to Zhenjiang (see Chapter 4), looked back on his team's work in a newspaper article in mid-1939, he was pleased to report that he heard the words *qinshan* ("feeling close"), *tixie* ("mutual support"), and *hezuo* ("working together") on everyone's lips.[9] This was the language of the new order, and it was not intended to signal anything to be ashamed of. Had Katō been able to eavesdrop on the conversations in Zhenjiang from which he was carefully excluded, however, he would have heard a different term, the one by which most Chinese still refer to collaborators: the bluntly unambiguous *hanjian*, "traitor to the Han Chinese," an all-purpose term for evil, deception, and treason. The term leaves no middle range between innocuity and damnation, no space in which ambiguity might arise, no reason to look back and ask what might actually have been going on.

With the flood of interest since the 1980s in wartime collaboration in Europe have come disputes as to where the boundaries of the word "collaboration" lie. At its broadest extreme, the word is allowed to cover all manner of cooperation, active or passive, shown to the occupier; anything, in fact, that enables an occupation to continue. At the far opposite extreme lies the narrowest definition that restricts the use of the word to supportive engagement in the tasks and ideology of the occupier, for which the more specialized "collaborationism" has been proposed.[10] The first definition has the disadvantage of leaving no alternative position for ordinary people who had no choice in the matter: everyone under the condition of occupation becomes a collaborator. The invention of "collaborationism" to tag willing collaboration protects most people under an occupation state from the charge of selling out their country, but it does not make the more usual type of collaboration—selling not to the highest bidder but to the only authority doing the bidding—disappear as a problem. Indeed, differently construed, this isolation of activists as a separate category has left the way open for a universal condemnation of everyone who survived the war, not just the occupied. Pushed to an extreme, all Germans become "Hitler's willing executioners," as one historian of the Holocaust has argued. The same logic could be used to charge the majority of French who accepted German rule as "Pétain's willing collaborators."[11] Widespread complicity gets totalized into an explanation for the Holocaust that looks in the mirror of the Final Solution and sees Germans as the Final Problem—and, if we look deeply enough, the Vichy French as well: pure victims getting the pure victimizers they require. To deem all guilty of the crimes that war permits is to erase any possibility of understanding the terrible ambivalences of living under war regimes and the tremendous ambiguities involved in making sense of everyday social action. When all distinctions among actions and motives disappear, we confuse how individuals acted with what we think they could have done, and so move to an absolute moral register where hindsight overlooks the contingencies and dangers that directed real-life choices.

Less aggressively phrased, however, this interpretation asks us to take seriously the day-to-day survival of a tyrannous regime as something that resulted at least in part from the work that the occupied did. As Michael Marrus and Robert Paxton have phrased this challenge, no occupying power "can administer territory by force alone. The most brutal and determined conqueror needs local guides and informants. Successful occupations depend heavily upon accomplices drawn from the disaffected, sympathetic, or ambitious elements within the conqueror people."[12] Here they lean toward the more limited definition of collaboration, without however limiting those who fall within the category to an extreme and evil few.

I have no desire to use the Chinese case to argue for or against any particular definition of collaboration. Dethlefsen's political definition, though serviceable, is somewhat hampered for having been formulated in relation to Denmark's rather unique wartime history, in which a foreign occupying power left the existing government in place when it took control. China's wartime experience was much starker than Denmark's or Vichy France's (at least before 1942 and probably after as well). A full military invasion such as Japan's ruled out any possibility of the "exercise of power" "continuing," and it stepped up the effect of "the presence of an occupying power" to something stronger than "pressure." All this placed collaboration in the Chinese case on a steeper moral gradient than in Denmark, where soft accommodation was mostly tolerated at the time, even if it came under retrospective moral condemnation later. On the Yangtze Delta in the winter of 1937–38, harder choices had to be made, and those who decided to climb that steeper moral gradient more readily found themselves exposed and compromised.

To push the Chinese who did work with the Japanese all the way to collaborationism may be to misconstrue the role of ideology in the Chinese setting. The leaders of the occupation state did indeed make statements expressing support for Japan's pan-Asianist pitch, but it is very difficult to find any genuine evidence that more than a few took Japanese war aims seriously. Those who were motivated to support Japan's claims did so generally from the desire to dislodge the National Government under Chiang Kaishek, not to embrace Japanese ideas for home use. Chinese collaborators appear to have been much more instrumental about their collaborationism than were the Japanese in their invitations to collaborate. Which is perhaps why the Chinese language has not gone to the trouble to create the same discriminations of meaning that the word "collaboration" has in English. No collaborator imagined China's relationship with Japan under occupation as anything but provisional, something to be waited out until full sovereignty fell back into Chinese hands—their own, that is.

The place to look for the complexity the Chinese case introduces is not among competing definitions derived from Europe's experience of collaboration. Better that we look within the plastic sphere of complicity with state power in the very broadest sense, regardless of whether that power is foreign or domestic. The creation and reproduction of a state under occupation is something more convoluted than a handful of morally aberrant puppets facilitating the imposition of an external authority. Its intellectual foundations lie deeper, in the understanding Chinese have developed over at least a millennium about how local authority and elite representation are constrained by, but must also coexist interactively with, state authority. Given the scale of the Chinese polity, state authority has always been positioned well outside the locality. If it often consisted of a ruling house and aristocracy that was Mongol or Tungusic, that was largely a matter of indifference at the local level, once conquest had been completed.

Whether this observation helps an understanding of what was at stake during the Japanese occupation depends less on the motivation of collaborators, which is often used as the litmus test for deciding whether someone was betraying "China," than on the structural environment within which collaboration had to take place. I suggested earlier that occupation creates collaboration. It does so by presenting certain elites with opportunities not available to them under normal political circumstances, whether for good or for ill. But such logic sends us off in search of motives and away from the broader issue of why collaboration happened in this context. More saliently, Japan's wartime occupation of China created collaboration by suspending the normal channels of political mobility and political communication and replacing them by an entirely new system, staffed by a mixture of old and new personnel. It is for this reason that I have chosen to approach occupied China not in terms of a collaboration state, existing purely to collaborate with the occupier, but as an occupation state: a political regime installed to administer occupied territory in the interests of the occupying power. Collaboration is a necessary part of occupation's political repertoire but is not coterminous with the structures and sanctions of the occupation regime, in which there must always be the occupiers' direct presence. Opponents applied such terms as "puppet" *(kuilei)* to the occupation state and its collaborators, banishing them into the netherworld of *hanjian* traitors, but this is not how the collaborators chose to identify their decision to *hezuo,* or cooperate, with the powers that be. Their self-identity may have been a fraudulent device to paper over the prestige and money with which the occupier rewarded them for their service, but venality was not necessarily the sole or defining mode that brought some people into a relationship of service to the occupation state. What some of those modes are will surface as we proceed through the five studies of local collaboration that make up the core of this book.

The analytical benefit of using the occupation state as a category resting on a more open understanding of collaboration is that it shifts the fault lines in the moral landscape of occupation from a small set of bad guys, isolated and idealized as a type, to a broader and more intricate pattern of interaction and accommodation without condemning everyone. The Chinese of the Yangtze Delta were never Matsui's willing executioners, even if many did end up going along with the occupation state. Whether this interpretation makes everyone, or no one, or someone, a collaborator is something that you, the reader, will want to think about as the multiple stories of local collaboration unfold in the chapters that follow. My own method will be to reserve the term for those who were actively engaged in promoting the creation and maintenance of the occupation state, while at the same time bearing in mind that what looks like collaboration from a distance may, on closer inspection, turn out to be something more complicated, even something entirely different. All I ask of the reader is to suspend judgment as to who is guilty for having worked with the Japanese until after we have seen them at work. We might consider suspending the expectation that we are called upon to judge at all, except in cases of self-advancement won at the blatant cost of the lives and dignity of others. Look not for who has dealings with the Japanese, but for the harm or good they do through those dealings; and as well for the wide areas where those who collaborated and those who resisted overlap.

When I began assembling the materials for this book, I expected the activists in the local collaborationist administrations across the Yangtze Delta to be the main characters in the story. The Japanese agents who aided and abetted them, I thought, would be playing lesser roles. It has not worked out that way. The Chinese who worked with the Japanese have proved to be an elusive lot. A few of the reports they wrote for the central government have survived, filed away in the national archives in Nanjing and the municipal archives in Shanghai, but that is the sum total of their leavings. None of the collaborators at the local level, to my knowledge, has left a memoir, or a diary, or even a letter from his time in Japanese service. The sharp shift in political winds during the civil war that followed the occupation meant that no one who worked for the occupation state wanted to write or preserve anything he had written. The search for collaborators' documents was in any case compromised by their relative obscurity and their postwar efforts to slip away unnoticed. The post-liberation purges in the early 1950s, when the Communist Party rounded up anyone who had collaborated in any sense with anyone other than itself, meant that those who might later have written about the war ended up publicly humiliated, shot, or lost in a labor camp.

The surviving documentary record does not endow the collaborators with much clarity of perspective or personality. There is the gaunt Su Xiwen, inaugural head of the Shanghai collaborationist regime, who studied at Waseda University (Chapter 6). His practice of distributing his identity across at least four aliases besides his own name nicely symbolizes just how difficult it is to know who he was, in any sense of the word. His membership in a Daoist spirit-writing cult in Shanghai suggests secret fraternities with connections we cannot even begin to trace, let alone interpret. There is Tao Xisan, the white-bearded philanthropist at the helm of the Nanjing government (Chapter 5). His benign grandfatherly appearance was completely at odds with the image projected by the crisply leather-jacketed Su Xiwen, but how can we gain access to what lay beneath the Confucian gown? Are we in any position to interpret who this man was from the image he projected, especially when we learn that his feeble political career was sidelined when he got caught in a corruption scandal a few years later?

The collaborator we get to know best, thanks to comments in the diaries and letters of the foreigners who knew him in Nanjing, is a Nanjing auctioneer named Wang Chengdian—"the famous Jimmy," as the American professor Lewis Smythe who oversaw the refugee camps liked to refer to him. Despite the many glimpses we catch of him through the writings of the Westerners who stayed in Nanjing to face the Japanese occupation, Jimmy Wang remains someone we see mostly from the outside: moving food supplies, recruiting prostitutes, facing down the Japanese in order to get things done, a man whose moral flexibility and whispered connections with the Nanjing underworld gave him distinct advantages in the chaos that invasion produced. His own reactions to what he saw around him we cannot know. Still, he is one of the few exceptions to the fate of most collaborators to remain as wooden as the puppets people saw them as being.

Not so the Japanese Special Service agents. These men went to China buoyed by their peculiar *mission civilitrice* to the backward masses of Asia and felt able to write with pride about their exploits. The fact that we can know them better than we can the Chinese they sponsored is a classic instance of the postcolonial predicament for writing colonial history: that the colonizers make themselves the leading characters in their own drama and tell the story more interestingly from their own perspective. Of course they manage to avoid answering the questions about collaboration that I want to pose, but some of the awkward dynamics of the collaboration relationship nonetheless glimmer through their accounts of themselves.

The Japanese appear as the main protagonists in two genres. The first is the reports compiled in the Shanghai office of the South Manchurian Railway Company. These were put together on the basis of the monthly work diaries which the Special Service pacification teams sent back from the field to Shanghai. Circulated to the appropriate vice-ministers, they were confidential and given the second-highest security rating for government documents. Ten of these reports produced in April 1938 for teams working in the Yangtze Delta survive in the archives of the Japanese Self-Defense Force in Tokyo. Seven from a second round of compilation, dated between August 1939 and April 1940, have also been preserved. Most of them give detailed and precisely dated accounts of the projects and issues that most mattered to agents in the field. They reveal little about the men involved, Japanese or Chinese; that was not their purpose. Even so, the personality and aspirations of at least the team leader come through in places.

Take the curiously naive Takada Mitsusaburō, head of the pacification team in Danyang county (he makes an appearance in Chapter 3). Oblique references in the January work report suggest that he did not fit well with the program he was assigned to serve. When Takada went on tour through the county and reached the village of Dengxiang, he discovered that it had been abandoned shortly before he and his entourage arrived. Takada was puzzled that the arrival of the 150 soldiers with whom he was traveling would frighten the villagers. A quaking villager found in hiding was dragged out and had to explain why that everyone had disappeared. He told Takada that the last time Japanese soldiers came through Dengxiang, they shot three people. Takada seemed genuinely surprised to learn that this sort of thing was going on. Somehow he had managed to find himself just behind the front line of a military occupation without having understood what the soldiers on his side were doing. Not surprisingly, Takada made little progress in getting the county in order and was removed from his post five months later. Thereafter he disappears from the record.

We discover Takada only through his team's work reports; he left no personal account of his experiences. A few others did. I have found three accounts written by pacification agents working in the Yangtze Delta and published during the war (those of Katō Kōzan, Yamazaki Kaikō, and Kumagai Yasushi), plus two postwar memoirs: the autobiography of a military officer attached to the Special Service Department (Okada Yūji) and a series of reminiscences by a pacification agent in the Nanjing Special Service Agency, written when he was in his eighties (Maruyama Susumu). These authors are concerned to testify to the good they thought they did, or hoped to do, however variously they interpret that standard. From our different perspective, their accounts do not always show their authors to best advantage, especially those written during the war. Yamazaki Kaikō's book makes him look like a bit of a buffoon. He is too eager to tell battle stories about hale young Japanese soldiers who give as good as they take and always have some pithy thought to share over a smoke. And he is too melodramatic about young Chinese men who surely would have led China on to a glorious pro-Japanese future had guerrillas not killed them. A posed photograph in the memoir showing the grinning author playing a portable organ for Chinese children in a school yard seems only to confirm this impression of a man who postured, condescended to those beneath him, and played up his own importance and perceptiveness whenever he could.

A very different personality emerges from Kumagai Yasushi's memoir. Kumagai tries to steer away from the tendency of the genre to overdramatize, speaking from the heart about what he thought he was doing and why he felt it had to be done, and at the same time revealing much about the difficulties of pacification. He went looking in China for what he could feel was irretrievably Asian and, therefore, a basis for building common ground with Japan. He found it, he believed, in the Chinese peasant. The peasants in his memoir are down to earth and sensibly aloof from the modern fashions that, Kumagai felt, were making Westernized parodies out of educated urbanites. The latter were a group that Kumagai could not stand; fair enough, since to judge from a failed meeting with some of them in Chapter 3, they could not stand him either. Despite occasional editorial outbursts, Kumagai gives the reader a carefully observed account of the work he and his team were trying to do. He also anticipates the contemptuous attitudes in which he fears his Japanese readers have been trained, reminding them that they have to change their way of thinking if they truly hope to get the people of China to unite with them in the struggle for Sino-Japanese co-prosperity. Kumagai published his memoir in 1943 when the prospects of achieving a transformation on either side were growing dim, and may have been desperate to explain to Japanese that they could not simply expect the Chinese to do what they wanted them to. Japanese had first to learn to love the Chinese before they could hope to change them. His is a remarkable, if hopelessly idealistic, voice. One wonders whether anyone was listening. One also wonders whether those who did had any inkling that Japanese soldiers may have killed as many as ten thousand people between the day in November when the army arrived at Kumagai's first posting in Jiading, and the day he left the county in April.

Memoirs by Chinese proved more elusive. Aside from five eyewitness accounts of the occupation of Nanjing, which have been reprinted and widely used to reconstruct the Rape of Nanjing, none came to my attention until I was reaching the very last stage of research in Shanghai in the autumn of 2001 and happened on two. Zhang Yibo was a small-scale industrialist in Zhenjiang who elected to remain as the Japanese army approached his city. His *Zhenjiang lunxian ji* (A record of Zhenjiang under occupation), which I use extensively in Chapter 4, is an eloquent statement of the bestiality of war and the cruelty of victory; of China as a nation victimized and Japan as a nation unrepentant. Zhang Yibo recorded these events not for their own sake but to produce a larger political effect, as instances of military atrocity that he could use to convince Chinese that they should not accept the invasion and had no choice but to resist. The first edition of the book appeared in the summer of 1938. In the third edition the following November, he appended the account of the Rape of Nanjing that American missionary John Magee had published in a Shanghai newspaper. From Zhang's perspective, one set of atrocities flowed into another, each enlarging the next. It did not matter if the stories occurred in different places: what was important was to create a seamless portfolio of evidence against Japan's conduct. He wanted actions, not archives. "The ancient adage from our Spring and Autumn period was that vengeance could last nine generations," he writes in a note on the last page of his book. "Now I say that avenging this national humiliation can go on for a hundred generations, if that is what it takes. The depth of our anger at Japan—in the past, in the present—is utterly bottomless."[13]

Another informative memoir of the occupation of the Yangtze Delta is Li Helu's *Chongming lunxian ji* (A record of Chongming under occupation), the basis for Chapter 7. Like Zhang Yibo, Li Helu narrates the experience of occupation from below. If his account differs in tone, it is in part because he composed it after the war. His concern was not to mobilize resistance but to single out Chongming Islanders who took advantage of the situation, whether as agents of the Japanese or as self-proclaimed guerrillas who posed as heroes in order to prey on the rural populace right through the war—and for whom the dismissive Japanese label of "bandit" was an apt description. Li's closest brush with danger during the occupation came not from Japanese soldiers but from such guerrillas, who stormed into his family's compound to "fine" him for failing to support the Anti-Japanese Movement. Li turned the tables and wondered aloud why these guerrillas were pillaging someone who had chosen not to collaborate. (The real collaborators all had bodyguards.) The gambit could have gone badly, but didn't. The bandit leader could see the irony and, fortunately for Li, chose not to be offended. Laughing that "this bookworm is no skin off my nose," he departed with his gang, leaving intact Li's life, property, and the opportunity for him to write the story down.

What the memoirist writes is not what the pacification agent reports. In the case of Li Helu's Chongming, there is no Japanese account to set against his own. In the case of Zhang Yibo's Zhenjiang, however, there are three: two Special Service reports, from 1938 and 1939, and a short memoir that team leader Katō Kōzan wrote and published in Nanjing's official newspaper in 1939. When reconstructing the occupation of Zhenjiang, I started with the confidential team reports. These led me to conclude that the Japanese Army had not devastated the city as badly as elsewhere, that atrocities were few, and that recovery went relatively smoothly. I followed this with Katō's newspaper memoir. Katō insisted that Zhenjiang was not badly hit by the invasion, and that the main challenge for him was the political one of getting a satisfactory collaborationist administration in place. Then I read Zhang's harrowing descriptions of what the city's residents suffered at the hands of the Japanese soldiers: elderly men cowering in storerooms shot, eight-year-old girls raped, houses stripped of everything that could be pried loose down to the lightbulbs. It was as though he and Katō were talking about different places—which in a sense they were: Zhang's fury had been set alight by the opening onslaught of the takeover, whereas Katō did not arrive until after the first five weeks of the occupation and was freer to tell a story of reconstruction, not destruction. The two could not be expected to share a common perspective in any case. Those who worked for the occupation state needed to conspire in the illusion that things were getting sorted out. Those who did not, spoke from other assumptions and had no need to whittle their anger down into some innocuous emotion.

One of the challenges I faced in writing these case studies, with the partial exceptions of Zhenjiang and Nanjing, was to learn to see the relationship of collaboration from both ends of the bargain. This is difficult to do when sources do not exist in equal measure from both sides. Part of the solution was the makeshift one of keeping all the other cases in mind as I worked on the one before me, hoping that the others would furnish me with context and help me stay alert to the gaps and refusals built into the sources. Differently put, this was the challenge of maintaining some distance between what the sources, whoever wrote them, were telling me and what I understood as having actually happened. These never coincide under the best of circumstances, and in a partisan conflict they can diverge hugely. The other part of my method, therefore, was to look for the surprises, for the departures from what one would expect a source to say; for the moments when the author recognizes that the project to which he is dedicated, or the purpose to which he is devoted, or the story he must tell, is incomplete; that with those who help there are those who harm, that among those who do damage there are those who seek to do good.

Zhang Yibo's memoir of Zhenjiang contains a few such moments. One comes a month into the occupation, after the worst of the disorder has passed:

On 9 and 10 January, soldiers were billeted in the factory dormitory. I saw one of the employees having a pen conversation with the soldiers. One soldier wrote "Let China and Japan make peace as soon as possible" in the notebook he kept in his breast pocket, then quickly rubbed it out as though afraid someone else would see it. Another in idle conversation pulled a picture of his wife out of his breast pocket and showed it to the other man, then got talking about home: how many oxen he had, how many chickens, how much bamboo grew in his grove, which showed he was a wealthy peasant. Yet another got talking about the burning of the South City of Shanghai, phrased in a way that showed he regretted what had happened. Hoping for peace, disgusted with war, wanting to go home: it all came pouring out.[14]

Chummy conversations with the occupied expose elements of Japanese soldiers' subjectivity and help to deconstruct the hero-and-villain accounts of popular lore. Yet these vignettes do not cancel out the unequal relationship between occupier and occupied that war created. Japanese with the best of intentions were constantly thrown up against this barrier, however they reached across that inequality, and the national difference on which it was based, to find common ground with Chinese. At the same time, though, the willingness of a Chinese observer to record such moments alerts us to the complexity of the occupation experience.

Japanese propaganda tried to make the same move by appealing to the notion that they and the Chinese were culturally and racially the same, invoking such formulas as *tongwen,* "people of the same script," and *tongzhong,* "people of the same type," literally "of the same seed." The latter was a modern term, but *tongwen* had a textual history that went back two millennia and celebrated the power of the written script to unify all people under the Chinese throne. Stretching the phrase to propose that Chinese and Japanese inhabited a natural condominium of culture could only be a disingenuous construction in the context of war and occupation. At a deeper level of self-identity, the invocation of *tongwen* reinforced Japanese anxieties regarding their cultural derivation from China, a notion that they had been strenuously resisting ever since Japanese modernization programs had placed Japan in accomplishment far beyond backward China. For Chinese, who found themselves in Japan's shadow, the rhetoric had little appeal. They felt no imperative to unify with other Asians when those Asians came in violence, no inclination to suppress one difference in favor of another that hid itself as sameness.

A few collaborators were willing to invoke the proposition of racial commonality with Japan as a higher principle than racial difference with the Westerners. It gave them a convenient logic for using Japan's presence as a lever against Western concessions and unequal treaties.[15] And yet the sentiment did not find general expression, except in propaganda materials. Take, for example, the manifesto adopted in May 1939 by the Greater Shanghai Youth Corps. The text of its manifesto speaks of sharing script and race as the basis for an Asian anticolonialism:

> Ever since China was subjected to the Red policies of the Communist Party and the economic and cultural encroachments of England and France, East Asian brothers have been propelled into regrettable interne-cine conflict. China and Japan share script and race, look after each other in suffering, and are as close as lips to teeth. England and France have driven our peoples to impoverishment and our finances to exhaustion.[16]

The Youth Corps was a Japanese propaganda operation to which Japanese intellectuals were assigned to run projects intended to naturalize Japan's presence in China. The manifesto is, then, a Japanese text masquerading as a Chinese text—Chinese lips over Japanese teeth, to invoke the text's central (and very "traditional") metaphor for strategic closeness. It speaks only for Japan.

Zhang Yibo adopts a different classical phrase than the lips-and-teeth trope to model his racial conception. His phrase was coined two and a half millennia earlier, when the cultures north and south of the Yangtze River were felt to be vastly different. Someone living north of the Yangtze could not imagine having anything in common with those living south, and expressed this difference by saying *fei wo zulei*, "they are not of the same kin-category as us." "*Fei wo zulei*," Zhang declares several times in his account of Zhenjiang's occupation.[17] The phrase does not express the modern eugenic concept of race—transposed into modern English, *zulei* might be closer to "species" than "race"—but the point is clear: Chinese and Japanese have nothing in common. In fact, resistance to the claim of racial commonality did not come from the Chinese side only. It was built from the Japanese side as well, and would be there so long as Special Service agents such as Kumagai Yasushi insisted that his army was waging a war for China's own good. There can be no equality in occupation, and no brotherhood in condescension. The barrier would keep going up so long as Japanese soldiers and officers saw nothing wrong with killing noncombatants. One of Zhang's employees, who had taken shelter with his wife's family while she was recuperating from a wound, was the first person a Japanese soldier saw when he barged into that family's house. The soldier fired and killed the man. Asked how he could do this, he answered that shooting a Chinese was no different than killing a dog.[18]

The only way to escape from this impossible situation, as the Japanese soldiers billeted in Zhang's factory implicitly understood, was to end the war. The peace Chinese wanted may not have been the peace that the Japanese soldier surreptitiously espoused to the factory worker. Peace could be imagined on many terms, not all of them equally favored. There was the peace that ended the bloodshed but included a continuing Japanese military presence: a peaceful occupation. Better than that was the peace that ended the open military presence by having Japan withdraw its troops from China, though perhaps not its influence: a neocolonial peace. By 1940 this option had gained support within the military leadership and was advocated by the Wang Jingwei government that had come to power in Nanjing, but it never prevailed. Best of all from the majority Chinese point of view was the peace that removed Japanese presence and influence entirely from China: an unconditional peace, which would come only with Japan's defeat in the Pacific.

The most that the people of the Yangtze Delta could expect between December 1937 and August 1945 was the armistice of stalemate. Within a year or two of being occupied, they understood that little could be done without pressure elsewhere forcing the Japanese to withdraw. Even Zhang Yibo grew to regard his internal exile as counterproductive, especially once order had been restored in Zhenjiang. As he put it, "I spent more than four years north of the Yangtze. Conditions there were peaceful for the first year or more, but it got dangerous later on. I ended up drifting about from one place to another, leading an extremely unstable existence. Even after Zhenjiang had become peaceful relative to north of the Yangtze, still I did not return home. It seemed as though safety and danger had changed places, yet the reasons why I could not do otherwise still applied." Eventually Zhang chose safety and stability, though not collaboration, and returned home. As late as July 1945 he was fighting off a hostile Japanese takeover his factory, slated for conversion into an alcohol distillery to serve the war effort. The Japanese could confiscate it, Zhang declared, but he would never sign a contract making the transfer legal. His refusal, as he put it, "was like throwing an egg against a stone."[19] Fortunately for him, Japan surrendered before the egg was smashed.

Resistance of the weak could not drive the Japanese army out, but it did make the occupation an ongoing headache for the Japanese civilians sent in to restore order and revive the economy. From the beginning, as the reader will see in almost every chapter, these agents found themselves in situations they did not relish. They had to put up with whoever came forward to work with them, many of them the worst of opportunists with no visible qualifications to serve. A mountain of distrust loomed before them at every turn. Nor could they simply hand down orders and expect their collaborators to follow them, for each foothold they thought they had gained seemed only to slip away under their feet when they tried to take the next step forward. They too had to work out realistic accommodations between their ideological sense of mission and their uneasy understanding that China was not theirs to control. If occupation creates collaboration from below, collaboration demands compromise from above: both are unstable arrangements, and neither leads to a satisfactory outcome. The pompous Yamazaki Kaikō and the avaricious Su Xiwen may have enjoyed the occupation, but none of the other characters in this story, Chinese or Japanese, found much satisfaction in what he was doing. Some acted out of duty, some, self-interest; some thought they did what they did to resist, others, purely to survive. Always the uncertain future hung heavily over everyone, a fog that nothing but the invaders' withdrawal could lift.

The attentive reader will have noticed that every person named thus far is a man. This imbalance is in part because this book focuses on the early, invasive phase of collaboration when the decisive realms of action were military violence and political dealing, realms in which women have not traditionally played a visible role. This invisibility did not protect women from the effects of invasion, of course. During the first assault, both sexes were equally vulnerable to aerial attack, bombardment, and fire. Thereafter gendered mattered, for Japanese soldiers treated the bodies of Chinese men and women differently. Both could be damaged, but for different symbolic purposes.

Men of fighting age were shot or conscripted for labor because they were, or stood in for, the soldiers of the nation. Women of childbearing age were raped or forced into prostitution because they were, or stood in for, the body of the nation. So rape was widely performed as a gesture of conquest, but not simply as a release for male sexual starvation; it was an act of humiliation. Japanese soldiers performed this act on the bodies of

Chinese women, but the target of the humiliation was Chinese men: it was proof of their impotence in all ways. This symbolism is acted out in the most gruesome story in Zhang Yibo's *Record of Zhenjiang under Occupation.* He tells of a husband and wife who came into Zhenjiang from the countryside with a basket of cucumbers to sell and were stopped at the city gate by Japanese guards. The guards stripped them and forced them to kneel naked in public for hours, until one of the guards raped the wife with one of her cucumbers. He commanded the husband to eat it, and when the man refused, he shot him. The woman was the object of violence, but the man the object of humiliation; and one could extend this equation by identifying as the object of scorn the Chinese nation. Zhang tells the story at second hand but believes it to have happened.[20] His belief is possible because this particular incident rings true to the experience of bodily harm that both men and women were made to suffer, in their different ways.

The violation of bodies produced a higher rate of sexual assault against women, but a higher number of deaths for men. One estimate of fatalities at Nanjing gives a male-to-female ratio of three to one.[21] Concomitantly, the chance that women, losing fathers, husbands, or brothers, would find themselves in households without income, was higher than it was for men. This difference is reflected in the gender proportion of residents of a homeless shelter in Nanjing a year after the assault, where women outnumbered men two to one.[22]

How women were affected by occupation, rather than invasion, is more difficult to sketch. Hanna Diamond has observed in the context of Vichy France that women under occupation "had to make choices in circumstances which were very different from those of men, and women were not on an equal footing in terms of collaboration or resistance either with each other or with men."[23] As we have not yet even begun to write the social history of occupied China, the social and economic lives women led under occupation, and the choices they faced and made, remain out of ken. We might consider adopting Diamond's argument that French women who formed groups to lobby for their husbands' release were encouraged to accept occupation rather than resist it—women in Nanjing did just this in the spring of 1938 under the guidance of the American missionary, Minnie Vautrin[24]—but this remains purely speculative until we know more about the lives of women under the Japanese occupation. What we can conclude, though, is what Diamond decided with regard to French women,

Children waving the flag of the Great Way Government, Shanghai, December
1937. From Mōgi Kikuo, *Shanhai shi daidō seifu shisaku hōkoku* (1938).

which is that collaboration was more a male temptation. "Although there
were some gender-specific forms of collaboration, relatively few women
joined groups and became involved in explicitly political forms of collaboration. Men, on the other hand, appear to have been more involved
with collaboration on an organized level." Men's training for public life
drew them into the possibility of collaborating, whereas women's exclu-
sion from political life and ideological jousting saved them from entanglement.

Women are not the only social group which has little visibility in the
story of local collaboration. Even less present are children. Parents with
other places to send their children did so. Most children lacked such opportunities to flee the war. Many came through the experience unscathed,
other than having their innocence exploited for propaganda photographs.
But many others suffered dislocation, loss, and trauma. Reports on refugee camps occasionally note their presence; otherwise, records of what
happened to them during the first wave of invasion appear not to exist.
The China War Orphans Relief Commission early in April 1938 an-

nounced that a total of 37,253 had been orphaned. The number covered only the greater Shanghai region, and it excluded orphans taken in by other families.

Children who suffered directly would carry their memories of the occupation through their adult lives. In one brief memoir of the occupation of Zhenjiang (Chapter 4), Li Zhizhong's strongest memory of being twelve years old was the night of 27 November 1937, when he huddled in a leaky bomb shelter with his brother and sister during the first massive aerial bombardment of the city. He remembers being too scared to cry, remembers shrapnel exploding directly over the shelter and some of the children—perhaps he is remembering himself?—peeing their pants. When they emerged from their muddy bunker after the raid was over, the children found the remains of more than sixty bodies scattered in the wreckage above ground. "So many of the things I went through are still right before my eyes," he recalled half a century later. Something this terrible "you carry through a lifetime and still are not be able to forget."[25]

It is not my purpose to document Japanese atrocities. Rather, it is to probe the processes by which collaboration arose: how Chinese came forward to collaborate, and what Japanese did to elicit and control it. Instead of conducting a search for collaboration backward, as the nationalist narrative does, from the regime it left behind at the national level, we will enter the process from below and from the start, when no one knew how broad the invasion would be, how far the occupation would go, and how complicated the intersection of Chinese and Japanese interests would become. War and occupation were conditions that Japan imposed from above, but collaboration happened when individual people in real places were forced to deal with each other. My method has therefore been to work from case studies at the county level, the grassroots of the occupation state, where we can find all arose the misunderstandings, false starts, and awkward compromises that characterize collaboration.

I made the selection of the sites for these case studies after an extensive survey of the holdings of Chinese, Japanese, and North American archives and libraries. Once I had pored over the materials I was able to locate, I chose seven cities and counties across the Yangtze Delta for intensive study. This selection was not based on whether the sites were typical or unique (some would prove to be one, some the other, and some both), but only on whether the documentation was sufficiently dense to allow for a more than superficial portrait of what local people did in the face of military occupation and the attempts of Japanese agents to recruit and guide them. After the case studies were written, I chose to include in the book five that were sufficiently distinct in terms of the themes that the sources allowed me to explore, and omitted the other two, which largely repeated what the other case studies demonstrated.

The first site is Jiading, a small county toward the east end of the Yangtze Delta at the edge of Shanghai, one of the first that the Japanese army invaded when it launched its assault on Nanjing. I selected it because this is where Kumagai Yasushi, who wrote the most interesting memoir of any pacification agent, was first posted. There is little about Jiading that is unique, so this first case study may serve to show what was typical of the process of pacification in county seats across the delta. The second case study is of Zhenjiang, a mid-sized county toward the west end of the delta downriver from Nanjing. Zhenjiang was the last important city to fall to the Central China Area Army before its attack on the capital. It was the capital of Jiangsu province up until 1937, but what makes it particularly attractive for the historian of collaboration is the memoir that Zhang Yibo wrote from the Chinese side of the conflict.

The third site of research is Nanjing, unique for being the national capital at the time, and unique as well for the presence of two dozen Westerners who intervened in the occupation process and recorded the intricate politics of collaboration more candidly than any other observers elsewhere on the Yangtze Delta. The sheer scale of troop misconduct in Nanjing sets it apart from other sites of invasion, though many have chosen to see it as archetypical of the violence of the conqueror and the abasement of the conquered.

For the fourth site of collaboration, we move back east to the city of Shanghai. Shanghai is a complicated case, in part because of the fractured jurisdiction of the city before and after occupation, in part because of the density plus inconsistency of the archival materials that have survived. In the winter of 1937–38, only the part of the city outside the foreign concessions was subject to a collaborationist administration, while smaller agencies proliferated in the suburban towns. This patchwork process created a quilt of competing jurisdictions and overlapping authorities that I have chosen not to reconstruct in their entirety, but to exploit selectively in order to explore important aspects of the collaboration experience in an urban setting.

The final research site is an island county in the mouth of the Yangtze Estuary, Chongming. Although Chongming had close links to Shanghai, these were the links of a periphery to a core. Being at the economic and political edge of the Yangtze Delta, Chongming presented a unique situation for occupiers and collaborators both. It is also unique in having produced the only account of occupation written from a rural Chinese perspective. Li Helu in his memoir is no less scathing of collaborators than Zhang Yibo in his account of Zhenjiang, but a longer time frame allows him to be more skeptical of those who claimed to represent the forces of resistance, despite (or because of?) the fact that Chongming was one of the few places on the delta where resistance continued throughout the war.

As I worked on the history of collaboration on these five places, five themes emerged. "Emerged" does not overstate the process by which the themes forced themselves on my attention. My analysis of collaboration first developed in tandem with my reading of the rich literature on collaboration in Europe, but the particular themes around which I have framed the book emerged inductively from what I found in the Chinese and Japanese sources. They were not the themes I went looking for, but they gradually suggested themselves as the most appropriate to capture the tensions and problems that arose within and around the occupier-collaborator relationship. They do not map the entire terrain of that relationship, but they do point to much of what is ambiguous and troubling about collaboration.

The first theme I call appearances. Appearances are what all parties in the collaboration relationship must strive for, initially and quickly. Invasion suspends the normal functioning of things. The first task of any collaboration is to reverse that situation, to transform the occupier's aggression into the appearance of normalcy and to disguise the collaborators' sudden ascent to power as legitimate authority. Both sides of the bargain need to make a regime appear as quickly as possible, which often means falling into makeshifts and compromises that neither side wants. Appearances is how I have chosen to frame answers to the question of why collaboration is often unable to generate a legitimate regime and a functioning administration. Kumagai Yasushi's candid reflections on his difficulty getting these appearances in place in Jiading, despite his own best efforts, is why this is the theme of the first case study.

The second theme is costs. The Japanese military had the clear expectation that the occupation should be financially profitable to them. But invasions are expensive: armies have to be equipped and fed, the destruction they cause has to be repaired, and the taxation systems that normally support the state yield no revenue. The collaborator is in the position of having to restore the local economy, rebuild the tax systems, and meet the occupier's demands for matériel. The popular expectation is that the collaborator derives benefit for himself for doing this work, which thereby imposes another cost that the local economy has to bear. Costs is a way of asking the question of whether the occupation was financially viable, and for whom. Financial records of the early occupation are scarce, but some data survive from Zhenjiang, which is why this is the case study where the theme of costs is addressed.

Collaboration is one clearly tagged possible relationship that Chinese could have with the Japanese, but those who chose not to collaborate did not therefore free themselves from entanglements with either party. Complicities, the third theme of this book, addresses the complexity of ties that inevitably arose among all actors in the local setting. Collaborators by definition are obliged to work with the occupier, and vice versa, but noncollaborators end up working with both, however indirectly. The occupier needs material support and at least a willingness not to resist, which noncollaborators have to give to survive, and on which collaborators in turn must rely to function. Those who refuse collaboration are nonetheless obliged to work out some sort of accommodation to the occupier's presence, as they have to do as well with those who collaborate. Everyone, even those active in the resistance, get woven into the web that the politics of collaboration spins. The theme of complicities is most directly addressed in the third case study, Nanjing, where the noncollaborationist Western community ended up working with Chinese and Japanese all across the local political spectrum.

These complicities invariably produce situations in which individuals and interests compete with each other for the power, resources, and protection that the occupier claims to provide. The fourth theme, therefore, is rivalries. This theme is a way of getting at the question of how the politics of collaboration actually get played out. Collaborators competed with the occupier, among themselves, and with noncollaborators in order to tap or control scarce political and economic resources. From the materials available for 1937–38 from Shanghai, the case study devoted this theme, I often found it impossible to distinguish who collaborated and who only made it seem as though they did, since both swam in the same pond of political opportunities and adopted the same language and gestures to get things done to their advantage.

My fifth theme is resistance. Resistance is what all prior studies of the

Japanese occupation lead us to look for, and indeed it was there on the Yangtze Delta, a more or less constant backdrop to everything the collaborators tried to do. Resistance did not achieve much by way of weakening or dislodging the occupier, but it did put pressure on Chinese by reminding them that there was an alternative to collaboration. This theme I address in the case study on Chongming, whose peripheral location on the delta meant that the resistance could operate with greater impunity than elsewhere in the region. My purpose in that chapter is not to reconstruct the full range of resistance on Chongming Island, nor even to assess its effectiveness, but rather to ask what impact ongoing resistance had on the work of collaboration. Did it weaken the will to collaborate, or did it force collaborators into a closer relationship with the occupier than they would otherwise have had?

In the course of writing the case studies, I discovered that what transpired in any one place occurred in much the same way elsewhere. This is because the occupier faced more or less the same challenges in every location. Japanese pacification agents were working roughly to a plan, which I reconstruct in Chapter 2, but they improvised heavily to carry out their duties. Although pacification got worked out in ways contingent on the particularities of each place, the process tended to be the same everywhere. What I found startling in this history is not the uniformity of the pacification project, however, but the consistency with which, in every county that came under Japanese control, a fragment of the local elite—however loosely we ascribe that status to these businessmen—came forward to make deals with the new authority. Every negotiation produced its own arrangements, yet the outcomes were consistent enough to produce the occupation state. Still, the details are significant. Only in the details can we detect the efforts local elites had to make sometimes to comply with, and sometimes to resist, an invading authority that was unwilling to be placated in the usual ways. Only in the details will we learn to doubt prior certainties and realize that the stark polarity of resistance and collaboration describes very little of what actually went on.

The close scrutiny that historians of wartime Europe have applied to the topic of collaboration since the 1970s certainly turned this familiar polarity into something troublingly ambiguous. A decade into the controversial new research, Roderick Kedward gingerly proposed that "perhaps the thickets of ambiguity are really the heart of the wood, representing the very stuff of the occupation experience." Perhaps the main markers on the landscape are no longer "the familiar trees of collaboration and resistance for which the woods are primarily known."[26] His hypothesis has been borne out by subsequent research. Historians producing local studies of German occupation in Europe have revealed a world far more complex than the heirs of the wartime generation have realized, in which ordinary people struggled to make do with compromises and smaller gestures somewhere between the two extremes of collaboration and resistance, and in which even collaborators tried to strike a balance.

The study of wartime China is a much earlier phase,[27] but what I have found in the Chinese and Japanese archives suggests that the ambiguity Kedward proposed for Nazi-occupied Europe applies equally well to the realities on the ground in Japanese-occupied China. There was collaboration, there was resistance, but there was much else besides. Even what looks like collaboration ends up being far more than resistance's simple opposite. These two insights—that collaboration occurred, and that collaboration is not necessarily nor always the destructive response to occupation it is assumed to be—erode the truths that national historiography holds dear, a matter to which I return in the Conclusion. I focus on collaboration not to exonerate or condemn those who chose to work with the Japanese, but to displace the resistance narrative of the war and show that the occupation experience is as much a part of China's history during the years 1937 to 1945 as the more familiar story of resistance. Wandering in these thickets of ambiguity, we will discover that what people did, and what they said they were doing, come quickly into focus only when we close our eyes. Better to keep them open and see what was actually going on.

— 2 —

The Plan

Japan's occupation of the Yangtze Delta in the winter of 1937–38 was one piece in a larger project to strengthen Japan's access to resources and markets and drive imperialist competitors from East Asia. The project had its roots in Japan's incursions against Korea late in the nineteenth century, but the pace of incursion onto the continent intensified in 1931, when the Japanese military occupied China's northeastern provinces and sponsored a client state there under the last Manchu emperor. Unlike Japan's earlier colonies, Taiwan (acquired by treaty in 1895) and Korea (occupied in 1910), Manchuria was not absorbed into the Japanese empire. The Wilsonian doctrine of the right of nations to self-determination had such authority after the first global war of the century that Japan could not simply reduce Manchuria to the status of a Japanese province or protectorate. Instead, it was obliged to sponsor a separate state, which it shopped in the English-speaking world under the confused romanization of "Manchukuo."

The ploy failed. No state body, other than the Vatican, accepted that "the new Manchurian State was formed as a result of a revolution of the people themselves, and that the Japanese are here only as advisors," as the head of the Japanese Special Service in Manchuria phrased it in 1932.[1] Universally regarded as a puppet regime owned and operated by the Japanese, the fiction mattered nonetheless to Japan, enabling it to act as a colonial power while keeping up the appearance that it was not. Even the Lytton Commission sent by the League of Nations made no meaningful dent in the facade. Japan deflected the mild censure it received, and the Chinese who lived in Manchuria found themselves under a reenthroned Manchu emperor pretending he was a head of state.

The occupation of Manchuria in 1931 was the first of a series of incursions into Chinese territory that would broaden out into a full-scale invasion of China six years later. The first assault was at Beijing in July 1937, the second at Shanghai in August. Beijing fell almost without a fight, but the troops committed to the defense of Shanghai held out against superior Japanese firepower. The battle for Shanghai was fought mostly to the north of the city itself and lasted until the first week of November, when Japan landed flanking forces first to the south along Hangzhou Bay, and then to the north along the south bank of the Yangtze Estuary. The Chinese line at the outer perimeter of Shanghai collapsed on 11 November, and the defense turned to a rout. The way to Nanjing was now open. The Shanghai Expeditionary Army, reorganized now as the Central China Area Army (CCAA), pressed westward across the Yangtze Delta from county seat to county seat. Its still undeclared target was Nanjing. The invasion might not have made the jump to occupation had the Chinese government capitulated to Japan's demand that it place its administration and economy under Japanese trusteeship. But the leader of the Nationalist Party and China's head of state, Chiang Kaishek, stood fast. Military defeat forced him to withdraw his government west into the interior, but he did not submit to these demands.

Debate intensified within the Japanese government and army through the autumn as to what course Japan should now follow. Success on the battlefield swung the consensus from limited operation to total war. The Supreme Command in Tokyo handed down its fateful orders on 1 December 1937: one to the North China Area Army to found a political regime in Beijing, and one to CCAA commander General Matsui Iwane to capture Nanjing.[2] With these orders, the conflict was converted from a punitive invasion, designed to force concessions from the Chinese government, into an occupation committed to removing that government and replacing it with a regime under Japanese direction. At least one officer attached to the Special Service Department in Shanghai regarded the order to attack Nanjing as a complete about-face of military policy up to that point, robbing the moderate faction within the military of any ground from which to counsel constraint or advocate a peaceful solution to the conflict.[3] Japanese political ambition and Japanese military violence were simultaneously unleashed: there would be no going back.

Invasion is one thing, occupation another. An invasion mobilizes massive force to drive a military opponent into defeat; an occupation means turning attention from soldiers to civilians and establishing institutions through which the conquered territories can be administered. But what sort of occupation would this be? Another Manchuria, where Japan set up the administration themselves and installed Chinese and Manchu puppets to front a colonial state? Getting involved in such fictions had not been the original intention of the Japanese government. The Japanese navy in particular was resistant to the idea of fielding yet another puppet regime on the Asian mainland, given the huge commitment of military support and the weakening of Japan's capacity to act elsewhere that this would entail. As late as March 1938, the commander of the China Area Fleet in Shanghai was telegraphing his vice-minister to warn that the Japanese army was bent on turning North China into a "second Manchuria" and that something should be done in Tokyo to restrain this ambition. To go this route, the commander insisted, would lead to "calamity."[4] Japan should stick to its goal of removing Chiang's government and seeing it replaced with one amenable to Japan's demands, not embroil itself in propping up more puppet regimes. With the National Government in retreat rather than in surrender, however, the Japanese army in what it designated as "Central China" had a political vacuum on its hands.[5] The vacuum had to be filled if China was to get back on its feet. As no faction in the Nationalist Party emerged to assemble an alternative regime, Japan would have to take matters into its own hands. The Yangtze Delta would be the first place in China in which the Japanese army simultaneously waged a full-scale war and recruited collaborators to build a new, compliant civil regime.

On 8 December 1937, thirty Japanese employees of the South Manchurian Railway Company arrived in Shanghai by ship from the port city of Dalian in Manchuria.[6] Their assignment: to take up what the Japanese were calling "pacification work." These men (there were no women, either as employees or as wives) were to be sent out over the following days and weeks into the cities and larger county towns of the Yangtze Delta to rebuild civil order. Fragmentary comments in the work reports they sent back to Shanghai over the next few months suggest that they had little idea of what was in store for them, and little knowledge of the devastation the army had wrought and that would be theirs to clean up. Three weeks before the men arrived in Shanghai, the Central China Area Army had broken Chinese defenses around the city. As it steadily enlarged its zone of occupation in the hinterland, the army needed people who had the skills imperialism in

China required: a knowledge of China, experience of Chinese society, and an ability to speak the language. The North China Area Army (NCAA), based in Beijing, had officers who had gained these skills in Manchuria, and was able to use them for pacification work. The CCAA did not. Instead, it turned to the South Manchurian Railway Company for its pacification agents. (The SMR is its English abbreviation, but I will use its common Japanese acronym, Mantetsu.)

The South Manchurian Railway Company was a Russian business which Japan acquired in November 1906 following its defeat of Russia and its assumption of the Russian-built railway in southern Manchuria. In time the Mantetsu grew into a full-scale development corporation engaged not just in operating a railway but in providing a wide range of transportation services, production, investment, and economic research. At its height in the 1940s, the Mantetsu employed some 200,000 people, two-thirds of them Japanese.[7] This was the company to which the CCAA subcontracted the work of rebuilding state, society, and economy in occupied China. Its employees had the competence, training, and ability to work on the ground, which the army required. Also, they were civilians, and remained so throughout the period they were seconded for pacification work. The army regarded their civilian status as an asset, for it meant that they could appear to the Chinese as being at arm's length from the Japanese army. They did not go about in uniform but wore plain white shirts, the front pocket of which was embroidered with the Japanese/Chinese character *sen/xuan* ("announce"), the first part of the two-character phrase *senbu/xuanfu,* "announcing comfort," translated as "pacification."

The CCAA placed the task of organizing and monitoring pacification personnel in the hands of the Shanghai office of the Mantetsu. This office set up a Pacification Department for the purpose in November 1937. The entity to which both the agents and the department were ultimately responsible was not the company, however, but the CCAA's Special Service Department (SSD, Tokumu bu). All Japanese expeditionary forces, on the mainland as in Manchuria, had a *tokumu bu,* to which were assigned a range of noncombat activities. The main concern of the Special Service in Shanghai in December 1937 was to reconstruct political order in the vacuum that the army's invasion was creating across the Yangtze Delta. At the lower end of state administration, the SSD had to rebuild administrative operations at the county level, which is where the pacification agents were placed. At the top, it had to cultivate prominent Chinese politicians who

Japanese pacification agents outside their office, 1938. From *Shina jihen gahō* (1938).

could organize an alternative regime to the National Government. (This it was able to do by the end of March, when a putative "national" regime called the Reformed Government [Weixin zhengfu] was inaugurated in Nanjing.) With the task of designing a new order came the responsibility for securing it, which meant gathering intelligence and securing finances. The latter task would lead the SSD in Shanghai into the opium trade, among other money-making ventures, as a profitable short-term device to raise revenue for its clients. Recruiting collaborators, wholesaling drugs, running intelligence operations, and doing so under a cloak of secrecy have earned the Special Service a nefarious reputation. Even scholars tend to confuse this agency with the notoriously brutal Military Police (Kempeitai), with whom the SSD often had to work.[8] Although Special Service personnel could be involved in security operations, the SSD in Shanghai was in fact a locus of moderate opinion and moderate action within the military establishment. Members of its later avatar, the Asia Development Board (Kōain), would be the only military officers to speak out in 1939 and 1940 against broadening the conflict in China and advocate that Japan cede genuine sovereignty to the collaborators' regime. Several of its officers would end up under either investigation or arrest on the charge of being soft on China.[9]

The newly arrived agents spent their first day in Shanghai with Major-General Harada Kumakichi, head of the SSD. Harada was a career officer whose intelligence and dynamism had recommended him for the intricate work of building the occupation state. At the reception that evening at the Palace Hotel, they were received by Itō Takeo, the recently appointed director of the Shanghai office of the Mantetsu. This office was the base from which Itō oversaw a large number of civilian operations in support of the invasion, of which pacification was only one. No record survives of what Itō told the newly arrived employees in his speech that evening at the Palace Hotel. Indeed, little survives of what he did at this point in his career. Itō wrote a memoir after the war, but in it he manages to avoid disclosing what he was doing in this early phase.[10] His sketchy, ambivalent account of his first months in Shanghai suggests that the pacification program was not a project that engaged his attention, but perhaps it was because he did not wish to recall how actively he was involved in the Japanese project to occupy China. He says of the army's decision to hire Mantetsu people that "it was, I think, a brilliant way of proceeding," and he praises these employees in passing as "conscientious staffers." Yet of the 250 employees who would become involved in the project, of whom one-quarter went to the field and other three-quarters worked in the Pacification Department in the Shanghai office, not one does he refer to by name.[11] Nor does he show any interest in their subsequent careers. They were too junior and insignificant to justify his notice or concern.

Though Itō's remarks that evening no longer exist, it is reasonable to suppose that he touched on the fine traditions of the company for which they worked, the unprecedented victories the Japanese army was enjoying as it cut a wide swath across the Yangtze Delta, and the heavy responsibilities the agents were about to assume in building Sino-Japanese cooperation at the grassroots. To sketch the challenges they were about to meet, he could well have quoted, as did his office in its major report on pacification work the following March, from a November 1937 Special Service document entitled "Outline for Pacification Work." This document explains that the purpose of pacification was "to make clear to the Chinese masses in the combat zone the true intention of the Imperial Nation in this Incident, to get rid of anti-Japanese thinking and the spirit of relying on EuroAmerica, and to make them aware that they should now rely on Japan, which will be the foundation for living in peace and taking pleasure in their work." This passage expresses the two themes that Special Service propagandists would beat into the occupied population for the next year. The first was that they should abandon the idea that "EuroAmerica," the imperialist bloc from which Japan was rescuing China, would ever help them. The second was that they should give up thinking about such divisive matters anyway and return to living the way good, ordinary people should, getting on with their daily lives and getting back to production. Normality here is phrased as *anju leye* ("living in peace and taking pleasure in one's work"), a traditional Chinese adage that Japanese propaganda assumed had some kind of pull on the Chinese heart.[12]

Itō might have quoted as well from another document, "Outline for Carrying Out Pacification Work in the Occupied Areas of Central China," fragments of which his office copied into its March report:

> To get the common people to return speedily to their rightful occupations, we have to guarantee their life and property. To first settle their minds, we have to restore order. And we have to get them to trust the gracious benevolence of the Imperial Army. As we do this, we must encourage them gradually to separate themselves from the anti-Japanese National Government and go along with the formation of a new regime. To gain their allegiance, we must use ideology, politics, and economics to nurture into being from the roots a pro-Japanese atmosphere.[13]

The Special Service officers who authored this document were reasonably clear that the agents would be up against massive dislocation and anxiety generated by the failure of the Imperial Army to exhibit the "gracious benevolence" that it was supposed to. They tag the National Government under Chiang Kaishek and the Nationalist Party (Guomindang) as anti-Japanese, but they are realistic enough to understand that the popular opposition to Japan was not just something whipped up by Nationalist Party propaganda. It arose from the conditions that the invasion had created. Agents would have to address these conditions not just ideologically, but politically and economically as well, if they were to turn the situation around in Japan's favor.

The SSD report in which this and the preceding passage are embedded goes on to translate these sentiments into practical instructions for the newly arriving pacification agents:

- link up with the local Japanese garrison as soon as you arrive;
- coordinate your work with the army and the Military Police;
- treat the creation of new political organs as the core of your work; and
- handle refugees by first organizing aid, then resettling them and returning them to work.

Itō would not have gone into the concrete details of pacification work at the Palace Hotel reception. That would have been Harada's responsibility, yet Harada's access to these trainees was brief. The first to be sent out were in Shanghai for barely two days before being handed their assignments. The army's pressure to get the agents into the field as soon as possible outweighed the luxury of preparation. The brevity of their briefing in Shanghai might indicate that these agents were not well acquainted with the tasks that lay ahead, but this is unlikely. An organization as thorough and as well run as the Mantetsu would not gamble on the wits of its operatives over the advantages of adequate preparation. I prefer to assume that their training in pacification work began before their ship ever docked at Shanghai, probably taking the form of reading Mantetsu pacification reports from North China, where such work had been going on for several months. The North China office of the Mantetsu had compiled several such documents the previous month, and two have survived in the archives of the Japanese Self-Defense Force in Tokyo.[14]

The first of the North China reports is the minutes of a pacification team liaison meeting held in Tianjin on 8 November 1937.[15] It consists mostly of summaries of the reports made by each of the leaders of the twenty-nine pacification teams *(senbu han)* in Hebei province, which started working in mid- to late October. These summaries provide quick sketches of the difficulties the teams faced handling local collaborators, settling displaced populations, and dealing with economic disruption. They would have given the prospective agents heading to Shanghai at least a sense of the range of problems they could expect to encounter in the field.

More comprehensive in its presentation of pacification work is the other surviving November report, a planning document for extending pacification into the region north of Beijing.[16] The document was finalized in the North China office of the Mantetsu on the first of that month, but it was based on a draft that the Special Service Agency in Zhangjiakou, the major rail nexus north of Beijing, had drawn up at the end of October. ("Special Service Agency" was the nomenclature for regional suboffices of the SSD; it would be the term used to designate the regional pacification office that the Shanghai SSD set up in Nanjing.) This report begins by setting out the two general objectives of pacification work. The first is organizational: to create a unified civil administration that reaches to all the counties and localities of the region. The second is ideological: to win sympathy for Japan by bringing stability and order. It then interprets these objectives in relation to the tasks pacification agents should take up. Organizationally, they should work closely with the "self-government committees" (SGCs), the new leadership groups that Chinese collaborators were being induced to form. Ideologically, they should focus on promoting anti-Communism and encouraging "the concept of reliance on Japan" in order to combat "the concept of reliance on EuroAmerica." This procedure for challenging Western imperialism was the ignored-suitor gambit: try to erase sympathy for the rival by replacing it with sympathy for oneself. In practical terms, it meant implementing a Japanese version of the social gospel: insinuate your way into the grassroots of Chinese society and win people's affections by helping them become more secure, better off, and healthier. The adage *anju leye* ("living in peace and taking pleasure in one's work") is again invoked. Assure the Chinese people that this is all that Japan wants on their behalf.

What threatened the ability of the erase-and-replace approach was the principle of equivalence on which it rested. If one reliance was being replaced by another, then the imperialism of the Western nations was simply being transferred over to the Japanese nation. The attempt to forestall such logic was to speak in euphemistic terms of "reliance" rather than "colonial subjection." Still, the notion that the one could be substituted for the other created the danger that Japan would name what it was desperate not to name: its own colonial posture toward China. The agents would painfully discover that Chinese did not find it difficult to name what the agents themselves could not. As Zhang Yibo, the voice of resistance from Zhenjiang whom we met in the opening chapter, reminds compatriots who might be tempted to go along with the occupiers, how can one still think it possible to *anju leye* when "the enemy has turned your locale into a city of the dead, where the sounds of the market have stopped and the day's noise been reduced to the silence of night, and what rings in your ears are military commands barked in a language not your own, the terrifying rumble of tanks, sporadic gunfire, the crash of doors being kicked in, and the howling of the damned to the stomp of their leather boots"?[17]

The Zhangjiakou pacification plan strikes a note of anxiety about Soviet influence on Chiang Kaishek, but the main focus of the report is on organizational matters. The plan explains that each pacification team will consist of several agents, at least one of whom should be a staff member of the NCAA's Special Service Department and therefore a military officer. Then it addresses the work the agents were expected to do to get the self-government committees to the point of assuming administrative and security responsibilities for their areas so as to free up Japanese personnel. Once the SGCs were stable, the next step was to mobilize village headmen to set up a pacification network in the countryside. The teams should appoint special assistants to help the headmen carry out this work. The tasks of pacification at the local level included the registration of all households into five- or ten-family units to function as component parts of the *baojia*, the traditional neighborhood watch system that Chinese states had been using for centuries. The document also advises setting up branches of a mass mobilizational organ along the lines of the Concordia League (Xiehe hui), which the Mantetsu launched in Manchuria in 1933 (and relaunched the following year) to recruit popular support for the occupation state there.[18]

With what knowledge this amounted to, thirty-four agents (the original thirty were joined by four, including Kumagai Yasushi in Chapter 3, who were recruited locally) were sent out from Shanghai in mid-December. They were not the first pacification agents on the Yangtze Delta, however, nor were their SGCs the first. The earliest agents had been mobilized three months earlier to work in Baoshan, the county north of Shanghai where the Shanghai Expeditionary Army, as the CCAA's forerunner was called, landed in August. There the army sponsored a local Chinese committee as early as 23 September, and a pacification team was sent in during October to guide its work. Next in line for pacification was the South City of Shanghai, the heart of the old walled Ming city south of the French Concession. A team of eleven Japanese agents plus four security personnel began work there on 15 November. Another team was formed secretly about the same time to rebuild the Shanghai city government, the subject of Chapter 6. Yet other pacification agents went out to Songjiang on the 26th, Suzhou on 1 December, and Wuxi on the 7th. Each of these interventions was done on an ad hoc basis and is not documented; thereafter the work of pacification proceeds in a more systematic fashion.

The pacification team of Baoshan county near Shanghai, October 1937. From *Shanghai tebieshi zhengfu chuzhou jinian tekan* (1940), opposite p. 406.

Of the new agents leaving Shanghai on the morning of 10 December, the first two were bound for Nanjing, rushing to catch up with the Japanese army and be on site when the capital fell. The rest were given their team assignments later in the morning. That afternoon and over the next four days, they fanned out into the counties in the immediate hinterland around Shanghai. Some ran into problems soon after they set off. The four men sent out on the morning of the 13th to Qingpu, directly west of Shanghai, were turned back that afternoon by Chinese military activity. A week later the situation in Qingpu still had not improved, so the four were reassigned to Hangzhou, where they were joined the following day by two more and their team was elevated to the status of a Special Service Agency. The three-man team sent to Kunshan on the 14th faced a different impediment: they found that the Japanese garrison commander had already appointed a pacification officer, so two of them were reallocated to work further inland, in Zhenjiang, for which a team had not yet been formed. The rapid advance of the Japanese army meant that the initial supply of Mantetsu personnel could not keep up with the demand from the field. A

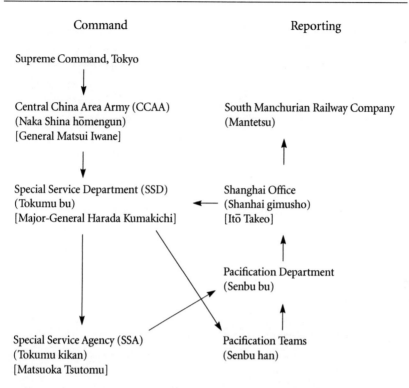

Figure 2.1 Organizational chart of Japanese pacification agencies in central China, January 1938.

second cohort of agents was assembled in Shanghai at the end of the third week of December and sent out on the 24th. Many of these went down into Zhejiang province. A smaller third cohort of agents was dispatched to fresh locations in the second week of January.

We will get to know some of the men who volunteered to be pacification agents better as we read through the case studies. They cannot be reduced to a single type, though many did share qualities often found among volunteers: an enthusiasm for the task to which they were being assigned, an energy to be proactive, and a belief in the rightness of Japan's mission to reconstruct East Asia. The chief pacification agent in Zhenjiang (Chapter 4), Katō Kōzan, communicates this subjectivity in a reminiscence that appeared in two parts in the *New Nanjing Daily* in July 1939.[19] A year and a half after first arriving in Shanghai, Katō could still recall the excitement that the war created among civilians like himself—"an ordinary person

holding an ordinary job with the South Manchurian Railway Company"—
who would otherwise have never had the chance to be assigned to on-the-
ground work of such importance. Here was an opportunity "to get close
to the Chinese people the Japanese army was helping by destroying the
Nationalists and the Communists," as he puts it. For the ambitious and
unadvantaged, it was an opportunity for career advancement that did not
normally fall to people of their modest social position.

Katō arrived in Shanghai from Dalian as one of the second cohort of
agents. He passed a dozen days living in the Mantetsu offices over the
Seikin Bank on the Bund. While waiting for his assignment, he went out to
tour the city, hoping to get a feeling for the situation he was about to enter
and the conflict he thought he had come to help end. Seeing the bombed-
out district of Zhabei, he claims, taught him everything he needed to know
about pacification work even before he had departed for the field. The lesson as he understood it was that war would be banished from China not by
conciliating the Nationalists and Communists, but by drawing the people
away from their teachings of hatred and war and into the relationship of
co-prosperity that Japan was offering. Katō left Shanghai on 23 December
in the company of another agent, confident of the righteousness of his
mission. Or at least that is how he chose to present himself to Chinese
readers of the official newspaper published in the capital: embarking upon
the glorious work of pacification.

Katō's subjectivity was not unique among the Japanese civilians who
went out to serve their country's cause. Kimura Hisao, recruited by the
Asia Development Board in 1940 to work in Kalgan, recalled that he went
off to China as an "innocent and idealistic teenager with a sense of adventure." Writing in the 1980s, Kimura was not defending that idealism so
much as trying to get readers of another generation to understand the
thinking of people who volunteered for Special Service work. "There were
at the time good reasons to think that we had something to offer. Ours was
the only country in Asia to have not only remained uncolonized, but to
have successfully conducted its own industrial revolution." These successes
gave Japanese the confidence of imperialists, though that was a term they
were educated to apply only to Caucasians. "Why should we not lead the
way against the evils of Western imperialism by promoting the same pattern in other parts of Asia? It seemed the most natural thing in the world
that the downtrodden nations of the East should look to us for leadership
and inspiration." In fact they were not looking to Japan for that leadership,

and Kimura was willing to admit later that this illusion was the most destructive feature of his subjectivity. But that was the subjectivity with which he and many others, "incredibly innocent and brimming with idealistic fervor," were equipped as they set out for China. "Few of us knew at the outset of the cruelties of war, but there was no excuse for not knowing the truth by the end. The great tragedy of the war for Japan was not that we lost, but that we learned so little from our defeat, and emerged with no real identity."[20]

The vision that the Special Service Department encouraged its agents to have was an impossible one: to create a genuine government of the people that would also respect Japan's legitimate economic needs and security concerns. Here was the condition that built the fundamental contradiction into the entire project from the word go, the compromising contradiction which it could never dissolve. As the project of creating the occupation state evolved, both sides would try in different fashions to engineer ways of escape. They might have succeeded had the occupation state become the government of all China. But it did not, and so long as it did not, there was always a more legitimate government waiting in the wings to push its compromised competitor off the stage.

The Mantetsu employees the SSD sent out into the field in mid-December were being dispatched to create the grassroots of the regime that the SSD wanted to see built from the ground up to replace Chiang's regime. Swept up in the romance of colonialism, none of the few who later wrote about their experiences betrays any inkling that the core contradiction of the occupation state rendered the project in which they were involved impossible. A Special Service officer who took part in the victory ceremony in Nanjing on 18 December, Okada Yūji, admits in his memoirs that he completely gave way emotionally to the feeling that this was a great turning point for Asia.[21] Okada was not an expansionist, but at that particular moment it seemed to him that Japan's mission to save China from itself, and so to act above its national interests on behalf of all of Asia, was not only honorable but feasible.

This misconstruction was one that every pacification agent had to make out of the circumstances into which he walked. It depended vitally on keeping one's eyes trained on the horizon and not seeing the suffering and destruction close at hand that the Japanese invasion had caused, whether directly or indirectly, and for which, therefore, Japan might be held responsible. That reality could not but intrude, and on rare occasions Special Service documents do make reference to the reality of military misconduct. The North China Area Army's "Outline for Implementing Peace Maintenance in the Areas Occupied by the Army" of 22 December, for instance, goes through the usual list of responsibilities for pacification teams, among which it candidly includes the instruction that the teams should coordinate with the local garrison to engage in police work. At the end of the document, in a final observation that comes across as an afterthought, the NCAA advises the teams to pay attention to the policing of Japanese soldiers, noting that their bad conduct can be a great impediment to pacification work.[22] As indeed it was, obliging one set of Japanese to plaster over the cracks in the normal functioning of everyday life that another set of Japanese had opened up. The job of pacification was not easy. As I shall note in Chapter 8, many Japanese were psychologically undone by their experience.

The effort of assembling the occupation state at the local level fell not just on the occupier but on the occupied as well. Occupation is an imposition, but it is also a relationship: dramatized and prejudged by the term "collaboration," but a relationship all the same, and one that exists only to the extent that both sides engage in creating it. Occupation nonetheless involves abrupt alterations. As Swiss historian Philippe Burrin eloquently describes the French experience of German occupation, "foreign occupation constitutes a massive, brutal intrusion into the familiar frameworks of a society. It imposes authority and demands obedience founded upon neither tradition nor consent. It disrupts the networks and routines of collective life and confronts groups and individuals with choices which, in such circumstances, are very grave."[23] The monumental tasks then arise of creating a new political order in the face of the "break-down of the old system of local administration"[24] and of constructing a plausible ideological apparatus that can make the occupation work in the face of widespread popular opposition. All the while the occupiers must pretend that the new regime of discipline they seek to impose rests not on violence but on the political assets of "tradition" and "consent," assets their intrusion has banished. If the occupiers find that difficult, as they invariably do, it is because they are obliged carry out their state-building project at a time when, as Burrin notes, "the networks and routines of collective life" no longer function as they did. The choices the occupiers make in this sort of situation are important: by shaping the grassroots of the occupation state, they can affect the viability of the overall occupation. Ultimate victory or defeat is likely to be determined elsewhere, but the arrangements that sustain day-to-day administration have to be worked out locally. That means finding, among the people whose lives the occupiers have disrupted, prominent individuals who will permit themselves to be drawn into participating in these arrangements.

The initial task of pacification was therefore the political one of finding Chinese who would enter into the relationship that occupation demands. The Mantetsu's 16 March 1938 report from Shanghai, from which I have already quoted, describes the first stage of a team's political work succinctly:

> When a pacification team arrives at its site, it first carries out a survey of the residents within the pacification district. Together with the army, the Military Police, and security personnel, it devotes its energy to getting rid of bad elements and encouraging the people to come back. At the same time it investigates the people on whom it sets its sights [as collaborators] as well as their resources. It issues "loyal subject certificates" to residents and compiles a residents' register. Anti-Japanese posters in the area it tears down, in place of which it posts and distributes our side's announcements, flyers, and the *New Shenbao* [a Shanghai collaborationist newspaper] in order to settle the people's minds. It also cleans up any leftover weapons, ammunition, and corpses.
>
> Then it investigates and imposes its leadership over whatever peace maintenance committee or other entity of that sort the army or other agency has formed. Should there be no peace maintenance committee, it works in coordination with the military authorities to set one up directly.

Pacification agents usually arrived at their first posting to find that the local garrison had already started recruiting collaborators, following the procedure established in North China. This was to get local people to form a "peace maintenance committee" (PMC, *zhian weichihui*). This nomenclature the Japanese in Manchuria had already adapted from the practice in North China of forming local elite control committees when central administration was weak (the first collaborationist PMCs in the north appeared in Beijing on 30 July 1937 and in Tianjin two days later).[25] According to the CCAA's "General Outline of Future Political Strategy" of 4 December 1937, pacification agents were to set up such a committee, if one did not yet exist, by contacting prominent local figures who might be will-

Office of the Peace Maintenance Committee, Jinan, Shandong, 1937. From *Shina jihen gahō* (27 January 1938), p. 29.

ing to extend their established authority to a new regime.[26] The common ground for enticing local leaders to collaborate was anti-Communist solidarity. The goal was to attract men of substance and reputation. The CCAA outline recognized that this might be difficult and allowed that political unknowns might have to be used if prominent figures are not available. As it turned out, almost all PMCs were made up of political unknowns, dependent for their survival on funding from the army.[27] Given the inevitable instability of the process, the CCAA stressed that the rebuilding of local organs had to remain firmly in Japanese hands. Peace maintenance would not become a formula for relinquishing power to local interests, however much those interests would have to be engaged and accommodated in the transition from military to civilian rule.

Not surprisingly, Japanese and Chinese expectations did not coincide. The army hoped to use the PMCs to capture the local elite. Those who came forward to inhabit the PMCs hoped to capture the army as their weapon for restructuring local power in their own interests. Almost every pacification team inherited the problems this difference in aims created. Having a PMC on site gave pacification agents something to start working with, but they quickly discovered that the PMC was usually filled with marginal elites, the very people with whom they would have preferred not to work. As we shall see in most of the case studies to follow, the teams had to expend much effort on bringing their PMCs to heel and weeding out their personnel in hope of recruiting better men. Finding oneself with the "wrong" collaborators was a side-effect of rule by violence, which opens up political opportunities no one anticipates or desires. The occupier finds himself working with the oddest associates in the hope of reaching normal ground, and realizes that he is unlikely to manage that task so long as these associates are involved.

With fragments of the local elite on side, the occupation state at the local level must then bring statelike means of coercion into play: conscription, recruitment, and relocation; expropriations, levies, and corvées; policing, propaganda, and administrative restructuring. All are standard devices of control and extraction that state builders use under any conditions, not just occupation, to mobilize or discipline a population to its support. In taking up these devices, an occupation state is unlike an indigenously constituted state in at least one crucial aspect. Dependent on foreign military power and staffed by whomever the foreign power is lucky (or, often, unfortunate) enough to recruit, it lacks a strong relationship to the routine functioning of society—Burrin's "networks and routines of collective life." The occupier is caught in the conundrum of demanding recognition of his legitimacy while having no means through which to project a convincing claim to legitimacy. Without this legitimacy it appears only as what it is, externally imposed and unwanted. This conundrum is self-generated, of course, for the physical and symbolic violence of military invasion creates the legitimacy problem in the first place. There are no military solutions to this problem. Political solutions have to be found, which means entering the open-ended sphere of politics and negotiating outcomes that the occupier would have preferred to legislate but lacks the means to do so.

No documentation survives to reveal what actually transpired when a unit of the Japanese army, as opposed to a team sent by the Special Service Department, set up a PMC on the Yangtze Delta. There are, however, two documents in the Shanghai Municipal Archives that sketch the terms within which Japanese officers expected PMCs to operate.[28] They concern a PMC in an unnamed town in the vicinity of Shanghai. The head of this PMC was named Yang Xueqiao, the commander of the garrison surnamed Ōmoto. The first document is the minutes of a meeting attended by the leadership on both sides dated the 13th, though of what month the document does not say; probably December 1937, possibly January 1938. The eleven items listed in the minutes touch on three areas of concern. The first of these is the functioning of the PMC. In his opening remarks, Ōmoto reprimands the local merchants and people for failing to take the initiative to set up a PMC, doing so only at his insistence. He reminds them that they have permission to travel to Shanghai so long as they wear an identifying armband. Their initial tasks, he says, are twofold: to clean up the streets and buildings, and to make sure that commoners know to bow respectfully to Japanese soldiers and not go about in disguise.

The second issue is communication. Ōmoto says that people should report any problems they are experiencing to the Japanese army. Improprieties should come to him directly for the moment, though later reports can go to Murasei, a junior officer otherwise unidentified. Problems arising from language misunderstanding should be reported to someone identified as Officer Yang—the garrison's Chinese translator?—and he will pass them on to Ōmoto. Linguistic misunderstandings come up with some regularity in local reports back to Shanghai. To mention one example, a soldier stationed in the suburban town of Gaoqiao outside Shanghai went into a watch shop in the evening of 22 January to get his watch repaired. Unable to understand each other, the soldier and the shopkeeper got into a loud argument. When a Chinese policeman heard the noise and stepped in to help sort this out, the soldier struck him on the head with his bayonet. The policeman's hat protected him from injury, but that did not stop him from reporting the attack to his superiors, who complained to the unit's commanding officer. The commander conceded that the soldier was in the wrong and had him transferred out.[29] A hat deflected this moment of anger from deadly consequences, but the outcome of frustration could have been much worse.

The third area of concern expressed at the meeting between Yang Xueqiao and Ōmoto had to do with economic issues. Ōmoto declares that the merchants must reopen their businesses as soon as possible, assuring them that "our soldiers hereafter will not have bad conduct." (My awkward English phrasing attempts to replicate the oddness of the Chinese text; the diction of the entire document is so odd that I suspect it was written by a Japanese.) Two items in the minutes reveal that Chinese merchants have been fleecing Japanese soldiers: the PMC is warned that goods offered for sale should have their prices clearly marked, and that Japanese who cannot understand Chinese should be allowed to pay in yen at a fixed exchange rate. The last two items in the minutes note that Japanese soldiers should acquire military provisions through the PMC, but that for personal items they may make their purchases in other towns. This last item seems to indicate that local merchants regarded the garrison's presence as profitable and were anxious to keep military supply orders in the local economy and not have the garrison spend its money somewhere else.

The document that follows the minutes of the 13th in the Shanghai Municipal Archives file is a list of ten demands, undated and unsigned. All ten are written in both Chinese and Japanese. The Chinese text uses awkward phrases and the occasional incorrect translation for terms in the Japanese text. Add to these the northern rendering of "village" as *cur* rather than *cun* (though villages on the Yangtze Delta were rarely called *cun* in any case) and it seems that the author was a Japanese who learned his Chinese in the north. The text, phrased as coming from the Japanese garrison commander and directed to the residents of a "street" or suburban village, lays out the terms of the occupation. The first task is to set up a PMC, with a Self-Defense Corps optional at this stage. The second is to issue armbands to members of the PMC and those locals whom they recognize as "loyal subjects." (The term, *liangmin,* was one the founding emperor of the Ming dynasty used in the 1380s to designate obedient commoners; the Japanese revived it to serve much the same purpose.)[30] The third is to clean up the streets, houses, and riverbanks. Fourth and fifth, residents must show sincere respect for Japanese soldiers and respond to their demands. There then follow the serious infractions of martial law. Anyone stealing military property will be severely punished (the slightly incoherent Chinese phrasing of this sixth regulation suggests that decapitation will be the punishment, but that is probably a faulty translation). Those traveling without authorization by land or water will be arrested. Residents from other villages will be allowed entry only if a local can vouch for who they are; upon arrival, they and their boats must be reported to the garrison. The last rule of occupation is that anyone wishing to cut grasses or reeds may do so without authorization. This seems like an odd provision to write into the rules of occupation. I can only speculate that a dispute over such resources must have arisen, and that the garrison commander saw a need to reaffirm that what had been held in common prior to the Japanese invasion would continue to be regarded as such, and that no one could use the Japanese presence to unfair local advantage.

These few documents provide the only accounts I have found showing the terms of occupation the army imposed on the PMCs. The minutes indicate that the committees were formed to restore order, monitor the activities of the local people, and provide channels of communication and exchange that would allow the army to gain access to local resources with a minimum of conflict. Although conflict could arise between the army and its local collaborators, the PMC had little power to resist army control. The ten demands suggest how thorough that control could be. Indeed, it was so thorough that many assumed, as a Canadian missionary in Henan did, that the PMCs were actually Japanese military teams, not committees of Chinese civilians.[31] The documents also expose the extent to which the occupation relationship was mediated through language, a site of interaction that constantly reasserted difference between occupier and occupied. As the awkwardness of the relationship got replicated in the awkwardness of language, those reading these Chinese texts were reminded that they were being spoken in a foreign voice.

The setting up of the PMCs was only the first in a series of steps that pacification agents were to take in reestablishing local government on the Yangtze Delta. The next step was to replace the peace maintenance committee with a self-government committee (SGC, *zizhi weiyuanhui*). The Mantetsu's 16 March report on pacification work on the Yangtze Delta describes what this stage involved:

> From this point, to create local self-government organs, the team first identifies powerful people in every town and village, and taking them as the core, chooses the people it wants to organize a self-government organ. As part of this policy, it gradually links these organs up with an administrative self-government organization it has already created and set up at an important location, enlarging and strengthening it and eventually forming a local self-government committee (or united self-government committee) which has the character of a county government. This it directs and supervises in such a way that, as the new regime is set up, it will be brought under its control.

The language of "self-government" was a popular Republican double-speak that conceded to local elites the right to run local affairs—and indeed expected them to take on this responsibility—without allowing them to arrogate fiscal powers at the expense of the central state.[32] So too for the Japanese planners, the creation of a self-government organ was a step up a

Standard Stages   Optional Stages

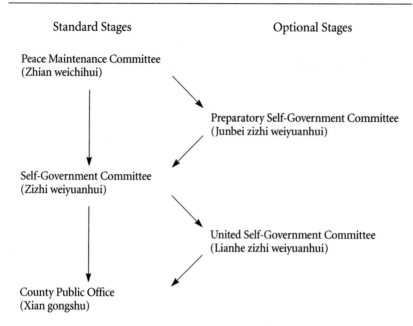

Peace Maintenance Committee
(Zhian weichihui)

Preparatory Self-Government Committee
(Junbei zizhi weiyuanhui)

Self-Government Committee
(Zizhi weiyuanhui)

United Self-Government Committee
(Lianhe zizhi weiyuanhui)

County Public Office
(Xian gongshu)

Figure 2.2 Stages of constructing local government on the Yangtze Delta.

one-way ladder in a complex process of state building that started in every village and culminated with a regime in Nanjing at the apex of the occupation state. As the Mantetsu report describes it, it was a process of both recruitment and reduction. It started with recruiting village-based elites to the Japanese cause, then reducing their number to those it selected for village-level organizations. There followed a second round of selection that recruited these village entities into relationships with a county organization that in turn reduced them to a subordinate status. Mobilizing village elites as the grassroots of this state was a way of forcing an engagement between those men and the Japanese-sponsored regime, at the same time placing them under a control that appeared to emanate from the new regime but was kept in the hands of the Special Service agents.[33] The occupation state had to be a joint Sino-Japanese project, but that did not make the Sino-Japanese political relationship an equal one.

Among the elites that an SGC absorbed were those members of the preexisting PMC whom the pacification team either judged acceptable or could not manage to get rid of. To them were added whoever else of importance the team managed to recruit. This cobbling together of different, sometimes mutually competing, constituents could be difficult. One way of mediating the difficulties in easing out objectionable members and wooing more attractive figures was to create an SGC preparatory committee, which then negotiated the transition from PMC to SGC. In the process, the pacification agents might be able to shunt political liabilities aside into other functions or organizations, especially those where tact and fiscal responsibility were less important, such as the police or militia. This might also buy them time to enlist elites who were resisting involvement. The better educated felt particularly vulnerable, as a Canadian missionary in northern Henan noted in June 1938. Their preference, if they could exercise it, was not just to stay aloof; it was to flee: "One reason for men of education leaving and especially those with Western training is that they fear that when the Japanese arrive they may be forced by them to take part in the local government under the direction of their conquerors."[34] The fear was justified, as Japanese pacification agents regularly canvassed such people and pressured them to collaborate.

For all these reasons, the work of forming a satisfactory SGC could be lengthy. The period between a team's arrival and the inauguration of the SGC might be as short as a week, as it was in Taicang and Danyang. Or it could take over four months, as it did in Songjiang. Much depended on local conditions. Nonetheless, the Japanese had the factors of military control and popular distress to force the outcome they desired, and so the process usually moved relatively quickly. When the chief of staff of the Central China Area Army filed his report on pacification on 20 January 1938, he was able to report that twenty-seven pacification teams were at work in the main locations throughout the Yangtze Delta, and that "as many as fifteen or sixteen main cities have already set up self-government committees, with self-government organs gradually being formed in the villages as well." These achievements indicated that, as he hopefully phrased it, "order is being restored and the people are feeling settled."[35]

Superior as SGCs were to PMCs, the Japanese regarded them as provisional as well, to be superseded by regular administrative organs once regional stability had been achieved. They were bridges to something else rather than destinations in their own right. This is stated explicitly in the CCAA's eleven-point "Plan for the Direction of Political Affairs in Central China," dated 18 January 1938. The tenth point states: "The self-government committees will be removed in connection with the preparation of administrative organs."[36] The SGCs were put in place so that the SSD had something with which to work, but it was made clear from the start, at least on the Japanese side, that they could not be expected to provide an effective or even compliant local foundation for the occupation state. It is not clear that those on the Chinese side were aware of this limitation when they were recruited. Would that knowledge have dissuaded them from acting? Given the scale of the gamble they were making, probably not, but it meant that this hurdle would be followed by another on the long path to local power.

Pacification agents stayed on the scene to direct the administrative work of the SGCs, particularly in the key areas of security, revenue, and the resuscitation of the economy, as a larger program of county government was being readied. Their formal designation as a "pacification team" tended to be dropped over the next few months in favor of the vague and generic "team." Whenever possible, after the first few months, or even weeks, pacification teams and agents did their best to fade from public view. Their ongoing authority was common knowledge, however. When Interior Minister Mei Siping declared at his trial for treason in 1946 that the pacification teams had been the supreme power in the occupied counties, overseeing everything that Chinese officials did, he was offering a reasonably accurate description of where power rested in these counties.[37] For Mei, "self-government" was a Japanese fiction: a name put on something that was in reality its exact opposite. Whatever the court's evaluation of Mei's claim that the local organs of his regime were powerless, it chose not to accept his implication that Japanese control absolved him of responsibility for what went on at the grassroots of the occupation state.

With political arrangements in place, the pacification teams were then to take up the practical challenges of repairing the tears in a war-torn society and reestablishing a basic stability that would allow people to get on with their lives and, more important for an occupier concerned to turn occupation to its benefit, with their labor. The headquarters of the NCAA produced a chart entitled "Kōsaku yōryō" (Outline of work) that lays out the full extent of the work in which pacification teams could be involved. Calibrated to conditions in North China, it includes some provisions, notably those regarding horses, that did not apply to pacification work in Central China. As I have found no comparable outline of work from the archives of pacification work in Central China, this document provides the best summary of the range of tasks that a pacification team had to undertake after the initial cleanup of corpses and debris, jobs that this outline conspicuously chooses to leave unmentioned. It is translated here in full:

1. Political maintenance work:
    (i) encouragement of the population that has fled to return: loyal subject certificates, travel passes, identification of who is politically and economically powerful
    (ii) stabilization and reassurance of the population
    (iii) collection of land registers, household registers, and tax rolls
    (iv) organization and training of self-defense corps: self-protection corps, neighborhood watch system *(baojia)*, anti-Communist youth corps
    (v) win the people's hearts
2. Social policy work:
    (i) care for refugees: refugee reception centers, soup kitchens (salvaged rice), giving out school supplies
    (ii) provision of medical care, dispensing of medicine
    (iii) home for the elderly, orphanage, former prostitutes' home
    (iv) opening of an information booth: employment office, dispute resolution office, people's tribunal, opinion box
    (v) circulation of a newssheet
    (vi) protection of the property of absent owners
    (vii) protection of the property of loyal subjects
    (viii) public recognition of moral exemplars
    (ix) comfort for those who have lost family members or have been injured by war
    (x) punishment of bad people and criminals and public notification of such
3. Economic restoration work:
    (i) encouragement of the circulation of military scrip and Preparatory Bank notes
    (ii) distribution of spring rice seeds
    (iii) distribution of tree seedlings (encouragement of tree planting)
    (iv) encouragement of agricultural harvesting: harvest banners, pawn redemptions, warnings
    (v) peasant granaries
    (vi) opening of markets: stores, restaurants, markets, popular credit institutions (pawnshops, native banks), fixed pricing, arrest of overcharging merchants

     (vii) buying and selling of agricultural products, negotiation of commodity purchase prices: provision of civilian rolling stock, setting up of commodity exchange offices

    (viii) rural cooperatives, commercial cooperatives

4. Propaganda work:

     (i) wiping out of anti-Japanese Communist education: bookmobiles, penny libraries, displays of reading materials, newspaper reading rooms, public posting of newspapers

    (ii) dissemination of Japanese language: dispatch of lecturers, kindergartens

   (iii) introduction to Japanese affairs: inspection tours

5. Public welfare work:

     (i) repair of roads and bridges

    (ii) recruitment of soldiers

   (iii) energetic forwarding of military matériel

   (iv) self-provisioning of housing and horses

    (v) recovery of weapons and ammunition

6. Work with villages protecting important installations and transportation routes:

     (i) formation and strengthening of a leadership network in the protecting villages

    (ii) organization and leadership of youth and children in the protecting villages

   (iii) leadership of road protection weeks

   (iv) pacification and leadership directed toward railway employees

    (v) cutting down of tall vegetation along railway lines[38]

The closest analogue to this document from the Yangtze Delta is the report on pacification that the Shanghai office of the Mantetsu prepared on 16 March 1938.[39] That report distinguishes three categories of work, rather than the six in the NCAA chart:

- "political work," under which it places the care of refugees;
- "economic work," which includes the restoration of public utilities; and
- "the work of moral transformation and propaganda," where it slots medical care.

What the NCAA marked off as "social policy work," the Shanghai office distributed between politics and propaganda. What is missing from the Shanghai report, when compared with the North China document, are indications that the teams were involved in organizing militias (1 [iv]), setting up road and railway protection schemes (6),[40] or, most remarkably, recruiting soldiers (5 [ii]). Some of these tasks were not yet envisaged, though the first two would be taken up here and there on the delta later that spring. What is missing from the NCAA outline, to look the other way, are the restoration of public utilities and the revival of local industries, as well as the replacement of existing textbooks with those used in Manchuria or Japan.

The differences between these two outlines reflect the different economic and educational contexts of the prosperous Yangtze Delta and the less-developed North China Plain, where rural schools were rare and public utilities and local industries nonexistent. The commercial character of the delta economy meant that the teams there got involved in a range of activities that would not have concerned their North China counterparts.[41] But rather than ask only what is missing from either report, consider what is missing from both documents: any mention of the military duties of pacification teams. It is the case that the teams on the Yangtze Delta were staffed by civilians, yet in both regions the agents were engaged in discovering and disposing of Chinese soldiers and guerrillas, as well as intelligence gathering and counterterrorist operations carried out in coordination with the Military Police. The teams were also involved in attending to the noncombat needs of Japanese soldiers.[42]

After the first pacification teams had been in the field for a month, the Shanghai office of the Mantetsu compiled a comprehensive outline identifying all the teams and arranging them into a proposed structure of eight regional Special Service Agencies. The plan as it stood at the end of January (with some additions inserted as late as mid-March) appears as Table 2.1, a slightly emended translation of a chart accompanying the 16 March pacification report. What is striking at first glance is the low number of the Japanese agents assigned to the task of rebuilding civilian order across a region ravaged by war. The table projects something of an illusion, however, for just behind the pacification agents stood a far larger number of soldiers garrisoning the places where the agents worked and providing them with the coercive authority to convert their plan into practice. The numbers do suggest, nonetheless, the thinness of Japanese control. This in

Table 2.1 Structure of pacification teams on the Yangtze Delta as outlined by the Shanghai office of Mantetsu, January 1938

Branch office	Pacification team	Start date	Number of pacification agents	Agents who are Mantetsu employees	Additional security personnel
Shanghai	South City	11/15	11	0	4
	Pudong		0	0	2
	Jiading	12/12	5	5	0
	Baoshan		4	0	0
	Chongming	[3/18]	3	0	0
	Zhenru	12/14	4	4	0
	Kunshan		3	0	0
	Taicang	12/13	4	4	0
	Qingpu		5	0	0
	Western District	Not yet			
	Chuansha	Not yet			
	Nanhui	Not yet			
	Fengxian	Not yet			
	Subtotal		39	13	6
Suzhou	Suzhou	12/1	3	0	9
	Changshu	12/12	3	2	0
	Wuxi	12/7	4	2	0
	Wujiang		4	0	0
	Jiangyin	Not yet			
	Subtotal		14	4	9
Jiaxing	Jiaxing	12/16	8	8	3
	Songjiang	11/26	6	4	4
	Nanxun		6	0	0
	Jiashan		3	3	0
	Jinshan	Not yet			
	Pinghu	Not yet			
	Subtotal		23	15	7
Zhenjiang	Zhenjiang	12/19	6	5	0
	Yangzhou		5	5	0
	Danyang	1/9	5	5	0
	Changzhou	12/19	2	0	0
	Jintan	[11/26]			
	Subtotal		18	15	0

Table 2.1 *(continued)*

Branch office	Pacification team	Start date	Number of pacification agents	Agents who are Mantetsu employees	Additional security personnel
Hangzhou	Hangzhou	[12/27]	7	6	6
Nanjing	Nanjing	[12/24]	5	5	12
	Jurong	Not yet			
	Jiangning	Not yet			
	Lixian	Not yet			
	Subtotal		5	5	12
Huzhou	Huzhou		7	4	0
Wuhu	Wuhu	[1/6]	6	5	0
	Taiping	Not yet			
Total	37		119	67	40

Note: Dates in square brackets were not in the original chart and have been added from other sources.

turn points to the paucity of material and human resources that Japan could afford to dedicate to the work of occupation; and perhaps as well a willingness to accept the appearance of pacification over its substance—indeed, to desire only the appearance.

As the Japanese army ranged beyond the Yangtze Delta, the Pacification Department had to keep up with the expansion and get teams into the field on short notice. By March, another sixteen teams were being readied for service north of the Yangtze. But the Mantetsu was running out of personnel it could afford to funnel into pacification work, forcing the Shanghai office to recruit new agents outside its own ranks. The company started with non-Mantetsu employees working in an official capacity in Manchuria, then turned to personnel in the East Asian Economic Investigation Bureau (Tōa keizai chōsakyoku, a semiautonomous research entity within the Mantetsu, based in Tokyo); then to recent graduates from China programs in institutes of higher education. Lastly the Mantetsu went scouting among Japanese employees of the consulate or of textile firms in Shanghai, looking for anyone with some experience in China. As the system grew, so too its structure evolved. By the beginning of 1939, the system consisted of seven Special Service Agencies: three in Suzhou, Nanjing, and Hangzhou, the rest outside the delta, in Nantong, Bengbu, Anqing, and Wuhan. By October 1939, the Shanghai, Suzhou, Nanjing, and Bengbu agencies were running teams in fifty-nine counties.[43]

But this is to look too far forward from the evening of 8 December 1937, when Itō Takeo addressed the first cohort of company employees to be sent into the Yangtze Delta. These young men had no intimation of what awaited them at their posts. They set off with only the roughest of plans, confident in their mission but prone to misconstrue what they were to find in terms of what they had known in the far less brutalized and polarized environment of Manchuria. What some discovered upon arrival would be worse than they could have imagined. The agents who went to Zhenru at the northern edge of Shanghai found Zhenru almost uninhabited. It was worse for the teams sent further west—to Taicang, Changshu, Jiaxing, and Changzhou. All four teams reported back to the Pacification Department in Shanghai that the cities to which they had been assigned were completely empty. Pacification barely qualified as a plan. How was it to be carried out when there were no Chinese people there to pacify?

— 3 —

Appearances / Jiading

Japan's military invasion suspended all existing political arrangements on the Yangtze Delta. The Central China Area Army ruled wherever it arrived, negotiating its authority with no one. Once the army had canceled the jurisdiction of the National Government by occupying its territory and shutting down its administration, the goal was to replace that regime with a new authority. The teams that the army sent in to do this work of pacification, as the previous chapter notes, were not military agencies. They did not operate through violence to bring their authority to bear on the population, although the local garrison was always there to back them up if need be. Their means were politics, persuasion, and payment. As we shall see, the payments were never large and they soon dried up, which left politics and persuasion: politics to maneuver Chinese into positions of collaboration, and persuasion to convince collaborators and noncollaborators alike that Japan would succeed in its project to control China, and that this control was in China's long-term interests.

The time frame for this case study as for the later ones is short, principally the three or four months after the first arrival of the pacification team. The available documentation has largely imposed this time frame, but it serves my purpose, which is to show what the haste of reconstruction meant for the process of collaboration. Given enough time, an occupation can come to be seen as simply one event contributing to the way things are. In the short term, however, occupation appears most abusive and the new regime it ushers in, most illegitimate. The first concern of the pacification team had to be to project the appearance of stability and good government—ironically, the very social goods that the violence of their invasion had shattered—even and especially when they did not exist. The pacification process must cause the violence by which the occupation authority was imposed to disappear and make the new arrangement appear to be other than abruptly imposed. It must project the idea that a state structure exists where it does not; it must construe nominal submission as engaged support. Not only that, but the agents in charge of this process must do their job as quickly as possible. Time is on the occupier's side only in the very long term.

Indicators that the new regime was having local success in imposing its control mattered hugely to the collaborators. If collaboration names a relationship that rests on an inherently unstable balance of power between an external power and its local representatives, then the first task of the new local bosses must be to camouflage that imbalance. Collaborators must claim that they adhere to the highest principles of public service and good order. They must appear to hold real power and not simply to be lackeys of a foreign occupier. And they must represent themselves as standing for the best interests of the local people, or at least better interests than the regime they have replaced. These appearances are important because, in the absence of more stable claims to legitimacy, they can have practical consequences. If the local people cannot be convinced that the new administration is the effective replacement of the old county government, who will bother to register themselves, pay taxes, or heed the collaborators' directions, except when they are coerced to do so? This was the practical question that Japanese agents and local elites faced during the winter of 1937–38.

In a sense, there is nothing unique about the inequality of the relationship that occupation imposes between local and extralocal power, nor in the joint willingness of center and locality to represent that inequality as though it were based on a genuine interaction between central and local interests. All states exist by such inequality, and all political regimes obscure it in the service of winning mass support. What is different in the case of occupation is the impossibility of an alternative power asserting itself within that relationship or even evolving into other arrangements that might enable the local to influence or even invade the center. Most of the power relationships under an occupation flow one way, from the top. And yet, as we shall see, this flow does not give occupier or collaborator the freedom to act as he chooses. This unfreedom of political action from below is what makes collaborators appear to be puppets.

We are able to explore facets of this challenge in Jiading county because

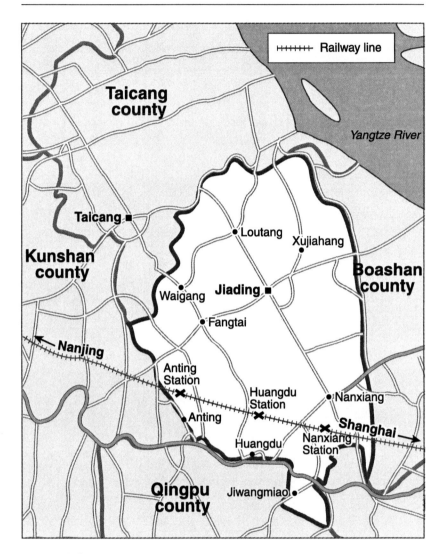

Map 2. Jiading county.

Kumagai Yasushi wrote two accounts of his experiences as a pacification agent. These accounts do not just show what he tried to do to create a local collaborationist regime, but reveal the makeshift measures he had to settle for to claim any degree of success. One is his team's work diary, which survives in the form of extensive excerpts in the classified report that the Jiading team, like every other pacification team, was required to send back to the Mantetsu's Pacification Department in Shanghai in April for their report to the army's Special Service Department.[1] The other is a memoir he wrote about his experiences in Jiading and later in Bengbu, north of the Yangtze. Published in 1943, the book was intended as wartime reading for Japanese back home. The memoir is a historian's dream, for it gives a "subjective" account of the experience of pacification from the Japanese side coming from the same author of the "objective" account lying in the archives of the Self-Defense Research Institute in Tokyo.

The two texts are as different in tone as could be. The Mantetsu report consists of terse entries typed in katakana, the script of official wartime communication, intended only for those who had clearance to read "top secret" documents. The other is an expansive and emotional reminiscence printed in the more common hiragana script for the Japanese public. In the one, Kumagai chronicles his team's work following Special Service guidelines. In the other, he evokes the experience of working in the Chinese countryside. His purpose for doing so, he tells his readers in the preface, is so that they might better appreciate the integrity of rural Chinese life and accord the Chinese the respect they deserve if "co-prosperity" is to mean what it says. In the one, he is an agent of the colonial state; in the other, a man on a civilizing mission. The team report avoids the personal, whereas the memoir tells the occupation as a first-person travel/adventure story. Some of the facts in the work diary are there in the memoir, but in the latter the tone is more important than the facts: Kumagai the adventurer facing an ominous world awaiting discovery and salvation at his hands, Kumagai the hero braving the uncertainties of a hostile countryside in order to bring security, enlightenment, and peace to sturdy, reliable peasants. His two voices do not contradict each other so much as tell different stories, or tell the same stories in different ways. Kumagai's memoir is of course not just a history of his experience but a validation of his actions, a script smoothing out the reverses and confusions of his own conduct. Like the work diary, it is an affirmation that the policy and methods of pacification were right and just. In the absence of Chinese documentation on Jiading during the first half-year of occupation, Kumagai's writings are our only record of the process of creating the occupation state's grassroots in Jiading. They are also our only record of the recurring gap between what he hoped collaboration could provide, and what it did.

On the morning of 12 December 1937, Kumagai Yasushi set out from Shanghai in the back of an army truck with the four other pacification agents. Their assignment was to reimpose order on the county of Jiading.

The county lay directly to the northwest of Shanghai, and the county seat was one of several that ringed the city. Kumagai describes their arrival:

> It was a terribly cold day, colder than anything in the last few years. By the time we got down out of the truck that had brought us the ten kilometers from the pacification office in Shanghai to the county seat, our hands and feet were numb with cold.
>
> There were five of us together on this assignment: myself, Furukawa, Kawase, Yukimoto, and Yamanaka. We were in a state of some agitation as we walked through the West Gate, but once we looked about us when we were inside, we didn't see a living thing. It was a desolate scene: roads torn up, houses collapsed, not a shadow moving. We found five or six Military Police standing around a fire, and they were surprised by our sudden intrusion.
>
> "Who the hell are you?" they wanted to know.
>
> "We're the pacification team," I replied. A kindly look immediately lit up their faces.
>
> "Is that so? We're glad you made it."
>
> These soldiers had come through a tough battle and that very day had been assigned as Military Police for the area. For whatever reason they seemed relieved to see familiar faces. They were all a little older than regular soldiers.
>
> "I'm Kumagai," I told them when they asked my name.
>
> We went off directly to call on the head of the Military Police unit, then looked for a suitable house in which to set up our base camp for pacification work. The next morning we got right down to the tasks at hand.[2]

With this little story, Kumagai Yasushi launches into his account of bringing order to Jiading. Kumagai was one of the South Manchurian Railway employees sent out from Shanghai in the second week of December to lead pacification teams into the interior. Kumagai was anything but a long-time Mantetsu employee, however, for he had only just been hired the previous week, recruited specifically for pacification work. What his actual background was, he never reveals, only that he had spent several years in China before the war. He knew Chinese well enough to eavesdrop on conversations and tell from dialects who was local and who was from elsewhere. As the author of two texts in different genres, Kumagai is the best witness we have to the first steps the Japanese took to bring the counties of the Yangtze Delta into the occupation state.

As an object of Japanese pacification, Jiading was not greatly different from the other counties in the Shanghai hinterland that the Japanese army swallowed in its westward assault in mid-November. If Jiading had any particular military significance, it was being the first county on the rail line between Shanghai and Nanjing, and hence the first territory across which the Japanese army had to cross on its crusade to destroy the government of China. The county seat where Kumagai and his men alighted on 12 December was not on the train line, but three of Jiading's larger towns—Nanxiang, Huangdu, and Anting—were close by the first three stations on that line. These were the first places in Jiading to fall to the Japanese army in the second week of November. The county seat was occupied last, on the 12th, after being thoroughly bombed from the air. The aerial bombing of civilians was a tactic the Japanese military had innovated during its aborted attack on Shanghai in 1932. It was used more extensively during this second invasion.

Jiading was a small city of 30,000, clustered around a famous pagoda that dated from the Ming dynasty. The bombs missed the pagoda but destroyed a third of the other buildings and virtually emptied the town of people. Casualties were severe. According to a report that the head of the Jiading Burial Society made to the Japanese authorities, his group had disposed of 4,570 civilian and military corpses by the end of February. A countywide survey of casualties compiled by the county government after the war determined that Japanese soldiers were responsible for the deaths of 8,031 Jiading residents in 1937, and 3,720 in 1938, with another 332 people left unaccounted for.[3] The striking of civilian targets was common Japanese practice elsewhere as well. When another pacification team reached the nearby seat of Taicang county the following morning, for example, they found over half the buildings burned and the rest looted: the state granary and salt depot stripped clean, the Public Security Bureau gone, the city library in ashes. "Not a shadow moved" is how their work diary describes the city when they entered.[4] Further west along the railway line, the much larger city of Danyang had the misfortune to lie directly in the path of the Japanese advance toward Nanjing. The first wave of aerial bombing on 27 November ignited a conflagration within that city that spread quickly and burned for three days; a second wave two days later started fires in places that had managed not to burn the first time, reducing Danyang to utter devastation.[5]

No Chinese document concerning the conquest of Jiading survives. There is, however, an SGC report dated May 1938 from neighboring

Taicang that describes the situation there. The anonymous Chinese author of this report lingers on his account of the destruction in order to ensure that the central government understood what local administrators were up against. "Wherever the conflict reached in the county seat and along the river and highways," he wrote, "the greater part of the shops and houses were reduced to ashes. The population of the entire county abandoned their homes, and those who fled in fear from the armed soldiers numbered at least 100,000. Since the beginning of recorded history our people have not suffered through a disaster as extreme as this." And this was a collaborator writing! Jiading could not claim the same absence of historical precedent for suffering, as we shall see, yet it presented a comparable picture. Even after order had been restored, as the Taicang writer goes on to note, "the great majority of those on whom disaster was visited nonetheless have no homes to which to return. It pains the heart to hear them cry from hunger and dazes the eye to see them shiver from the cold"—stock phrases, though no less true for being so. "In all the adjacent towns and villages, the damage has been severe. Wherever cannon shells reached, houses have been reduced to wasteland and nothing but toppled ramparts and shattered walls greet the eye." [6]

The only comparable description for Jiading is what Kumagai wrote the following day, and it tallies with the impression of the Japanese military violence in Taicang:

> What a sorrowful scene of desolation it was. As soon as we arrived in Jiading, we walked through the town from the West Gate to the East Gate, and then from the South Gate to the North Gate. Houses had collapsed, roof tiles were scattered over the roads, and snapped electrical wires were strewn about, making it hard just to walk. Here and there were holes probably caused by bombs dropped from airplanes. Oddly enough, the towering pagoda standing in the center of town was the only thing to survive unscathed. Not a soul was to be seen. All we saw was the occasional doddering elder crawling out from one of the collapsed hovels and going back in again. Sadly, a third of the houses within the city wall had been destroyed. We found ourselves in a city of death, a mysteriously silent world in which the only sound was the tap of our own footsteps. Where on earth had all the residents fled to? One after the next, every uninhabited house was completely empty: no furniture to sit on and absolutely nothing to eat. [7]

The devastation allows Kumagai the memoirist to position himself in the story of Jiading's resurrection as facing a huge challenge in order to become the hero of his own story. The greater the devastation, the greater must be his own achievements. Yet the absence of anyone willing to be saved (except for the doddering elderly who don't seem to count for Kumagai, except as objects of pity) causes him momentary panic:

> How pitiable, we thought. Reviving the place seemed hopeless. We were supposed to pacify the people, yet there was no way to do our work if they weren't there. Standing in the midst of the ruins, we felt that our glorious dream had been completely shattered. We had absolutely no plan other than gathering and taking away the scattered timbers and tiles and getting the roads back in order.

In a later aside in his memoir, Kumagai notes that some agents succumbed to the temptation to carry out a Potemkin village–style cleanup that was nothing but appearances. What he disdains as "camera pacification" compromised the integrity of Japanese colonialism, and he would not do the same. In the battle for Chinese hearts and minds that Kumagai thought he was waging, objective results were necessary. This meant that appearances were important after all, since the only victories worth having were those that could gain credit with his Chinese audience. Indeed, appearances might be the most a pacification agent could hope for. Kumagai's insistence on correct subjectivity was intended for his Japanese readers, subjectivity being the colonizer's first and last resort. So the lack of a plan did not last for long. Kumagai quickly drew up seven tasks for his team: "get the residents who had fled to return first of all, set up local self-government organs, work diligently with the army to maintain security, help revive the economy, enlighten people through education and propaganda, devote ourselves to medical treatment and public health measures, and as well provide support for and liaison with the military."[8] The key to these tasks was the first, getting some sort of "local self-government organs" up and running; the other six would then follow easily.

The military unit that had captured Jiading a month before Kumagai's arrival had recruited locals to form a peace maintenance committee. Their leader was a man by the name of Sun Yunsheng. Nothing is known of Sun other than that he hailed from Baoshan county to the east, which had fallen to Japanese forces in September. An outsider, at the very least; beyond that, someone around whom lay the suspicion that he had cultivated ties with Japanese in his home county before showing up in Jiading. Sun may in fact have been brought in by the Japanese army. When the Yamada Unit pulled out of the county seat for service further west, it left behind the Uchino Police Corps to keep the peace and supervise the PMC. One of the first things the PMC did from its office in the ruined city was to set up a commodity-purchasing cooperative to try to get control of local grain supplies. The committee also set up a registration program that was supposed to involve checking everyone's identity and issuing loyal subject certificates to those who could verify that they were local residents. As far as the pacification team could figure out later, the PMC did nothing to actually confirm identities. It was interested only in the five pennies charged for each certificate.

Kumagai had no choice but to work with the PMC his military predecessor had created, but his first move was to cancel the PMC's registration scheme and set up his own Loyal Subject Inspection Post at the PMC office. The first results were modest: roughly 300 people a day showed up to register. But as those who had fled returned in greater numbers toward the end of December, that rate went up to 700 to 800 people a day. The certificates the team issued were a simple but reasonably effective policing device. If someone wanted to enter or leave the city or set up a stall in the market outside the West Gate, he had to show a certificate to the guards posted by the Japanese police. A loyal subject was one who held a certificate; a disloyal one did not. By 29 January, 16,541 people held loyal subject certificates, still only a quarter of the prewar population, the implicit benchmark by which the team assessed everything it did. (Breakdowns by age and sex are not possible for Jiading, but they are for neighboring Taicang, where three-quarters of the early "loyal subject" population consisted of people under twenty or over forty; males outnumbered females by a factor of three to two.) By the end of March, the registered population was 32,286.[9] The team judged that passing the halfway point marked a major political success.

Along with registration, the pacification team got busy early on with propaganda work. Within two days of their arrival, team members had gone around the town removing anti-Japanese fliers and replacing them with posters the Pacification Department back in Shanghai had given them when they left. On 15 December, they put up warnings against looting the damaged areas of the town or removing anything to the countryside. In his memoir, Kumagai says that a month into the occupation he was puzzled that many people were in the streets of the town during the day, but that everyone left at dusk. It took him a while to realize that they were combing the town for anything of value that they could carry off. This discovery becomes an opportunity for him to regret what he took to be a characteristic lack of community feeling and an absence of mutual assistance in Chinese life, rather than an understandable response to the community breakdown that invasion had caused and in which he was implicated. The New China he wanted to build would not be like this.[10]

Nine days later the pacification team issued regulations against theft, gambling, and arson. The rule against gambling is eye-catching. Why did the team consider gambling as having any effect on the security of the Japanese occupation? Clearly it could not have the impact that theft and arson would. The prohibition hints at something else: the nation-building intention that stands somewhat apart from, but always behind, the peculiarities of occupation. Just as the Nationalist regime recognized gambling as a vice that was not wanted in the new modern nation that it sought to create, the occupation state that was coming into being in Jiading was fashioning its moral order in relation to similar—possibly even the same—concerns. By identifying elements of popular practice as antimodern and subjecting them to legal sanction, the pacification team was assuming its role as the agent of a greater purpose, which was to transform at the grassroots the popular custom that might compromise the moral project of the modernizing state. In this, Kumagai was following the lead of Republican reformers.

The same nation-building intention was at work in the orders the local Jiading administration issued on 4 April for the registration of opium dens. More was at stake in this matter, however, given that the fiscal consequences of controlling the opium trade far exceeded anything that gambling taxes could furnish. Kumagai declares himself unable to understand why so many people in Jiading smoked opium. He put opium smoking and gambling together as two of the many faults he thought he detected among Chinese people. Tea houses, flower-drum singing, operas in the local dialect, and inappropriate sexual relations were some of the others he cites—just the sorts of vices that the reformist Nationalists had disdained up until 1937. Rural folk insisted to Kumagai that opium was the "best cure for all ills," but he was a radical modernizer who could not accept what he regarded as their "traditional" point of view.[11]

Kumagai's attitude was widely shared among pacification agents elsewhere on the Yangtze Delta, who marked opium and gambling as Chinese bad habits that Japan would erase. As his counterpart in neighboring Taicang county, Tamaki Hajime, phrased this way of thinking, "The revival of objective conditions through the reestablishment of stability and the restoration of the economy must be accompanied by the subjective renovation of the lifestyles of the people, specifically the suppression of opium and gambling. This team is committed to saving the people of postwar China."[12] It is hard not to see a gap between this sort of correct subjectivity and the actual practices that occupation unleashed. Tamaki reported that his team had "guided the SGC toward making preparations for setting up opium smoking centers, which opened on 1 June." At the very same time, the Taicang SGC member who authored the work report from which I have already quoted credits the Nationalists with greater success on this front than the Japanese:

> This county's management of [opium] suppression had been quite successful until the military incident, when the suppression system went by the board. Those who had not yet gone off opium went back to consuming it just as they had done, and those who had stopped found it difficult not to let the dead ashes spring back into flame. If suppression is not strictly reimposed, then the change will become even worse.

These accounts show that the Chinese collaborators and the Japanese agents could tell two very different stories about China's past and future.

A third project that the Jiading pacification team took up in the early weeks of the occupation was the provision of medical services. This aspect of the team's work is not highlighted in the work reports to the SSD, but is featured in Kumagai's memoir, probably because it gave him the greatest direct personal contact with ordinary people. He remarks on the poor level of the people's health, particularly in the countryside, and praises the team's work in bringing "civilized medicine" to Jiading. Between 13 and 25 December, the team treated 196 patients, most with some success. Although their medical work amounted to little more than rudimentary first aid and standard drugs, it impressed some peasants sufficiently that they thought the team members were doctors. Doctors were a rarity in the Jiading countryside: before the war there were roughly fifty in a county of a quarter of a million people, only two of whom were trained in Western medicine. Kumagai was using free medical work as modernizing cadres elsewhere have done, to build credit among people who never saw doctors.

He interpreted their gifts of chickens and eggs as signs of gratitude for what the Japanese were doing for them.[13] But is it not also possible to see their gifts as paying off a debt in the hope of terminating, rather than perpetuating, their sense of obligation to feared intruders?

These tasks were secondary to the main mandate of pacification, which was to create an effective local administration that would cooperate with the Japanese and serve as the grassroots of the new occupation state. The disreputable PMC had to be shunted aside and replaced by a more solidly grounded self-government committee. This topic is delayed in Kumagai's memoir, perhaps because it was an area in which the team's achievements had fallen short of his hopes. He opens the one chapter in which he talks about building a Chinese administration, bearing the rueful title "The Reality of Politics," with a frank admission of the depth of his difficulties:

> Among the most important tasks for those of us on the pacification team was directing the setting up of local self-government organs. I can say that this was one of the tough assignments. We had to discover who were relatively powerful in the area, then we had to get them together and hastily organize them into a "peace maintenance committee" or a "self-government committee." In many cases we proceeded by starting with a peace maintenance committee, developing that into a self-government committee, and then after many failures and reorganizations establishing the foundation for a county government.
>
> To carry out this work, in fact, we had to get over I don't know how many shoals. Over the course of our first two months, we were gradually able to get relatively powerful people to come forward and bring about the formation of a committee.[14]

The source of the difficulty the team had in "directing" a Chinese administration into being was its lack of access to "relatively powerful people," that is, the people of influence whom Japan wanted to collaborate. Kumagai's work report observes that as late as April, "unreliable elements" among the local elite were hindering what he called the committee's "development." In his memoir he phrases the problem more elaborately:

> The interpersonal relations were truly complicated, which got us into real difficulties. Some of them were busy plotting in favor of Nationalist Party interests, some were taking advantage of their positions to pursue private gain, others were gathering private retainers and arrogating police power,

yet others were secretly making contact with the bandits. Initially many people hid their real names and acted under various pseudonyms. We were fully aware of all this, but there was nothing we could do to counter it.[15]

Rather than raise this difficulty as an inevitable aspect of regime building under occupation, Kumagai chooses to take refuge in the concept of "interpersonal relations." He portrays the Chinese he tried to work with as prey to an undisciplined confusion of allegiances and alliances. This situation existed, he believed, because of their naturally devious character and their preference for putting petty self-interest ahead of community concerns. The Japanese presence in the process of local regime formation is left entirely out of his explanation. Again, just as with the absence of locals willing to be pacified on his team's first arriving in Jiading, Kumagai cannot allow his presence to be seen as the source of the problem he faced of creating a cooperative Chinese administration. The root of the problem, he reasoned, lay rather in the tumultuous environment that he had come to sort out, and as well in certain bad habits that Chinese themselves had failed to correct.

The PMC that had been thrown together "hastily"—Kumagai's term—in the first days of the occupation was his opening problem. The army unit had apparently agreed to take on whoever had come forward at that unstable moment and put them in charge. Its membership was a fait accompli that the late-arriving Kumagai had to work with. Sun Yunsheng, the head of the PMC, would prove remarkably tenacious. His alliance, or at least prior relationship, with Police Chief Uchino made it hard for Kumagai to bypass his candidacy, if indeed that is what Kumagai wanted to do, when creating the county SGC. The difficulty of having to deal with a preselected group of collaborators was embedded in the larger problem of elite recruitment under the condition of occupation. Those who came forward in the first days of occupation, as he observes in his classified work report, were "mostly unreliable and of dubious virtue and capacity"—not the sort of people he wanted for his project of building a virtuous occupation state.[16] He needed local elites of quality. His project to bring order to Jiading needed their reputation, their visibility, and their authority to command the acquiescence of the local people. Without the collaboration of at least some fraction of the established local elite, he could not hope to build an occupation state that would be anything but a massive sinkhole into which scarce resources simply disappeared. But anyone with status, education, or money had cleared out before the Japanese army arrived. They were simply not available. The matching problem from the other side was that the established elites had little to gain from working with the invaders, other than recovering homes that the army had requisitioned and perhaps recovering opportunities the army had closed down. They had even more to lose. Collaboration always begins as a short-term arrangement hemmed in by the moral pressures against it and the fear that it will fail.

Jiading residents had particular reason to cling to resistance as the moral high ground, for they all grew up with a memory of resistance to military takeover peculiarly their own: the heroic and futile resistance against the armies of the Manchu invaders in 1645. On that occasion, a consortium of elite and popular leaders held out against a siege that eventually failed, ending in the brutal destruction of the city and the massacre of those who defended it. Kumagai knew the story and tells it in his book as an excuse to explain why anti-Japanese consciousness was strong in the county.[17] He quite appreciated that the story of that resistance made it much easier for the other side to teach people the virtue of resisting an invader such as himself. He declines to mention a more recent event reinforcing the message of resistance, and that is the Japanese attack on Shanghai in 1932. The attack was a cynical attempt to divert attention from Japan's recent occupation of Manchuria. Japanese forces on that occasion not only leveled significant areas of the newly constructed northern section of Shanghai but bombed the railway into Jiading, forcing residents there and in Baoshan and Taicang to flee southwest away from the attack. The return of Japanese bombers in 1937 not only revived that memory, but sent people once again scurrying to the same places they had gone for refuge five and a half years earlier.

These living local memories may have inhibited some who wanted to cooperate with the invader. Those at lower levels of the local political heap, however, might view the situation differently, as an opportunity for personal advancement that had never before been in their reach. The boldly opportunistic were willing to forget 1932 and 1645 in order to slip in through the gates of power that, under ordinary circumstances, were shut to all but the privileged few from a narrow circle of locally dominant families. In the vacuum that occupation created, individuals with marginal claims to public authority could use the liminal moment between the old order and the new to step through—and onto—the PMC. Their opportunism placed Kumagai in a double bind. He had to use at least some of those who were already on the PMC, lest even that coterie renounce its newly formed loyalty to the Japanese. Their presence, however, made it more difficult to draw in those who earlier had abstained from any kind of involvement, and would continue to do so given who remained on the committee. As the Japanese had little they could use to force reluctant candidates into collaboration, nor any reason to suppose that popular support for a new elite would be forthcoming if they did, constant negotiation and compromise with whatever segment of that elite would negotiate with them was the only course. The grassroots leadership of the occupation state could in the end only be made up of those available and willing to serve in the face of counterattack from the other side. And that threat was made real soon enough. A team of assassins killed Chen Guiquan, a middleman with whom the pacification team had established profitable links. Then Zhang Liangui, a capable young Nationalist tax collector whom the team recruited to set up a tax scheme for them, was shot.[18] Collaboration could be a dangerous business.

Reorganizing the PMC was the team's main behind-the-scenes task in January, especially after the 18th, when army planners in Shanghai called for the gradual replacement of ad hoc local organs with regular administrations. On 21 January the team announced the formation of a nine-member Jiading Self-Government Preparatory Committee. The preparatory committee was charged with overseeing the reconstitution of the existing PMC into an SGC. The team's confidential report concedes that the preparatory SGC was in fact simply the PMC by another name. In other words, the PMC members had proved themselves impervious to purge. (Kumagai was not alone: the Taicang team leader was complaining in February that "the central figures on the current SGC are almost all third-rate types or worse.")[19] The only way to change things was to find new members among those who had fled the county. "The formerly really powerful people of Jiading," as the team report refers to the upper elite, had been among the first to leave before the Japanese attack. Some had headed west to Suzhou, while those who could afford it had sought shelter in the International Settlement in Shanghai, as they had in 1932. Some who had gone to Shanghai returned toward the end of January just as the new committee was being formed. The team hoped to entice some of these people onto the SGC, not only to improve the reputation of the committee but also to use them as a counterweight against the factions among the existing members who were fighting over the prospect (still largely imaginary) of making a quick profit. The team also hoped to entice the local wealthy into investing in the new order—which at this point meant paying for committee expenses.

The pacification team's concern to shape the SGC to Japan's purposes is signaled in the regulations the Preparatory Committee drew up at the beginning of February. (By the last week in February, that name got dropped in favor of Self-Government Committee.) The committee consisted of seven sections: General Affairs, Civil Affairs, Transportation, Relief, Finance, Security, and Economy. The first of the three responsibilities assigned to the General Affairs Section is specified as: "Liaison with the army and the pacification team, and mediation work of all sorts with the army." The section was thus tasked with coordinating with the Japanese military and, more specifically, with handling the contradictions that arose between the Japanese army and the local populace. These contradictions were numerous, to judge from the frequent but brief entries in the team's work diary for the first half of February that read: "Resolution of an incident involving conflict between army and people." The pacification team had been working with the same problem from the other side of the divide by lecturing Japanese soldiers as early as 10 January about not starting up conflicts with local people, but they were civilians and could not really expect to exert any authority over the military.

The Civil Affairs Section of the SGC was given three tasks. The first was to issue loyal subject certificates as their predecessor had done. The second was to run a census that would produce a complete registration of all households in the county and enable the Japanese to set up a neighborhood watch system. The third was to supply corvée labor to the Japanese army. Rates of corvée were high through the winter of 1937–38 as the Japanese army struggled to repair the damage it had done. Japanese interest was only in infrastructure, however. Damaged housing they left to the people to restore, and that took time. A provincial inspection in December 1938 found that the city and suburbs had suffered from "extremely severe" devastation from bombing and fire and that, even a year later, the damage had still not been cleared.[20]

The regulations for the other SGC sections have the same drift: tooling the committee's functions to the needs of the occupying power. The rules covering the Economic Section states, for instance, that until such time as merchants appointed by the Pacification Department in Shanghai arrive in

Jiading to engage in economic recovery, this section will buy up materials needed in the current emergency. It specifies raw cotton, the hinterland agricultural commodity Shanghai most needed. Without it the Japanese cotton mills in the city could not operate. Japanese mill owners were sufficiently anxious that their supply of cotton be restored that the Japanese Cotton-Spinning Association sent four representatives to Jiading as early as 28 December to investigate the situation. It was arranged that the SGC would appoint agents to buy up raw cotton from rural producers on a monopoly basis, then contract for shipping it to Shanghai. The military embargo on the use of inland waterways made this the greater challenge. The Jiading team was able to get the Tōyō Cotton Company to arrange shipping in exchange for a monopoly on the wholesale purchase of Jiading cotton. Local growers benefited from this deal. Brokers in 1938 paid them twelve yen per 100 catties (roughly 60 kilograms), an increase of 20 percent over the prewar price.[21] The price would go to twenty yen the following year.

The pressure to reopen trade routes pulled against the army's need to control the movement of goods and people for security reasons. This meant that the team had to maintain a tight embargo on illegal travel. On 17 February, for instance, and again the following day, it issued a notice banning boat travel at night. At the same time, the movement of goods and people was essential for restoring the economic well-being of the county. The team was particularly desperate to get the population of Jiading up to what it had been before the invasion, so it wanted every possible channel left open for former residents to return from Shanghai, bringing with them their resources and contacts. The team called a meeting with the SGC's Transportation Section on the 18th to figure out how transportation links might be improved. The section agreed to operate two boats to ferry people between Jiading and Shanghai. Only on these boats was it legal to travel to and from Shanghai. A month later, however, the Transportation Section found itself in conflict with Shanghai's Great Way Government over the taxation of these boats. The latter, it seems, was unilaterally imposing a stiff levy on the SGC's boats, which was impeding the flow of people and goods between the city and the county. The Jiading SGC brought this to the team's attention in late March, hoping that it might intervene. The team could only show an empty hand, for it had no clout to influence what went on in Shanghai.

Did any of this work lend the SGC administrative power? The pacification team report suggests not at all. The evening before the committee began operating on 3 February, the pacification team held a reception in the committee's headquarters with Japanese officers and prominent local people to encourage links among those who would thenceforth be running Jiading. The following afternoon, the team called all committee members to its office to, as reported in its diary, "give direction regarding the conduct of business."[22] In theory the team may have wanted a county administration that did not look like a puppet, yet it treated the SGC as precisely that. Its report gives the distinct impression that the pacification team initiated most of the SGC's projects, everything from getting the roads cleaned to enforcing the ban on public meetings by sending police patrols into teahouses. Indeed, the team not only made up the public orders but put its name on them. On 25 December, a proclamation against removing goods from the city went out over the names of both the PMC and the team. Thereafter, the pacification team disappeared as the posted voice of authority. So, for example, the public notice of 12 January listing punishments for crimes, which the team drew up, bore only the SGC's name. The team went on to compose many more public notices—banning the cutting down of electricity poles for lumber (early February), demanding that weapons be collected (14 February), ordering the removal of corpses (18 February), cordoning off a rifle range (22 February), outlining antiaircraft procedures (21 March)—but all appeared over the name of the SGC.

The pacification team was concerned to extend its administrative reach into the countryside, as was the SGC. The Peace Maintenance Committee that predated the team's arrival had set up branch committees in Loutang and Xujiahang. The team sponsored two more in January and another two in February (at Waigang, Sunbangqiao, Fangtai, and Anting). Four of these six affiliates were selected for branch status in a reorganization on 27 February that reinstituted the five-district jurisdictional system of Republican Jiading. That left one district without a committee: the railway town of Nanxiang. The invasion had damaged it too severely for any sort of leadership agency to be formed there for the first few months. Kumagai was finally able to oversee the installation of a branch committee in Nanxiang on 5 March. The resulting SGC structure consisted of a general committee overseeing five district committees in Xujiahang, Loutang, Waigang, Fangtai, and Nanxiang.

Kumagai reflects on the tortuousness of this process of committee proliferation in his memoir:

Subcommittees were organized in the various districts throughout the county. Because of the security situation along with various internal difficulties, we lost contact with these subcommittees on several occasions. Under certain conditions we had to "supervise" them into becoming healthy self-government organizations. More than a few times we were at a loss to know what to do. I won't write out in detail all the various situations and difficulties that arose, but at that time I didn't let the question of whether or not I lived up to the title of "supervisor" trouble me overly. The "supervision" or "work" I did was in fact simple work and supervision; what concerned me was whether it was of any use. More essential than any theory of political organization or economic work is one's "sincerity." The sincerity of really trying to save the peasantry and rebuild the villages is more important than any political work: that is true politics.[23]

Kumagai found it difficult to work with the opportunistic elites on the branch committees. "Rebuilding the villages" may indeed not have been high on their agenda; on the other hand, his complaint that these committees were unhealthy may signal that their perspective was not his, that passively accepting Japanese "supervision" was not their chief priority. Their first interests were local, and whenever the state appeared to encroach on these interests, they could be expected to create the sorts of difficulties that Kumagai only alludes to.

Once the five branch committees were in place, Kumagai could report back to the Pacification Department in Shanghai that the first stage in the construction of a countywide administration was completed. That is, appearances were in place. The second stage was now to "give substance" to this administrative system. Part of this task involved gaining control of self-government committees that were operating independently of the main committee and the pacification team. The head of the branch committee in Fangtai, for example, reported on 5 March that "bad elements" had formed rogue PMCs in the two railway towns, Anting and Huangdu, for the purpose of exacting illegal levies. The following day, Kumagai drove out with two other team members and several SGC members to Anting to take control of that branch committee and inspect its financial records. Would-be collaborators were increasing local instability, not defusing it.

Security problems only grew after the main Japanese force moved west. In late April, Chinese soldiers moved in across Jiading's western and southern borders from Kunshan and Qingpu counties and established contacts with town elites in these areas. When a man named Zhao Jitang set up an unauthorized PMC in Jiwangmiao west of Nanxiang toward the Qingpu border and started collecting weapons, the pacification team suspected that he was passing these weapons on to the guerrillas. The team's lack of control outside the largest half dozen towns where the authorized branch committees were located left local control in local hands. On one occasion when Kumagai was in Loutang, he discovered how ambiguous that control could be. He describes taking part in a predawn raid on a boat at Loutang in which four "bandits" were captured. With them was a girl whom he recognized as the daughter of a trusted associate of the local PMC. When he asked the girl's father about this, the man told Kumagai that his daughter had gone out shopping two or three days earlier and had not returned. It did not occur to Kumagai that he may have stumbled on a situation far more complicated than he realized, in which local families were doing what they could to appear to be cooperating with the Japanese while working with the other side.

These complications indicate that the occupation state was unable to operate reliably at the most local level. The first sign in the team's work diary that the SGC was not performing according to standards is an entry for 20 February stating that the team had drawn up a list of all employees of the committee, presumably with the purpose of vetting them. Two days later (22 February) the team convened all SGC members plus the heads of the branch committees in Loutang and Xujiahang to discuss what it politely termed "policies to strengthen the organization." A report four days later that SGC employees were mixing with bad elements in the teahouses —presumably selling favors—confirmed Kumagai's sense that the committee was out of control. Kumagai decided to take the initiative. On the 23rd he called in Sun Yunsheng and another leading member of the committee, Li Pinxian, to explain that he planned to appoint a former Nationalist district head to run the county's affairs. Four days later (27 February) he put forward a reorganization plan that the pacification team would impose on the SGC and its branch committees. Kumagai could not trust these people to comb out those elements in the new grassroots he considered liabilities.

The sense that the SGC was not meeting the team's expectations only grew through March. Li Pinxian removed himself with the excuse that he was ill—at least, that is how his sudden absence from the committee as of

27 February is explained, leaving Sun Yunsheng in charge of the committee. Kumagai met with Sun on 2 March to warn him that one of the original members, Wu Hongsheng, would be removed the following day for "illegal activities" considered damaging to the reputation of the committee. He also issued Sun with "strict orders" to set up the neighborhood watch system and a commodity purchasing cooperative, the two institutions the Japanese planners regarded as critical to making the occupation viable.

If creating the grassroots of an occupation regime seemed difficult, so too did financing it. Under the heading "Current Funds and Budget" in early February, the entry is simple and clear: "None," it states. "In process." The pacification team reported that the committee had only a few thousand yuan on hand, and recognized that secure funding was essential if the SGC were to continue to function. The Japanese were not going to underwrite expenses from above; these had to be met locally.

The only sources of income mentioned in early February are the fees for the loyal subject certificates (5 fen) and for boat passage between Shanghai and Jiading (1 yuan, or 100 fen). Other taxes were imposed on an ad hoc basis. Weak security outside the town of Jiading meant that no taxes could be collected beyond the wall. The assassination of tax collector Zhang Liangui further stalled the attempt. The main hope for fiscal income was urban business taxes. As people returned in greater numbers, the businesses that had shut down reopened (the only businesses operating in December 1937 were two tofu makers and a watch repair shop). Boys on bicycles were soon making the trip into Shanghai to buy things for local peddlers to sell—the older boys could do two runs a day—but this was business on a very modest scale. By mid-March, though, 268 businesses had obtained permits to operate. The SGC could now look forward to collecting fees on butchers, tea house proprietors, and, after they were registered on 4 April, opium retailers.[24]

The pacification team was painfully aware that the occupation state could never become stable without long-term funding sources. So long as the local regime could not afford such normalizing gestures as reopening primary schools, it could not begin to assert that it legitimately served the needs of the local community, and therefore had the right to tax. While the SGC took the only course open to it of taxing the urban businesses that could not avoid the collectors, the team took a different tack and decided to solicit financial and political support from the absentee local elite. The team in neighboring Taicang had already been to Shanghai three weeks earlier, hoping to use that county's native-place association as a bridge to the powerful people who might be coaxed into investing in their home county. On 16 March, two members of the Jiading team did the same. They went to talk to the leaders of the Jiading Native-Place Association in Shanghai, suggesting that they contribute to the costs of reestablishing order in their home county and invest in the economy on which most relied to do business in Shanghai.

The businessmen were reluctant even to meet the pacification agents. Eventually they agreed to share a meal in a restaurant in the French Concession. The Jiading team's bid failed, just as the Taicang team's had. In his memoir, Kumagai obscures his team's failure by picturing the businessmen they talked to as unattractively Westernized. He singles out the thirty-five-year-old who served as their spokesman:

> What came out of his mouth was not Chinese but a foreign language, surprisingly enough. He had an affluent manner and was dressed in the finest. The impression he made on me was of someone who wasn't Chinese, but had to be American or English. How could this sort of person, who seemed to have lost his feeling as a Chinese national, hope to make any contribution to Chinese or East Asian culture? It would be much better if Chinese looked and acted like Chinese.[25]

By pitting "East Asian" against "Western," Kumagai is able to transform his failure to engage the people he desperately needed to collaborate into an argument that they should have no role in sending China back to its peasant future. "The real strength of China lies in the villages after all," he concluded. The dialogic relationship these Jiading businessmen had with Western culture, common enough among those who lived in Shanghai, was a problem for Kumagai. It did not just set them apart from his stereotype of Chinese peasants; it nurtured an "unhealthy nationalism" that pulled them away from his bid that they should serve Japan's interests in order to serve China's. Kumagai probably believed his characterization of Chinese businessmen as culturally aberrant, though whether he did does not matter. It was useful to him as what John Dower in another context has called a "middle-level discourse" in the rhetoric of war ideology: "commentaries on the enemy—and the self" that skirt race prejudice but decline to acknowledge the policy calculations underpinning the discourse.

Kumagai wanted to rebuild New China along healthy Asian lines by creating a local administration that could help Japan achieve its political and economic goals in China. Although an SGC did come into being to create the appearance of self-government, the larger success he looked for eluded him. He decided to force the SGC onto a new course. Realizing that Sun Yunsheng was not going to build an effective or responsible administration on his own initiative, on 21 March he ordered him to carry out a complete reorganization: make new appointments, devise new regulations governing the main and branch committees and their members, order his rural appointees to get the neighborhood watch system going, and promulgate whatever other regulations were necessary to get control of the situation. Kumagai continued to hold out hope that prominent members of the established elite would join the influx of Jiading natives returning to the county in April and take over the reins from Sun. To the end he was unable to report any catches for leadership positions.

This hope was in any case more than outweighed by the guerrilla activity in the countryside that was challenging his claim that Jiading was returning to normal.[26] On 10 April he wrote in his personal diary (as redacted for his memoir):

> During the first ten days of this month as the crops have grown tall and the tree foliage has filled in, there has been a surge of activity by bad people outside the city wall. Every night the racket of gunfire becomes intense. It seems that they are taking advantage of the turnover of the garrison here. Information repeatedly reaches us of shootings and robberies in the villages, particularly attacks on wealthy farmers. Suddenly we are facing a dramatic worsening in the security situation. The level of alert is so serious that every night when the pacification team member on duty is relieved, his replacement is under orders not to sleep.[27]

Kumagai wanted to hear in the gunfire the sound of banditry, but he was beginning to hear the sound of political resistance. Guerrilla units were becoming increasingly active in the areas around Fangtai and Huangdu, and on two occasions actually occupied the SGC's branch committee offices in both Waigang and Loutang. The latter occupation, on 22 April, involved a force of forty soldiers and fifty irregulars of both sexes. The guerrillas were not simply engaging in shows of force to humiliate the collaborators. In Waigang they assassinated an SGC bureau head, along with a notorious bandit leader operating in the area. Committee members were becoming extremely anxious, according to Kumagai. The daytime successes that the committee could report for April—two schools reopened, thirty police-men in training, and one Japanese language school in operation—seem insignificant when set against the nightly reminders of armed insurrection and assassination.

The Japanese team leader in neighboring Taicang was facing the same instability in his rural areas. He insisted in a work diary entry in mid-April that "the pacification team, the garrison, and the SGC are in tight unity with each other, three bodies with one mind. Given the current arrests of destabilizing elements and the predations of bandits, we must devote our-selves thoroughly to winning the hearts and minds of the rural people." This hopeful gloss appears at the end of a frank account of the difficulties that pacification work faced that spring. It reads like a description of the situation Kumagai faced in Jiading:

> Within the county many continue to engage in ideological disruption. First of all we have a situation in which bandits continue to be active. Then there are these facts: those who constitute the SGC became its con-stituents during the most hectic phase following the Incident, and none of the administrators anywhere in the county is qualified for his post. On both the material and the psychological fronts it is extremely difficult to win the hearts and minds of the people of the county. On top of this, in almost all their undertakings, the SGC does nothing but wait to be di-rected by the pacification team. Especially as long as security in the county cannot be guaranteed, nothing can be done. It is because of this that the SGC is powerless to carry out anything.[28]

Tamaki and Kumagai both held out the hope that a successful campaign of military suppression would give the rural people what they wanted, peace and security from bandits and relief from the financial extortions of Nationalist guerrillas that, they assumed, were draining the last reservoir of peasant support for Chiang's regime. Ridding the people of their oppres-sors would give the Japanese those elusive hearts and minds—or so Tamaki insisted in his report back to Shanghai of the campaign he and the local garrison coordinated in May. The assassination of two SGC employees on the 30th of the month belied the claim.[29] In fact, a reasonable measure of security would not be achieved at least until the end of 1939, when a large operation involving both Japanese and Chinese troops drove the resistance forces out of these counties. Hearts and minds were another matter.

In the summer of 1938, the structure of the occupation regime changed.

The local committees were canceled and the grassroots approach of the pacification teams was abandoned in favor of a top-down "regularization" of local administrations. The SGC became a county administration, and the SGC head was replaced by a magistrate appointed by the province. A local named Feng Chengqiu took office as the magistrate on 25 June.[30] Feng survived the subsequent reorganization that converted the county of Jiading into a district of Shanghai. His actual authority commanded little, however. A year later, in a May 1939 work report to the central government, Feng candidly acknowledged that he had accomplished next to nothing in his first year in office.[31] A rural survey team the Asia Development Board sent in two months later to investigate rural conditions agreed. As they phrased their experience of rural Jiading, "It was so bad that when you took one step outside the city wall, you felt yourself in danger."[32] When Feng was required to convene a mass celebration on 16 October 1939 to mark the first anniversary of having becoming part of the municipality, he kept up appearances by putting together a morning meeting in the primary school, an afternoon parade, and an evening lantern procession. The article describing this event in the *New Jiading Daily* survives because a Jiading official made a point of sending it to the Shanghai municipal government to show that the order had been complied with. It is preserved in the Shanghai Municipal Archives along with other clippings and seven photographs, six of performances and parades and one of a meeting in the Confucian Temple.[33] A quick glance at the photographs reveals that the participants in the six pictures of performances and parades, as well as the audience in the seventh taken in the Confucian Temple, were all primary school children. Children, it seems, were the only constituency Feng Chengqiu could mobilize for the occasion.

There is no record of what happened to the old PMC/SGC cronies who, for a brief time in the winter and spring of 1938, thought they had taken the power of the state into their own hands. SGC head Sun Yunsheng disappears from the documentary record, though we should not read too much significance into this silence, given that no documents touching on administrative or political matters during the next few years survive in the Jiading District Archives. Not until 1943 is there anything to consult, and then only a roster of district heads from June of that year, on which not one of the early collaborators is named, and the minutes of the district affairs meetings in July and November of that year.[34] After two more purges followed by the removal of Magistrate Feng in favor of an outsider in February 1941, an entirely different group came to power. The "grassroots," such as it had been, was now twice gone.

In the course of establishing an occupation regime, the Japanese placed themselves under pressure to complete several tasks quickly. This short history of the early occupation in Jiading has sketched these tasks. We will come back to each of them in more detail in the following chapters as we watch pacification teams elsewhere on the Yangtze Delta apply the SSD guidelines to local conditions that often baffled their efforts. The first stage, after clearing away the rubble and the corpses and setting up some kind of temporary shelter for the homeless, was to build the grassroots leadership for the new occupation state, first in the county seat and then in the outlying towns. The second stage, though it was not always the second to get dealt with successfully, was to extract revenue. There were the costs of local administration to cover; beyond that lay the costs that the invader was bearing to occupy China, which Japan intended to recoup. The Japanese army might make one-time-only grants to local collaborators, but it had no intention of paying for collaboration. Nor did it have the funds to do so. The occupation was a low-budget operation that relied on windfalls, confiscations, and extralegal exactions. It was the pacification team's job to set up a no-cost administration by constructing a stable local revenue stream.

Consolidating the first two tasks dictated a third: sponsoring a regime plausible to ordinary people and sufficiently compelling to elites that they might be induced to support it. The undesirables who popped up as willing collaborators in the early weeks of the occupation proved, at this later stage of building the occupation state at the local level, to be the greatest liability. Some mismanagement and some theft of financial resources on their part would probably not be enough to scuttle an SGC, but gross misconduct and a complete lack of moral or political authority could doom a local body struggling to appear as though it were the legitimate government of the county. The real corrosive, though, was the lack of security. If the pacification team's political success rested on the unspoken military hegemony of the Japanese army, so too its effectiveness in bringing about a normalization of economy and ideology demanded the safety that only armed soldiers could provide. The administrative and economic affairs of the county could not be run without this protection. If tax collectors, teachers, and editors were vulnerable to assassination, no taxes could be collected, no schools opened, and no newspapers published to counter the propaganda from the other side. And if team members could not ensure this, it was unlikely that their puppets, to use an unkind but reasonably fair description of most of the men they worked with in Jiading, could do it for them. Ongoing instability in the countryside testified to the apparent impossibility of imposing the occupation state much beyond the county town.[35]

Working sometimes together, sometimes at odds, the pacification agents and their collaborators assembled what looked to be a functioning civil administration. If they could put little substance behind the appearance, it was because, each step of the way, they were dogged by the conditions that invasion produced. We have seen many examples of this effect: order restored early on, but no houses to inhabit; urban residents returning, but only to remove their belongings; loyal subject certificates issued, but to generate revenue rather than to produce a reliable census; the self-government committee replacing the PMC, but without any turnover in membership; rural elites forming SGC branches, but to pursue their own interests rather than to facilitate the operations of the occupation state. Despite Kumagai's best efforts, the result was just the sort of camera pacification that he despised. Best efforts were not enough to guarantee substance. That required an entirely different relationship with his collaborators, and one that, under these circumstances, neither was in a position to build.

Kumagai left Jiading at the end of April for his next pacification assignment north of the Yangtze River in Bengbu, the provincial capital of Anhui. Shortly after reaching his new post, he sent money back to a Chinese friend in Jiading, asking him to buy a gift for his godson, Guoshu. Guoshu's father was a member of the Jiading SGC who had pressed Kumagai many times that spring to enter into an adoptive relationship with his elder son. Commending a son to a friend was a common practice in Jiading, a device through which a father hoped to advance his son's social position. The adopted godson did not move in with his godfather, but he could expect help and favors in the future. Kumagai had been cautious, but the father would not allow the request to quietly lapse. Kumagai agreed at last to go through with the adoption ceremony. He was not so naive as to be blind to what the boy's father was doing, which was to secure a tight relationship with the most powerful person in the county. But Guoshu called him "Papa" and Kumagai was charmed.

Some time after sending the money, Kumagai received a letter back from Guoshu. It ended with these words:

A few days ago, Mister Zhang told me that you sent him a letter asking him to buy something for me to remember you by. I was really excited. Mister Zhang asked me what I would like. I thought that buying a watch would be good, because I would look at the watch all the time, and that would be just like seeing you all the time.

I won't write any more now. I wish you good health.

Your godson,

Guoshu[36]

After completing his assignment in Bengbu, Kumagai returned to Shanghai. Guoshu's father brought his son into the city several times to see him after he first got back. Then, without warning or explanation, the visits stopped. Kumagai could not understand why the warm connection with Guoshu and his father had gone cold. "Some profound change must have happened," he reasoned. "I kept thinking that I would see them."

They never came back, and he could not think why. The occupier should have been able to think his way through the barren calculations behind the relationship between himself and Guoshu and know better than to feel bereft. This too was just another gesture in the appearance of compliance that the occupation demanded. To admit that he was not dear to the boy would force him to rename his relationship with Guoshu's canny father as coercion, and the father's with him as collaboration, and that Kumagai could not afford to do.

— 4 —

Costs / Zhenjiang

Invasion is a costly undertaking. The invader must bear the costs of launching an overseas military invasion and maintaining an army of occupation on foreign soil, with little prospect of recouping any of those costs soon except through looting. The invaded suffer the deficits that warfare and disruption produce in the form of losses to property, infrastructure, and productive capacity, none of which can be restored rapidly. Farmers lose labor, draft animals, and access to markets. Industries in targeted urban zones are vulnerable to military bombing and confiscation; even those able to go back into production, as we shall see in the case of Zhenjiang, could shut down for want of raw materials and reliable systems of transport. Beyond the costs of repairing the damage of an invasion, there are the costs of resurrecting an economy in shock: reopening transportation arteries, guaranteeing the safety of investment, and providing replacement assets for what the war has destroyed. Without immediate investments, the state has nothing on which to depend for its financial viability, and in turn cannot afford to make the necessary investments to escape the vicious circle of revenue collapse. With no crops in the ground, there is nothing for the state to tax; with no funds to pay police to protect the tax collectors even if there were a harvest, the result is the same.

Japan had to shoulder the first costs of its invasion, but that subsidy could not continue. Pacification agents were therefore anxious that collaborators find their own sources of revenue and not expect to survive on handouts from the military. Helping the agents achieve that self-reliance brought them up against the core contradiction of armed occupation: the opposition between the rationality of destroying the capacity of the enemy to resist, and the rationality of protecting economic assets so that the enemy can produce for the occupying power. The collaborator in his turn was immobilized by the contradiction inherent in his own relationship to power, which derived from serving the economic interests of local people while also serving the economic interests of those who recruited him. Having to manage this contradiction was the price of entry into collaboration politics. Conventional wisdom has it that collaborators were motivated by greed and got rich from serving the enemy. Such may have been the case in some locations, but the evidence from Zhenjiang shows the leading collaborator paying a high price for his collaboration.

The financial predicament of the occupation state is that it must do all its cost accounting in the short term, when legitimate revenue has evaporated and the costs of reconstruction are high; and further, that so long as instability continues, losses cannot be set against gains even in the medium term. Toward the end of this chapter I will consider the question of whether Japan's conquest of the Yangtze Valley paid off. Though the available data is incomplete and unreliable, it does suggest that it didn't. What rewards then could there be for the collaborators? And yet many were willing to make the gamble.

The city of Zhenjiang would not be defended. As the county capitals to the east fell one after the other to the Japanese army, Jiading among them, the Interior Ministry ordered the evacuation of all transportation corridors through which the invaders were expected to advance. The city of Zhenjiang, at that time the provincial capital of Jiangsu, was where the Shanghai-Nanjing railway and the Grand Canal converged at the Yangtze River. Strategic and vulnerable, it was an important target for attack. The wealthy decamped first, either to Shanghai or further up the Yangtze River. Provincial and municipal employees followed in mid-November, most of them gone by the 23rd, when police presence was reduced to a few patrolmen at the city's main intersections. The last of the city's banks shut their doors the next day. Zhenjiang had already experienced intermittent bombing from the air, but intense bombardment three days later convinced those who had hesitated that it was time to leave. Boat passage across the river had become almost impossible to arrange by then, with the government and the military requisitioning anything that floated. For many the only option was to flee on foot into the hills to the southwest. It is impossible to estimate how many of the city's original 210,000 residents, or the county's prewar of population of 476,000, still remained at the end of November.[1]

Those left behind either had nowhere to go, or were too elderly to flee, or else stayed because they had something to protect. Abandoned in their midst were many wounded soldiers, casualties of the war further east. They had been coming in from Danyang to the southeast by rail and canal for several days. Now that there was no more transport to get them out, they were left to sicken, suffer, and die on the platforms of the train station and in barges moored by the city wall. Zhang Yibo, the manager of a mosquito-coil factory, saw some of them by the New West Gate on the evening of the 28th, begging to be taken to a hospital. In his moving memoir of the occupation of Zhenjiang, Zhang recounts what he did to ease their distress, though there was little he could do.[2] "By this time the rickshaws had long since disappeared, and besides, there were no hospitals to send them to. All that could be done was to help the wounded up onto the bridgehead and sit them down over by the food stalls." Zhang had food and water brought, but many refused to take anything because their wounds made it impossible for them to urinate. "Among them there was a child soldier so distressed that no one was there to care for wounded combatants like him that he could not stop the tears streaming down his face. It so hurt to see him." Zhang left the boy and the others at the New West Gate that evening, distressed over how little he could do for them. That night, the Japanese army shelled the gate. Zhang does not say whether the soldiers were there the following day, only that he saw bombed barges lying half submerged in the canal and several barge women in tears running along the banks of the canal. A day and a half later the city's garrison withdrew, leaving a small group of defenders to perform what everyone knew was suicide duty. The last Nationalist Party officials departed, leaving behind posters exhorting the people to "Defend Zhenjiang!" well after that was possible.

Nine days after Zhenjiang was abandoned, two units of the 13th Division (one of them under Major-General Amaya Naojirō, who would go on to take command of the garrison in Nanjing) entered the city through the South Gate. A clatter of gunfire at noon on 8 December announced their arrival. Residents sheltered indoors while the army pounded away at the few defensive posts that still held outside the city. Early the next morning, the looting began. Thoroughly and systematically, under the supervision of their officers, the soldiers entered each house in the city, stripped it of its contents, and ripped everything apart looking for hidden money and goods. Anything that could be lifted or pried loose was removed. Ancestor portraits were carried off as though they were valuable works of art. ("Only later," notes Zhang Yibo, "when collaborators pointed out to them

that these were not old paintings, did they stop taking them.") Light fix-
tures were smashed so that the light bulbs could be removed—an item the
Japanese army appeared to have run out of. Anything not wanted was
thrown into the streets and set alight. The soldiers entered the houses at
least half a dozen times every day from dawn to dusk for many days, just in
case anything had been missed the first, or the second, or the twentieth
time. "A river that flowed unceasingly" is how Zhang Yibo describes the
endless parade of soldiers passing through his home. "Thus, within just a
few days of the enemy army entering the city, every house was ransacked,
with things strewn about everywhere. Houses no longer resembled homes:
they were just trash heaps where there was no place even to step." The cru-
dity, filth, and wastefulness of the soldiers amazed him not just as deplorable but as going completely against type. He had been given to understand that the Japanese were a clean and aesthetically sensitive people; he
was wrong.

With the looting came the more serious attacks on persons. People were
killed if they refused soldiers entry or otherwise interfered with them;
those who had hidden themselves were shot just for being found; men who
either refused or helped soldiers to procure women were shot. Men and
boys were rounded up for labor service, and many did not return. Women
and girls who disguised themselves or kept hidden were raped upon discovery. As the Japanese soldiers were nervous about raping the women
who lived in the poor barrios for fear of being attacked, they burned them
out rather than go in and rape them in their huts. Some women chose
drowning when they saw no other escape. Many managed to get to the
shelter of the refugee camps, where they outnumbered the men two to one.
Even there, though, they were not completely safe. Zhang reports that
camp guards in three of the camps raped females in their custody, one of
them a thirteen-year-old girl. The wounded soldiers who were captured
fared worse than the women. Zhang did not himself witness them being
doused with gasoline and torched, but he heard about it from others. At
several locations around the South Gate, as these scenes were described to
him, "many wounded soldiers, who had been tied together in groups,
mostly face down, were burned. Their corpses had the sheen of black lac-
quer and their limbs were all contorted. Crawling on the ground they
looked like turtles. No one could bear to look." Had the boy in tears at the
New West Gate managed to survive the bombings, his wounds, and ne-
glect, this would have been his end.

Burying abandoned corpses fell to the Red Swastika Society. This voluntary organization, which had grown in popularity in the 1920s, was an indigenous alternative to the Red Cross Society. The Buddhist swastika replaced the Christian cross as the symbol of moral duty, allowing Chinese elites to take up Western models of civic modernity without doing so at the expense of their own traditions. It was a move that appealed to more traditionally minded elites in the Republican period, who chose to resist the fad of adopting Western models in all things that swept the younger generation. The head of the society's Zhenjiang chapter made his first report to the pacification team on 28 December, in which he stated that his burial teams had disposed of 292 bodies in and around city over the preceding ten days. This was only the beginning of their work. Zhang Yibo heard later that the Red Swastika buried between 1,400 and 1,500 that winter. After the war, the leader of one of the burial teams, Yang Fosheng, recalled the total as being between 1,500 and 1,600. Not all who died received a Red Swastika burial. A postwar investigation put the death toll in excess of 10,000.[3]

Zhang Yibo's analysis of the violence is straightforward: killing Chinese was a way for Japanese soldiers to indulge their pleasure at having been victorious in battle. It was simply "very satisfying."[4] He saw no need to go looking for any deeper psychological or cultural explanation. The explanation was war.

The burning of the city began a day or two after the first round of looting. For ten days the air was thick with smoke and the nights were lit by glittering flames. Zhenjiang's shantytown was gutted, though the poorest neighborhoods sought to protect themselves by hanging out more Japanese flags. In the more prosperous parts of the city, the burning was selective, though it included all the major commercial streets as well as many schools and five of the most prominent Buddhist monasteries in the province. For Zhang, these fires too were no mystery. They were set in order to destroy China's wealth and cripple its economy. "The main reason why the entire city was burned so extensively had to be their intention to destroy our property. Everywhere a fire was set, it was on their orders. Of course there were no firemen to put the fires out. Anyway, the enemy soldiers would certainly not have permitted that." Zhang later reports that "several people in fact were executed on the spot for trying to put out fires."[5] The Japanese army might have considered other needs, such as sheltering the population and getting the economy running to Japan's advantage, before

Zhang Yibo. From his *Zhenjiang lunxian ji* (reprint, 1999).

accepting the decision to burn the city. But again from Zhang's perspective, such thinking was less compelling than the pleasure of inflicting ruin. A pacification team report acknowledged that the arriving soldiers may have burned up to 60 percent of the commercial area of the city.

The atrocities are not irrelevant to the subject, inasmuch as the decision to collaborate took place in an environment of violence, rape, and destruction. To understand why some people decided to work with the occupiers one has to take this background into account, whether as a disincentive that collaborators had to reconcile in their own minds or as a goad prompting them to come forward and ease the plight of the defenseless. We are able to probe this aspect of the experience of occupation because of the survival of *Zhenjiang lunxian ji* (A record of Zhenjiang under occupation), the detailed record that Zhang Yibo wrote of the city's first two months of occupation. Zhang's memoir testifies that what Japanese soldiers went on to do a week later during the infamous Rape of Nanjing was consistent with previous conduct.

The military destruction bequeathed to the occupation regime economic as well as moral deficits. Fragmentary economic data in the two Zhenjiang pacification reports of 1938 and 1939 make it possible to sketch the financial burdens that invasion and occupation imposed on this county, and to track some of the initiatives that were attempted to get the local administration operating in the black. As we shall see, no viable solution was found.

As it did elsewhere, the Japanese invasion reduced civilians to refugees. In the city of Zhenjiang, ten thousand people without home or support ended up in seven refugee camps. Two were organized by Chinese, two by Zhenjiang's Muslim communities (all four of these were under Japanese supervision), and three by Christians. The camp at the power plant belonging to the Dazhao (Great Illumination) Company sheltered six hundred people, and the camp at the provincial teaching hospital provided refuge for another thousand. Of the Muslim camps, one was at the East Mosque, which housed two thousand people; the other was at the West Mosque, where four hundred sheltered. Muslims had been resident in Zhenjiang since the Tang dynasty, when Persian traders arrived and built their first mosque. When the Wahhabiyya or Muslim Brotherhood came to Zhenjiang to reform Chinese Islam in the 1930s, they split the community, which is why there had to be two camps. Unlike the other camps in the city where some grain had been stockpiled, the Muslim camps were chronically short of food (their leaders repeatedly came to the pacification office asking for grain). It is also striking that they housed a higher proportion of children (50 percent, as compared to 40 percent in the other two). Muslim families likely had fewer family ties to the rural areas where others were able to send their children for safety as the Japanese army approached.[6]

The remaining six thousand refugees appear to have ended up in three camps run by Christian congregations in Zhenjiang, though I have been unable to track down any information about these camps. The only report I have found on Christian philanthropy in the city comes from a 1939 survey of wartime conditions published by a group calling itself the American Information Committee in Shanghai. Their pamphlet, based on missionary reports coming from the hinterland, reports that six British and American missionary societies supported an International Relief Committee in Zhenjiang that fed fifteen thousand people a month between October 1938 to April 1939.[7] Presumably they were on site providing similar aid during the first winter of the occupation. There is an echo of the churches' presence in a report that the head of the pacification team made in December 1938. He wrote that he had become troubled by the degree to which their relief work had strengthened the "concept of reliance on EuroAmerica," and for this reason was asking his superiors in Shanghai for policy guidelines on how to diminish the Christian presence. The team reports contain no other information about these camps, probably because Westerners were under the purview of the Military Police rather than the Special Service, which dealt only with Chinese.

It is unclear when the pacification team arrived in Zhenjiang. A Mantetsu report to the SSD in March records its arrival on 19 December, though the team's own report dates the start of its work one week later, on the 26th.[8] The first entry that the Mantetsu report takes from the team's work diary, dated the 26th, records a meeting between the team and the garrison commander to determine where the food to feed the refugees was to come from. The following day, team leader Nakayama Yojirō led his five team members to the camp at the provincial hospital to investigate the situation on site. Zhang Yibo's wife was at the power plant that day. A Japanese officer whom she could not identify assembled the refugees there and gave them a talk about how disciplined the Japanese soldiers were and how much they deserved the refugees' respect.[9] This might have been Nakayama trying to make a good first impression, and failing.

The team's immediate task was to see that the refugees were fed, but that was only part of the larger objective of reestablishing civil order in Zhenjiang. The camps were necessary, but the camps were short term. The team's objective was to close them as soon as possible and get all refugees back into their homes. Given the damage and looting, though, this would take some time. Those who could leave, once they felt reasonably sure of not being molested by Japanese soldiers, preferred to do so rather than remain in the camps. By mid-February, the number of refugees under team supervision was down to 2,813, most of whom had no homes to go to or were too indigent to support themselves.[10] These people remained the indissoluble core of the homeless in Zhenjiang. In mid-March, the team washed its hands of the camps and passed them over to the Self-Government Committee.

The task of feeding the refugees was made easier by several fortunate circumstances. One was that the manager of the Great Illumination Company assumed all responsibility for caring for the refugees at the power plant. The other favorable factor was the store of 75,000 tons of government grain that fell into Japanese hands when the army captured Zhen-jiang. From this windfall the army could afford to siphon off the modest amount needed to feed the refugees. It did so strictly on a short-term basis, however. Rice never arrived in deliveries larger than 1,000 kilograms at one time, usually half that. Anyone leaving the camps was given only three days' worth of food with which to survive outside. Other goods that the military agreed to supply were made available only till the end of January. The brief notes in the team work diary indicate that support from the Japanese side was always short term, and intended to be understood as such by the Chinese side.

A visit to the refugee camp at the provincial hospital was one of three entries taken from the work diary for the team's second official day, 27 December, and included in the team's March report back to Shanghai. The second has to do with demands from the Japanese army that the team organize levies of matériel and labor. The entry records a meeting with a Japanese major-general to discuss how the team should serve the army's needs in these areas. Labor corvée in particular became a recurring burden for the pacification team during its first month of operation. Fifty coolies were wanted for transport work on 30 December; thirty for street cleanup on 4 January; another thirty for runway repair on the 11th; forty-seven to assist the Army Engineer Corps on the 12th, to list only a few of the requisitions the team was expected to meet. Refugees often filled these levies. Many hoped to earn a wage, though it is not clear whether they were remunerated. The army also went into the streets and dragooned labor whenever it was needed, without going through the pacification team, as Zhang Yibo notes:

> When the soldiers first arrived, forced labor was most severe; it got a little better once the city had been garrisoned for a while. Some laborers had to do transport work for the army that took them as far away as Yangzhou and Nanjing, others were put to work in the locally stationed military companies. They were taken without regard for age or status: anyone could be made their slave. In the middle of January, for instance, when order had improved and the noodle shops had reopened, a dozen men were rounded up while they were eating noodles and taken off. Even people working for the Self-Government Committee were dragooned; even children. My third son, only twelve and still immature, was ordered to

carry wood that soldiers had come to steal one morning. Only in the evening did he return, having been given nothing to eat all day.[11]

The pacification team's involvement in recruiting Chinese labor may also have extended to prostitution. Zhang Yibo reports that the Japanese army operated three brothels at Papa's Lane, Fuqiaokou, and the Little Wharf. These were staffed by Japanese subjects, presumably Koreans. There was also a Chinese brothel operating on Zhongzheng Road. Officers preferred not to go to such places and made private prostitution arrangements. So too, Zhang alleges—and it is the only such allegation I have encountered—did the pacification teams:

> Many officers have taken people's wives, either forcing them to live with them or renting them out for sex. Under the most terrifying threats, one kidnapped woman is made to service several soldiers in turn. The political organ attached to the Japanese bandit army is called a pacification team (they have created the puppet organizations everywhere and operate as the local super-government). When the team first arrived in the army's wake, its members brought with them not a few Chinese women, who allegedly had been grabbed in other places because of their beauty. When superiors are addicted to sex, their inferiors imitate them, so there was no way these officers could control their subordinates.[12]

The third entry in the pacification team's work diary for 27 December, after feeding refugees and organizing labor, touches on the matter of collaboration. The entry records that the team went that day to the garrison commander's office to ask for permission to set up a peace maintenance committee. They must have got it, for the sole diary entry for the following day reports that the team went out to recruit personnel for their organization. Unlike their counterparts in Jiading, the team did not have to spend their first months trying to get rid of the collaborators the army had already recruited. Nor had a group of Chinese already installed themselves as the new local bosses, as many attempted to do elsewhere. Thus unencumbered, the team went out on the 28th to troll among prominent people for eligible candidates for a PMC. The visits yielded success. By the end of the day, one man had been selected to become chair, and two others invited to serve as vice-chairs. They were given overnight to think about it.

The plan collapsed the next morning. Team leader Nakayama received a visit from Yan Zhu, otherwise unidentified, who the previous day had agreed to serve on the committee and then reneged. Yan thereafter disappears from the story, but he played a pivotal role on the 28th. He expressed to the team members grave doubts about the quality of the people they were putting on the PMC: "poor and weak," he called them. It seems that the Japanese agents had moved too fast and had been willing to make do with committee members they might later regret having engaged, creating just the sort of PMC that almost every other pacification team had to get rid of when they arrived, but this time without the army to blame. The team decided to follow Yan Zhu's advice and not install yesterday's tentative PMC. The excuse they used to get around the loss of face on both sides was that no PMC would be formed and that Zhenjiang would go directly to an SGC, which needed more time to assemble. Yan Zhu was likely working for or against someone's interests in making his intervention, though whose and to what purpose we cannot know. The pacification agents had not been in Zhenjiang long enough to know much about the political and social setting into which they had come, and this made them vulnerable to manipulation by one interest against another.

Having wiped the slate of candidates clean, the team started again, casting about for new people. The person they fixed on was someone whom they had met when they went out to inspect the refugee camps. Guo Zhicheng was the manager of the Great Illumination Company's power plant and the self-appointed benefactor of those stranded there as refugees. Team leader Nakayama seems to have liked and trusted Guo. He called on him on his fourth day to ask that he step forward. Guo promised to consider it, and was in line to take on the job the next day when someone else put forward a rival candidate, Yin Gongfu. Of this man nothing is known other than that he was wealthy. The team decided to go with Yin and have Guo serve as the number two man. The spare comment in the work diary entry for 30 December—"it was decided that Yin Gongfu would be installed as committee chair and that Mister Guo would provide support from within"—suggests that Nakayama regarded Guo as "his" man, someone he could rely on to steer the PMC in the right direction regardless of what Yin did. Let Yin play the public role; the real power would rest elsewhere. They met the next day at Yin's home to finalize the committee's membership. The team now felt confident enough of the group they had put together to upgrade the PMC to SGC status.

Between that meeting on 31 December and the SGC's inauguration on

10 January, the team's work report goes blank. The sole entry is a note on the 6th to say that the army had asked the SGC and the team to give up their quarters at the former Police Administration College. But something went on during those ten days, for when the SGC was made public, the line-up had changed. Guo was still number two, but Yin was now just an ordinary member and the leadership had shifted to a new figure, Liu Zhaoqing. The fifty-three-year-old Liu was a graduate of a Japanese police academy, which presumably meant that he could speak the language. Japanese records show him active in legal affairs in Nanjing in the 1910s, but reveal nothing of his subsequent career, nor indicate how he came to be the new head of the SGC. The only account that reveals hints of the process, which shows a different politics in play, is what Zhang Yibo reports in his book:

> The Zhenjiang SGC was inaugurated on 10 January. In the latter half of December, someone surnamed Yin met with others to discuss matters at the Great Illumination Power Company. At that time, Great Illumination was paying out a high salary to someone surnamed Xu, who was hired as a Japanese interpreter. Xu came from a lowly background, but being an interpreter he figured that great power was now in his grasp. He was so full of himself that even the two Guo brothers had to suck up to him. Later, the Japanese side decided that Yin was too old and muddled, and so they declined to support his becoming SGC head. After prolonged discussion and negotiation, which produced several personnel shuffles, the Japanese at long last settled on Liu in early January. It was already more than a month since the enemy army had arrived, yet the locality was still unstable and people continued to be fearful. Liu presented the Japanese side with eleven requests, the first of which was that they stop the raping and plundering. When Liu emerged to take office, he was committed to getting something done and rescuing the people from their calamity.[13]

Zhang's account and the pacification team's report diverge on a number of significant points. Yin Gongfu, whom Zhang did not know personally, comes out here as an old dotard, rather than, as in the team's report, as a wealthy rival pushing Guo Zhicheng aside. Indeed, one wonders why the collapse of Yin's candidacy did not open the way for Guo Zhicheng. It seems that the Japanese, and Guo himself, found it better to keep Guo behind the scenes. Even more intriguing is the modicum of sympathy that Zhang shows for the man who actually emerged to head the SGC, Liu

Zhaoqing. Zhang allows that Liu attempted to use his position on behalf of the people of Zhenjiang to mitigate Japanese excesses. He goes on, however, to reveal that Liu was powerless to outflank Japanese control, becoming caught in a bad situation:

> When he went to the refugee camp at the provincial medical college and addressed the assembled refugees, he wept openly and said, "I took office for your sake." The people of Zhenjiang had been facing danger for over a month and were still terrified. When they saw that Liu had come forward to restore peace, they were relieved that at long last someone was in charge of local affairs. Yet the day Liu took office, the celebratory notices that were posted up were dated to the [Japanese] Shōwa era, and the guests attending the opening ceremony had to submit to inspection by the enemy army. Then, when Liu went on parade, the person leading the way for the cavalcade carried a Japanese flag. All this showed that he had put himself under their implicit control. No longer his own master, he had let himself be pushed around. So that day when he expressed his feelings, it was as though he were asking for forgiveness.
>
> The SGC organization has been growing rapidly ever since, creating all manner of new organs. Traitors have rushed forward like ants to mutton, resorting to all sorts of devices to defraud people, so that now my compatriots are even worse off. This was not what Liu originally intended, yet he has become so enmired that he is not able to extricate himself.

Zhang's disgust with collaborators was not enough for him to condemn Liu outright. He presents the man as a tragic figure rather than an opportunist, though he gives no hint as to why he appreciated the difficulty in which Liu found himself. Liu was eventually allowed to resign, officially on 4 May, although the man who stepped in as acting head for the rest of May, Sun Zhao, was already serving in Liu's place by the end of April.[14] At the end of May, the position was finally turned over to the power plant manager, Guo Zhicheng, after the judicious three refusals.

Guo clearly wanted the job. He seems also to have been an efficient administrator, for when the SGC was reorganized out of existence on 1 August Guo was able to stay on as county magistrate. In fact, his career as a collaborator lasted longer than that of any other local SGC leader I have encountered. He survived several reorganizations all the way down to the autumn of 1944, when he finally disappears from the record. This is a remarkable run for someone recruited in the opening days of occupation.

It may signify nothing more than that he honed his ability to please the Japanese to a fine art. Given what happened in other counties, though, incompetence eventually torpedoed the careers of even the most obedient of collaborators when efficiency was at stake. Guo's managerial experience running the power plant must have provided him with at least a satisfactory level of administrative capability not to be vulnerable on that score.

Zhang Yibo refused to give Guo Zhicheng the benefit of any doubt, however. Before his book went to publication that summer, Zhang went back to his manuscript and added this passage:

> Weary of the puppet's life, SGC head Liu has left his bogus position. On 1 June the leadership switched to Guo, the manager of the Great Illumination Power Company. Guo has recently been promulgating bogus announcements regarding taxes on land, houses, lots, butchers, restaurants, hotels, and theaters, in addition to his many other harsh exactions. He is sucking the marrow out of the people's bones and leaving them wailing in the streets.[15]

Zhang indicts Guo and his younger brother for being active from the very beginning forging ties with the Japanese, evidence of which was their willingness to swallow their dignity and put up with Translator Xu. Guo Zhicheng's capture of the leadership was the payoff.

Guo Zhicheng was a great favorite of team leader Nakayama, but Nakayama could not stay long enough to work with him. Thirteen days after the SGC inauguration, Katō Kōzan arrived to take over the team leadership from Nakayama, who was transferred to Songjiang. A change in team leadership can signal that pacification was not proceeding smoothly. The team in neighboring Danyang, for instance, went through three leaders in a period of ten months, each replacement coinciding with a rise in insurgency. This seems not to have been the case when Nakayama left for Songjiang. Although pacification had begun early in Songjiang, that county proved to be one of the most intractable to pacify. A brief report in early February declared that "pacification work there was proceeding relatively smoothly,"[16] but all the weight is on the qualifier "relatively." The county experienced more turnover in Special Service personnel than any other county on the Yangtze Delta, going through two different PMCs before ever getting to an SGC. That SGC then took a long time to get up and running, and then only after stiff negotiations between Nakayama and the local Japanese garrison commander.[17]

The agent who replaced Nakayama in Zhenjiang is the other reason, besides Zhang Yibo, that it is possible to reconstruct the pacification of
Zhenjiang. In July 1939, a few months after leaving Zhenjiang, Katō Kōzan
published a two-part memoir in the *New Nanjing Daily*.[18] This memoir
lacks the detail and frankness of Zhang's, but it does at least provide both a
voice for the Japanese side and some critical observations about the pacification process in Zhenjiang. Katō was a Mantetsu employee who transferred down from Dalian to Shanghai in the second week of January to
join the second cohort of young men being sent out into Central China as
pacification agents. He received his appointment to head the Zhenjiang
team on 14 January, arrived nine days later, and slipped into Nakayama's
policies and methods with ease.

In his memoir, Katō recalls Nakayama telling him that Liu Zhaoqing,
Zhang Yibo's tragic collaborator, had been the people's choice. This strikes
me as an odd reference, in the sense that there was no need to comment on
the popularity of the SGC leadership unless there was a problem. Indeed
there seems to have been, for Katō does let slip the observation that the
SGC he inherited from Nakayama was "not terrifically ideal." Once again, a
pacification agent found himself working with people he regarded as liabilities. Katō's remark at least confirms Zhang's observation that Liu was
out of step with his Japanese handlers; perhaps it also indicates that the
Japanese were finding Liu too reluctant a collaborator to be of any real use
to them. Katō goes on to note that "the people were of one opinion"
in supporting Guo Zhicheng to take over the SGC leadership in June—
though this is not the impression that we got from Zhang. But then Katō
wants to assert that every collaborationist appointment was a popular one:
that the pacification agents were simply responding to the popular will.
Zhang Yibo rejects the entire illusion.

Katō and Zhang thus provide us with contrary versions of the Zhenjiang
occupation. At the end of the first installment of his memoir, Katō tells a
story that hints at an awareness that there could be two ways of looking at
the occupied world he oversaw. The story has to do with the pacification
team's arranging for medical services in the rural areas. This was the sort of
project that pacification teams thought would garner them popular support. In this case, however, it generated the rumor that the drugs the medical clinic was dispensing to the Chinese were addictive. The involvement of
Japanese in the contraband drug trade in occupied China gave the rumor
the ring of truth. Locals differed over whether to believe the rumor, Katō

observes, and this was because the Chinese have "two concepts of the Japanese." The difference between Katō's and Zhang's accounts of Zhenjiang under occupation stretches across just this polarity. While Katō calls for the unity of "same-race" people, Zhang declares that Japanese *fei wo zulei*, "are not of the same kin-category as us." Katō complains that Chinese should stop thinking of themselves as people of a defeated country, whereas Zhang asserts that this is exactly what they must never forget, that if Chinese "submit halfway along the course, trade war for peace, and willingly become slaves of a fallen country," they will never get their country back. Zhang speaks of "freedom,"[19] Katō of "co-prosperity." The difference between their two perspectives—their "two concepts of the Japanese"—is polar. Both have helped me to write this chapter.

Katō did not share Zhang's view of Guo Zhicheng. In his confidential work report for May 1938, he presents Guo as an ideal SGC head who had been able to attract mostly good people into the organization, a claim that Zhang flatly contradicts. The SGC's sole failure under Guo's leadership, from Katō's perspective, was its inability to ensure rural security. Katō is careful not to lay this failure at Guo's door, pointing out that wherever the countryside was stable, it was well administered. The biggest challenge to Guo's success as a collaborator would come in July, when the process of dissolving and replacing the SGC with a proper county administration got under way. (The name of the county was changed at this time to Dantu; for consistency I will continue to use Zhenjiang throughout this chapter.) Katō recommended to the provincial government, which had since been moved from Zhenjiang to the Japanese military headquarters in Suzhou, that Guo be permitted to stay on and serve as the new county magistrate. To Katō's dismay, he learned that the provincial authorities intended to parachute one of their own into the post. Katō was so keen to keep Guo in place that he went to Suzhou to plead his case in person, and to ask that the head of his secretariat be retained as well. He succeeded, though all the other committee members were removed, possibly a trade-off for allowing Guo and his assistant to keep their posts. A year later, Katō wrote in the *New Nanjing Daily* that the best thing he had done for Zhenjiang during his sixteen months there—a period during which "heaven and earth changed places," as he put it—was to get Guo appointed as magistrate.

Guo had Katō's backing; given the scale of difficulties he faced, he needed it. His first task upon taking up the magistracy in June was to attempt to consolidate the SGC's presence in rural Zhenjiang. The task had two sides, and the two sides could not be pulled apart. There was the need to recruit good people to develop the local institutions that the occupation state mandated, particularly tax collection and the neighborhood watch system. There was also the need to end insurrection. The one task could not be resolved without the other. The Japanese army feared that Chinese soldiers would infiltrate behind the lines into the Yangtze Delta in large numbers after the battle of Xuzhou in May, and put the entire region on high alert. The infiltration did not happen as quickly or as widely as was feared, but through the summer the Japanese garrison's ability to guarantee the security of rural Zhenjiang weakened. The army suspected by the end of the summer that the resistance was running a network of several thousand spies throughout Zhenjiang, Danyang, and the surrounding counties, and that this network was making it impossible to move troops without these movements being immediately detected by the other side. Japan could not continue to conquer China if it had to leave large garrisons wherever it passed, however, so Chinese would have to provide for their own security. The solution was to promote what was called "self-reliance," that is, to hand over security operations to the Chinese. As the Danyang pacification team phrased this arrangement in its work diary for April, "The fundamental approach to security should be that Chinese in the occupied areas defend the security of the occupied areas as a foundation for cooperation between Japan and China." Handing over security responsibilities would be a long process, and one in which the Japanese side was unwilling to invest much trust. The Zhenjiang pacification report for December 1938 could only offer the hopeful comment that the first step in that process had been taken with the local hiring of ninety-nine policemen.

Against this backdrop of constant disruption, Guo Zhicheng put together an administration that was supposed to extend across the entire county. He and Katō decided in his first week as magistrate to call a meeting of all sixteen district heads. They were to come in to Zhenjiang city toward the end of June, and were warned that anyone who failed to attend would be deemed an opponent of the newly founded government. Two were unable to attend because it was unsafe for them to travel, but the other fourteen showed up for the two-day meeting on 24 June. Guo's chief goal was for his subordinates to get the land tax system up and running. The reports the district heads gave at the meeting made it clear that this would not be possible: 70 percent of the county's population had fled when the Japanese army arrived, a third to a half of rural residents were still suffering deprivation, the spring wheat crop had been poor, oxen were scarce (a postwar survey of Zhenjiang claimed that the Japanese army killed or confiscated 3,490 head of oxen, horses, and donkeys),[20] rural credit was unavailable, and the district offices were working overtime on no budget to handle all the tasks that were handed down to them, including protecting the army's telephone lines.

As the resistance gained strength through the summer, the ability of the district heads to do anything but protect themselves, particularly those in the eastern and southwestern portions of the county well away from the county seat, dwindled. Information on their difficulties is scarce. Katō insists in his report for August 1938 that all that stands in the way of the people coming over to the Japanese side are the disturbances that bad elements whip up for their own benefit. If they only learned Japanese, he was sure they would abandon the anti-Japanese habits of mind that they had acquired under Nationalist tutelage. This is far too simple, especially when he had to put in his report for September that guerrillas had captured the district office in Dagang, the largest river town in eastern Zhenjiang and a major nexus for waterborne trade, particularly the lucrative trade in salt. The guerrillas did not hold Dagang for long, but the loss was a setback for the local reputation of the occupation state. This was more than simply bad elements acting up. The goal for the autumn therefore became to create a security network across the rural areas to prevent this sort of thing from happening again. In November, Katō tightened the neighborhood watch system. Zhang Yibo confirms this did have an effect, for as of the first of that month, every watch head was required to report in person to a member of the Military Police every night on every person in his watch.[21] Katō also hoped to better integrate the rural district heads near the city into the neighborhood watch system by getting them to form Self-Defense Corps militia units.

It is difficult to gauge whether this program made any difference. The following February, the resistance assassinated two of Guo's district heads on two consecutive days, one of them in Dagang. Possibly the latter was in response to the stepped-up security measures that had been put in place around Dagang in November to try to break the flow of contraband salt through its harbor. Selling at less than a twentieth the price of official salt, the contraband represented a bad leak in regime finances. Katō bluntly admits in his subsequent report that the assassinations were a "huge blow for our work." His long-term solution was to build rural institutions that would bring the people over to the Japanese side—but how could this be done as long as it was not safe to do so? Katō had no answer, other than to demand greater vigilance from his collaborators. District heads would continue to be vulnerable through to the end of the occupation. In December 1944, the parallel Communist government operating in eastern Zhenjiang grabbed one and put him on trial for working for the occupation state. He was convicted of treason and executed.

If the tasks of pacification were large, the expenses of self-government were equally huge, made more so by the fact that security was expensive to provide, and insecurity even more expensive to deal with. The surviving documentation allows us to get an impression of the financial side of collaboration in Zhenjiang. The occupiers were not willing to provide anything but short-term support to tide the collaborators over immediate difficulties, as already noted. The expense of running the occupation state was for the Chinese to bear. It is not clear, at least in the early phases, where the profits in collaboration lay.

Zhenjiang was reasonably well situated for economic revival. The strength of the local economy rested on its position at a major nexus where river, canal, road, and rail transportation intersected. The war impeded traffic on some of these routes, but the occupation did not shut them down entirely. Servicing them was a major component of Zhenjiang's urban economy. It meant that laborers who would have gone unemployed and hungry in other county economies had the wherewithal to support themselves. Zhenjiang's other immediate asset was its former status as the capital of Jiangsu province, which furnished the Japanese with substantial loot. A postwar estimate claims that the Japanese army confiscated 60,000 yuan from provincial government coffers, besides the large stocks of grain already mentioned.

It is not easy to reconstruct the fiscal operations of an occupied county, in part because statistics were not always kept up, but also because much revenue went unreported and many disbursements took place off the record. Unlike most counties for which the omissions and inconsistencies in the fiscal records make them hopelessly unreliable, collaborationist Zhenjiang is marginally better documented than other counties because of budget summaries for the autumn and winter of 1938 that Katō included in his pacification reports. These contain information of varying quality and consistency: what, for instance, ever happened to the 100,000 yuan in relief funds that the team confiscated from the accounts of the former head of the Zhenjiang Chamber of Commerce, and which Katō handed over to the county office on 5 December 1938? But when put together with occasional articles on the Zhenjiang economy that appeared in the *New Nanjing Daily*, the information manages to hint at what the county government and the people of Zhenjiang were up against in their struggle for economic recovery and fiscal solvency (which are not necessarily the same thing). The story that can be told from this data unfolds as a tale of the Japanese army's provocation of armed resistance and its failure to provide the security an economy requires in order to function.

The economy of Zhenjiang before the occupation consisted of a highly commercialized agricultural sector in the countryside and a modest urban industrial sector. The pacification team did not at first grasp how this economy worked and what forms its resources took. They were distracted by the presence of a nascent modern industrial sector, which is where they expected to find the dynamic core of the economy. Katō inserts a brief analysis of the Zhenjiang economy in his August 1938 work report, observing that it took him some months to realize that Zhenjiang's prosperity relied mainly on the regional circulation of commodities. The industrial sector would be important to occupied Zhenjiang, as we shall see, but the key was trade. And trade relied less on what Zhenjiang produced than on the efficiency of the land and water transport networks that intersected there. A chart of commodities passing through Zhenjiang in November 1938, which Katō includes in a later work report, shows that Zhenjiang was a major transshipment point for goods moving between the lower reaches of the Grand Canal and Shanghai to the southeast, and the middle reaches of the Grand Canal across the Yangtze into Yangzhou and further north. Its main asset was its position between an urban metropolis and a deep rural hinterland. Southeastward from Zhenjiang to Shanghai went grain and other agricultural products produced in Zhenjiang and in the interior north of the Yangtze. Northward from Zhenjiang to Yangzhou moved industrial goods as well as some specialized processed agricultural products, most of which originated in Shanghai. Typical of this pattern was the tobacco trade from Shanghai into the interior. Sensing that the invasion had created a good business opportunity, a businessman named Hara Hachirō showed up in Zhenjiang before the end of December to secure permission to ship tobacco from Shanghai.[22] The team readily agreed. We otherwise have little information about early wholesale arrangements.

Katō's analysis of the Zhenjiang economy was not limited to the city's ties beyond its own boundaries. He also recognized that the immediate rural hinterland within the county's borders was an important component of the city's prosperity. The countryside consumed some of the goods that passed through the entrepôt, but more importantly it produced the agricultural raw materials that sustained the city's processing industries and some of its trade. The viability of Zhenjiang's economy therefore needed a good measure of rural security, infrastructural maintenance of transportation arteries, and mechanisms for providing rural credit. Without these factors the links between the urban and the rural sectors would snap, and in turn disrupt significant inputs into the larger regional economy on which the county depended. This was the perspective from the county seat, of course, a vision of political and economic control extending outward from that center to the periphery on which it depended.

The urban economy of Zhenjiang also rested on factors within the city walls. An important one was the presence of well-capitalized merchants handling and promoting the trade. Katō was keen to see Chinese businesses back in operation as soon as possible. Just as his barometer of re-population was the number of transit passes issued (which in turn, he declared in his report for September 1938, showed that the policy of "coexistence and co-prosperity" was working), so his barometer of business revival was the number of business permits that the SGC issued. These he regularly included in his work reports. As of the end of February 1938, 1,239 businesses had received permits, mostly small service operations. The largest single category, for instance, was tea houses (169). Next in size were small retailers selling oil, wine, and dry goods (87); after that, rice shops (65), hardware stores (34), and butchers (32); and beyond these, the mass of small peddlers who were the vast majority of Zhenjiang's men of business. These were not the big merchants and industrialists whom Katō wanted to rally to the collaborators' side to drive a major trading economy, however. At this early stage, he had to pin his hopes for reviving Zhenjiang's trading economy on Japanese businessmen. Already a few had arrived in February, but more came in the following months, setting up small retail operations in the city's commercial district. By May, when Katō was pleased to report that the urban population had risen to 150,000, he could cite the presence of Japanese businessmen as one of the three factors favorable to Zhenjiang's economic revival (the other two were the windfall of confiscated goods—in which many of the Japanese retailers dealt—and the improvements in transportation). But their numbers were not great. Four months later Katō could count only eighteen Japanese firms handling trade up to Yangzhou, plus another twenty restaurateurs and small retailers. They brought significant capital and contacts into the economy, nonetheless, and were Katō's hope for surmounting the grain shortfall that began to loom in the second half of the year.

To stimulate Chinese business activity, Katō lobbied hard among his better-placed Chinese business contacts for a chamber of commerce to be formed. He mentions the desired chamber in his August summary as an important element for completing the reconstruction of Zhenjiang's economy, and points to the promulgation of new regulations for chambers of commerce by the recently founded Reformed Government in Nanjing as an indication that the time was ripe. He declines to say that it would improve his access to the business community and his control over the goods they handled, but these benefits would follow. The prewar chamber was defunct and its head had escaped to the International Settlement in Shanghai, and the local butchers and hardware dealers who had stayed behind were unlikely to serve as the core of a new chamber. Prospects improved in September, when for the first time the file of business permits revealed that Zhenjiang now had one business with capital in excess of 5,000 yuan. By November there were five in that category, and nine by the following January. Here were the people with whom Katō desired to work. The trend was not quite pointing in the direction he hoped it would, toward an ever-increasing influx of big merchants back into Zhenjiang. Indeed, if we look at the number of businesses in the next category down, we discover that, with one exception, the increase was due to businesses just below the 5,000 yuan threshold crossing up into the higher category. Still, Katō thought he was getting his critical mass of businessmen, and through the autumn pushed them to form a chamber of commerce. He was able to get an application for a permit into the provincial government in November, though for reasons unknown the application got stalled in Suzhou. No authorization would come down for months. Katō went ahead anyway. By December, the Zhenjiang Chamber of Commerce was in operation, albeit without a permit, and claimed six hundred enterprises as members.

Katō's next stage after the creation of the chamber (in everything they did, Special Service agents were always looking to a next stage) was to form trade guilds. The declared motive was the Japanese ideal of "self-government"—each trade should supervise itself—but the real need was to have trade representatives available to help Katō discipline their activities and clear up problems in the economy. Their availability was especially important in a situation in which the Japanese army sought to control many of the commodities traded through Zhenjiang. Thirty-nine guilds had been organized by January 1939, but Katō felt keenly the lack of a boatmen's guild among them. A new set of regulations and institutions governing river traffic had just been published, which amounted to a partial lifting of the army's closure of waterways to private boat traffic. Katō understood that river shipping could resume only through coordination with the army, and chafed at the fact that he had no clear counterpart in the local economy to help set up a network of shipping agents at key points along the county's rivers and canals. The army would demand assurance from the boatmen that enemy personnel and contraband matériel were not moving by water, and Katō could only deliver that assurance by having a network of shipping agents at his call. He should not have been surprised that the boatmen were not among the first to form a guild, however. That sector of the local economy had been damaged by the initial evacuation in November 1937, then devastated by Japan's preparations for the battle of Wuhan further upriver through August and September 1938, when every boat of any size was confiscated to support the assault. (The city also had to quarter some sixty thousand Japanese soldiers at this time.) Putting money into a boat had become a risky venture under these circumstances, and yet without boats, the goods that Zhenjiang pumped through its trade arteries could not flow.

Katō had somewhat better luck with Zhenjiang's modest industrial sector, which consisted of two spinning factories, a match factory, a flour mill, and a small rice mill, plus over a thousand small-scale workshops—among them Zhang Yibo's mosquito-coil factory. Most of these enterprises processed agricultural products for the Shanghai market and manufactured light industrial goods for sale further into the interior, mostly north to Yangzhou. There were in addition a modern printing plant and Guo Zhicheng's coal-fired power plant. The pacification team intervened early on to ensure that the power station stayed in operation by negotiating with the Japanese navy to supply coal. By early March the team could report that power and water were available throughout the city. The printing plant was another Japanese priority because of its value for propaganda work. The pacification team was pleased to find it well stocked with raw materials when they arrived. On 1 February the plant started turning out the *New Zhenjiang Daily* at a rate of seven to eight hundred copies a day (not one of which appears to have survived). Fifty of these went across the river to Yangzhou, and another fifty copies were shipped back down to Danyang whenever the rail line was open. It was a money-losing proposition, as very few businesses could afford to place advertisements, but it remained a Japanese priority nonetheless. The team put up the initial loan to get the paper going, then obliged the SGC to absorb operating costs until it could pay for itself. A year later, the paper was still requiring a subvention of 200 yuan a month.

Of the five modern factories, the two spinning mills disappear from all records postdating the Japanese army's arrival. They must have been damaged beyond repair, or at least beyond investment. The failure of other bombed spinning mills on the delta to get rebuilt suggests that investors were not keen to put money into rural industries when the occupation could not guarantee that these areas would remain secure. The rice mill was not damaged, though, and only required its employees to return to their jobs to resume operation, which it did on 9 January. Between these extremes of complete damage and none at all sat the match factory and flour mill, Zhenjiang's two largest industrial concerns. The invasion had knocked both out of production, though the actual physical damage was light. Getting them back into production was a high priority for the pacification team; it would also be a recurrent cause for anxiety, as we shall see.

The Yingchang Match Factory was one of seven across the Yangtze Delta owned by the Great China Match Company. Before the war, it had produced over half a million matches a day (eighty crates of 7,200 matches each) and employed a workforce of 375 women and 350 men. The factory stopped production on 23 November in anticipation that the Japanese army would capture the city. As its buildings escaped damage, the plant was taken over to billet Japanese soldiers. The Chinese workers were permitted to remain on site, which would prove beneficial for getting the factory back in operation. Several other factors played a role as well. First of all, the local representative of the Great China Match Company, Zhou Yangqiao, was able to speak Japanese. Second, the parent company back in Shanghai was able to negotiate with the Japanese consulate for permission to reopen the plant,[23] although that involved reorganizing the company on paper as a joint Sino-Japanese enterprise. Third, the factory had a month's supply of raw materials on hand when Zhenjiang fell, which meant that production could resume while new suppliers were found. Finally, the pacification team got involved in negotiating with the army to withdraw from the plant, which it did on 27 February. By May the plant was employing three hundred men and women. Katō allowed Zhou to continue managing the factory on a day-to-day basis, having previously appointed him as head of the SGC suboffice on the east side of the city where the factory was situated. The continued viability of the factory was put in question, however, when Japanese military control in the region weakened during the summer. The factory had to close for several weeks in July for lack of raw materials. Supplies began flowing again in August, at which point Katō arranged for the management of the factory to be taken over by a Japanese concern. Production did not expand. By September, the workforce was down to two hundred, and supplies continued to be a problem. An Osaka firm signed a supply contract in November that boosted the plant's access to raw materials, but once again, toward the end of December, supply disruptions forced the plant to close, this time for well over a month.

The match factory was important to the pacification team for several reasons. It was the most consistent producer of an exportable commodity, and therefore a generator of revenue. It was also the largest employer of urban labor. And so long as it was in operation, it offered the strongest demonstration that the occupation regime was economically viable. Its place in the Zhenjiang economy is shown in the November statistics for goods shipped out of Zhenjiang, to which it contributed 11 percent of the total in terms of value and was singly the most important commodity after rice, which was just a shade ahead. (It is possible, though, to read the relationship between these statistics another way, as pointing to the inability of the authorities to get adequate access to rural grain produce). Its vulnerability to supply disruption meant that its share fell over the winter, though it was back up to 9 percent in February.

The match factory had yet another role to play in the pacification of Zhenjiang when it became a source of financing for the Great People's Association (GPA). The GPA was a tightly centralized "mass" organization that the Reformed Government brought into being in the summer of 1938, modeled on the similar New People's Association in North China and the Concordia League in Manchuria, to serve as the regime's ideological arm. Preparatory work to set up a regional branch of the GPA in Zhenjiang began in September, and the branch was inaugurated on 1 October under someone Magistrate Guo recommended for the post. The GPA got several projects going immediately. It turned out propaganda, set up a pawnshop to fund small businesses (that scheme failed), organized a Youth Corps, and opened a Japanese language school; other initiatives followed through the winter and spring of 1939. To pay for its activities, the GPA obtained preferential access to the match factory's output. It was allowed to buy matches at a wholesale price per crate that was one yuan below the retail value, then sell these for a profit at a small shop it opened near the factory. An article about this venture that appeared in the *New Nanjing Daily* the following April included one piece of information not in Katō's work report: the arrangement between the GPA and the match factory was negotiated by a Japanese agent named Tsunegawa. Tsunegawa is not listed among the members of the pacification team, nor does he surface anywhere in the team reports. The newspaper's use of the term "agent" suggests that he was with the Special Service, probably from the Nanjing agency, and that he was sent in as part of a central initiative to fund the GPA.

If the unsteady fortunes of the match factory disappointed Katō, even more troubling were the ups and downs of the flour mill. The centerpiece of the new urban economy, the mill was built in 1926 to process the abundant local wheat, which was otherwise harvested and shipped off to Shanghai for processing. (The war altered this pattern of surplus grain production: to take the example of Taicang county, whereas 76 percent of the wheat grown there in 1936 was shipped out for processing, in 1938 93 percent of the crop was retained, now that it had become difficult to guarantee that local consumption needs could not be met.[24] Under conditions of interrupted transport, Taicang's food prices in general remained low compared with those in Zhenjiang, which depended on food coming from sources elsewhere.)[25] The flour mill was expanded in 1931 to grind three-quarters of a million sacks of flour a year. The mill was a clear asset for an army that had just confiscated large amounts of wheat. The team was keen to get the plant up and running, just as it was keen to gain access to the army's confiscated grain stocks. It was hoped that proceeds from the flour could help cover the SGC's operating costs. Also, by accepting only Japanese military scrip for the milled flour, the team hoped to use the wheat as an incentive to get local people to switch over to this currency.

The pacification team found that some of the machinery in the mill was damaged and decided that new equipment had to be purchased from Shanghai. In mid-February they opened discussions with the Arai Trading Company, a Japanese firm working out of Shanghai, to come in as an investor. When they learned that not all the needed parts were available, the agents turned to the original owners in the hope that they could rehire the technicians and get them to put the machinery back in running order. The technicians had fled back to their homes in distant Ningbo when the Japanese army attacked. As a compromise arrangement, the Arai Company agreed to ship some machinery from Shanghai in March, and at least some of the technicians were brought back from Ningbo. Then there was the problem of getting the mill workers to return. Most were Subei people from around Yangzhou, north of the Yangtze. There was also the matter of finding wheat to mill. This the team was able to arrange with the army, which turned over its entire stock of confiscated grain to the team with the understanding that part of the proceeds would go to fund the SGC. By May the flour mill was working at close to full capacity, with a slightly reduced workforce of two hundred. Now that this and the match factory were back in production, Katō could declare to his superiors in Shanghai that the urban economy was well on the way to recovery.

Although he had brought in the Arai Company as a partner, Katō kept the actual management of the flour mill in his own hands. He did transfer the mill's assets to the county government in August, but this was a formal gesture that left the actual running of the enterprise unaffected. What he wanted to do was to turn the mill into a joint enterprise, a model that would demonstrate that Chinese and Japanese capitalists could benefit by working together. He did everything he could to encourage Chinese businessmen to invest, and also to encourage Japanese businessmen to bring their capital and trading connections into the city. By September, however, the flour mill began to suffer from the regional insecurity that was crippling the match factory. The fact that the spring wheat harvest in 1938 was only 40 percent of the previous year's crop was a problem, and it was made worse by the growing difficulty of getting the grain from the growers to the city. The mill operated on and off through the fall, though production declined. Katō's solution was to hand over the management of the mill to the Arai Company on the condition that the company guarantee a steady supply of wheat. It was the same sort of arrangement he had made for the match factory with the company from Osaka, and it produced the same mixed results, for it was beyond the capacity of any company to guarantee supply in wartime. The Arai Company might be able to find the wheat it needed in other areas, but it had no control over whether transport routes remained open. The mill was thus forced to operate at about 30 percent of its prewar capacity through December. It may have done marginally better in January, but then it had to shut down entirely when the transportation routes in and out of Zhenjiang were cut in February. Flour had accounted for about 10 percent of the goods shipped out of Zhenjiang in November. By February, it simply disappears from the statistics. A small amount of wheat continued to come in from north of the river, but it was shipped straight on to Shanghai to be milled there.

The county government relied on a share of the profits from the two factories, which contributed more than half of its income through the summer and fall of 1938. At its inception, the SGC had started out with almost nothing and survived by working out food resale arrangements with the Japanese army and charging fees for transit passes. (Zhenjiang issued transit passes rather than the usual registration certificates as a profitable form of population control, since mobility rather than residence was the key resource for economic activity in this busy transportation zone.) The SGC also tried to draw income from the regional salt trade that ran through the county. The SGC got the army's agreement to cooperate in mid-January 1938, and in February was able to secure salt from the Yangzhou SGC and sell it in Zhenjiang, but this did not turn out to be very profitable. By the end of February, the SGC was broke, despite unspecified financial aid from the local garrison. The team gave what it hoped would be a one-time-only supplement at the beginning of March to cover salaries. If, as many who worked for the occupation state liked to say, they did so purely out of financial necessity, then the SGC's inability to meet its costs could threaten local collaboration with collapse. For the next few months, the SGC managed to raise several tens of thousands of yuan a month, three-quarters from various taxes and the rest from the flour mill and match factory, but no records survive.

Financial records resume in September, when a brief budget summary for the county government reveals that monthly revenue had fallen to a meager 6,500 yuan, most of which came from a transit tax on goods coming in and out of the county. Expenses, by contrast, ran to 49,333 yuan. The huge gap was filled with the profits from the two factories: a lucky backup, but not the basis for long-term financial viability. The county office was able to function, but on a revenue base that was perilously thin, especially when the pacification team was trying to woo investors with the promise that their profits would not be garnished nor their property confiscated. What had to be done was to reestablish the prewar fiscal foundation for county operations: the tax on land. The pacification team decided to push its Chinese administrators by setting a goal of raising tax income to 10,000 yuan for October and having a land tax system functioning by the end of November. Imposing a tax on landowners would continue to be the great unreachable mirage on the county's fiscal horizon throughout the occupation. In frustration, Katō stressed to the district heads he assembled for a meeting in late November that the taxes they had collected in the previous four months amounted to a mere 1 percent of what had been collected under the Nationalists; he demanded improved performance.

Until that happened, the short-term solutions for covering administrative costs were two. One was to collect higher amounts of transit tax, which the county did by installing tax personnel at the east and south railway stations (the regime in Nanjing would ban that levy in January). The other was to tax opium. The idea of using opium as a source of county government revenue had been on everyone's agenda since the early summer. The National Government had placed opium under strict monopoly earlier in the decade in order to restrict use in the long term, but also to gain some financial benefits in the process.[26] The invasion had disrupted supply and distribution systems, leaving the new officials with no fees to collect. This is not to say that opium ceased circulating. A black market operated during the first months of the occupation, though smokers buying on that market were liable to arrest.[27] The pacification team broke up a flourishing opium smuggling business directly across the Yangtze from Zhenjiang city in mid-February with the help of Chinese police and Japanese soldiers, but smuggling could not be controlled when demand remained high. In some locations, small operators were able to gain access to Japanese opium supplies in Shanghai and move them into the hinterland, with the agreement of local pacification agencies, though no traces of such operations survive in the records of the Zhenjiang team.

Zhenjiang was one of the first two cities on the delta to receive authorization from the Reformed Government in Nanjing to set up a local opium suppression bureau (the other city was Songjiang). A director was appointed on 20 July, though not until 4 November did the Zhenjiang Opium Prohibition Bureau officially open its doors.[28] Presumably the time was needed to set up supply, with a source in Shanghai and retailers operating under government license in Zhenjiang. The revenue from the opium tax first appears in the October-November budget, contributing 3,760 yuan in one month to a two months' income of 34,801 yuan. The November figures cannot be disaggregated, but opium furnished at least 20 percent of county income for that month. Opium income stayed at that level through January 1939, when it brought 21,040 yuan into the county budget of 104,897 yuan. In February, opium revenue fell to 9,520 yuan, but the total earned income that month was only 29,554 yuan, which put its share of the total up to 33 percent. Opium revenue remained steady in March (estimated at 10,000 yuan) but earned income rose to 41,435 yuan, reducing its share to 25 percent. Here the figures come to an end.

Even with opium's contribution to the finances of Zhenjiang, the county office ran deficits through the winter of 1938–39. December's budget shortfall was 31,410 yuan. The match and flour factories contributed 40,000 yuan to make up for it. January shutdowns removed this income from the county budget, so the pacification team came up with 17,298 yuan, with no explanation as to where the money came from or why it was provided. Transit, opium, and land taxes yielded another 54,036 yuan, well above January's expenses of 47,725 yuan, which put the county back in the black. In February, though, the Reformed Government banned local transit fees, which knocked Zhenjiang's fiscal juggling act from the high wire on which it was attempting to walk. Expenses exceeded earned income in February by a stunning 57,171 yuan. The March shortfall declined to 16,840 yuan, but that was only because the match factory, which was up and running again, chipped in 25,000 yuan.

The ever-deepening fiscal hole in Zhenjiang was not due to mismanagement, corruption, or shortsightedness on the part of those who devised the administrative systems. It rested rather on the crisis that the occupation induced in the regional economy. The best evidence of the larger crisis is a set of statistics published toward the end of January 1939 in the *New Nanjing Daily*. These figures appear in an article the newspaper ran on Zhenjiang's grain reserves. The article contrasts the production and flow of grain through Zhenjiang before the war with estimates for the coming year. It presents this information in the most neutral tone, making no observations and drawing no conclusions. The attentive reader would have been appalled, though probably not surprised, at how bad things stood. A county that before the war had produced 300,000 piculs (roughly 20,000 metric tons) of rice was expected to produce *none* in 1939. A county that had consumed 500,000 piculs of rice before the war would see its consumption fall by 40 percent in 1939. A county that had exported one million sacks of flour before the war would ship out only 40 percent of that amount in 1939—and that estimate turned out to be an optimistic fore-cast, for the flour mill shut down in January for want of enough wheat to grind. It should have surprised no one to read that Zhenjiang was a net im-porter of grain, for the statistics made clear that before the war it had con-sumed more than twice what it had produced. That was not the problem. The real problem was that the flow of rice through the county had fallen by half, and the flow of wheat by two-thirds. Katō the previous summer had correctly understood the circulation of commodities to be the key to the Zhenjiang economy. That circulation had contracted to the point of plac-ing the local economy in a crisis it was incapable of resolving on the strength of its own resources.

Early in January 1939, Magistrate Guo dispatched the second-in-com-mand of relief operations to Suzhou to plead for funds from the provincial government. A week later he applied to the same authority for Zhenjiang to be given the highest disaster classification for his county. In the mean-time, desperate to deal with the hardships the winter season brought to the poor, Guo contributed some of his private funds to have a hundred suits of padded winter clothes sewn and given to the poor. He used his own gener-osity to leverage contributions from other local philanthropists, who paid for another hundred suits. These were no ordinary clothes, however, for on the back of each jacket he had a couplet printed in large characters:

> Work hard for intimacy between China and Japan
> Support peace in East Asia.

To complete his redecoration of the public landscape of collaboration, Guo had the old park in the center of the city replanted with cherry trees. The *New Nanjing Daily* promised its readers that the trees would bloom beauti-fully in the spring.[29] For whose eyes was this walking and horticultural pro-paganda meant, if not the Japanese?

I have told the story of collaboration in Zhenjiang as a dialogue of initia-tive between Guo Zhicheng and Katō Kōzan. I have done so on the basis of only one certainty—Katō's declared preference that Guo lead the county administration—and one supposition—that Guo's longevity in office tes-tified to his ability to work well with his Japanese advisors. It is impossible to go deeper into their relationship to see who led on which initiative and who followed, whether certain issues placed them in opposition, or how they resolved the differences that must have arisen between them in the course of doing county business. What we see comes from Katō's account of the relationship, in which he casts himself in the leading role. From Guo's perspective we have nothing. All we have is Zhang Yibo's declaration that Guo threw himself into the work of extracting revenue without regard for people's welfare. But that observation may be nothing more than the prejudicial assumption of someone deeply antagonized by the very idea of Guo's administration, especially in light of the apparent lack of success this administration had in generating an adequate revenue flow.

What then can we say of Guo's collaboration? His role as the organizer of the refugee camp in the Great Illumination Power Plant placed him in contact with the Japanese authorities, but the evidence indicates that he went out of his way to become involved when it came time to organize the Zhenjiang Self-Government Committee in December, and to get appointed as county magistrate when that post needed to be filled in May. The question of how he benefited from his collaboration is not so easily answered. The ongoing difficulty of raising county revenue prior to reopening the opium bureau suggests that there was not much wealth around for him to profit from. His ownership of the power plant gave him a source of private income that made him a wealthy man before the Japanese arrived, and a year into the occupation he was still wealthy enough to afford to have a hundred suits of clothes made up for winter relief, but he could not be expected to draw on his own resources indefinitely.

There is a glimmer that Guo Zhicheng was not in the happy position this gesture might suggest in "New Order in East Asia," the booklet that a group calling itself the American Information Committee produced in 1939 to counter Japanese propaganda about the good life in the occupied zone. The short chapter on Zhenjiang, dated 11 May 1939 and probably written by an American missionary, is entitled "A Pre-war Capital Now Destitute." The author stresses the devastation of the occupation experience, not just dwelling on the initial Japanese assault but highlighting the difficult circumstances in the present: economic conditions that are "deplorable," with 90 percent of the populace living in extreme poverty, opium available on the open market, and education "at a standstill." But what particularly caught my attention was this passage:

There is a general movement by the Japanese to take over public utilities and all business of importance. For example, the electric power company was "re-organized" in spite of the fact that the principal owner was the

puppet mayor of the city; his younger brother was imprisoned for proposing to the Japanese that they ought to pay the family $30,000 for the
plant.[30]

The "puppet mayor" in this passage is none other than Guo Zhicheng. If
this story is true and not just rumor, Guo was under occupation just as
much as everyone else, dictated to rather than dictating the terms of his
cooperation, to the point of being unable to protect his own brother.

Guo's failure to turn his collaboration to his family's benefit did not
bring that collaboration to an end, nor did it make any difference to those
who lived under his magistracy. His administration rendered them vulnerable to organization, extraction, discipline—and poverty. There is no evidence that he influenced the occupation in a way that shielded the people
from Japanese security impositions or revenue needs. Caught in this bargain between demands from above and resistance from below, the local
collaborator had to calculate where to place his loyalty. In occupied Zhenjiang, Guo resolved that tension in favor of demands from above. What
benefits he personally gained from collaboration are impossible to detect.

Once the pacification team disbanded in February 1939, the documentary base for a history of occupied Zhenjiang crumbles away. Katō stayed
on to guide the work of the Zhenjiang county government for a few more
months, then was called back to Shanghai for other work. After publishing
his reminiscence in the *New Nanjing Daily* in July 1939, he disappears from
the historical record.

Does conquest pay? In his book of that title, Peter Liberman has shown
that a nation can add resources to its economic base by occupying another
country. The degree to which these new resources become cumulative for
the occupier varies, depending on the development of the occupied economy and the willingness of the occupier to impose harsh controls. A pre-
dominantly agrarian nation that is able to revert to subsistence production
in time of war leaves its occupier nothing to extract. Some degree of modernization of the occupied economy is necessary—notably in the forms of
industrialization and an efficient transportation and communication infrastructure—for the occupation to yield benefits; otherwise, the surplus is
too low and the costs of extracting it too high. The level of destruction that
occurs during the invasion preceding occupation can also affect the prospects of profitability by imposing critical delays on the revival of the mod-

ern sector and therefore on the occupier's capacity to extract. As for the occupier, Liberman found that its limiting condition was the willingness to be ruthless in making its conquest pay. Extraction rates in an economy under occupation are invariably lower than in an economy under domestic control, and those rates can fall to close to zero if the occupier is unwilling to force compliance. The occupier must be willing to subject the occupied to harsh repression, especially when sentiments of nationalism are strong.

Liberman found the empire Japan created between 1895 and 1937 in Taiwan, Korea, and Manchuria to be a case of profitable conquest. The initial costs of repression were huge, but that investment paid off by eradicating effective political resistance. "Once the conquests had been consolidated, the everyday costs of control were too low to drain either Japanese budgets or colonial productivity." He attributes Japan's success in these regions to "a combination of coercion, repression, and incentives for collaboration."[31] Japan's occupation of China from 1937 to 1945, which Liberman addresses only in passing, was entirely another matter. The costs of maintaining the occupation were huge, and the prospects of ever extracting significant levels of wealth or resources from the shattered occupied economy were feeble, and remained so throughout the war. China's modern sector was too underdeveloped for investment to yield quick returns, its communications too weak to make coercion efficient, and the power of nationalism too great to enable Japan to exploit the economy without having to pay huge repression costs.

What we have seen of Zhenjiang under the occupation confirms Liberman's view that Japan could not make its conquest of China pay, though not for want of ruthlessness. By every indicator, the local economy was less productive under conquest than it had been before the occupation. Most sectors of the local economy were either in collapse or under subsidy, depending on how important that sector was to Japan's perception of its war effort. It is impossible to determine how costly the occupation of Zhenjiang was for Japan, but the evidence suggests that Japan derived little economic benefit. The test is not perfect, since this chapter covers only the first year of occupation. A year may not be enough time to consolidate a conquest. But consolidation was not forthcoming in the years to follow, as the evidence of ongoing instability reported sporadically in the *New Nanjing Daily* attests. The newspaper assured its readers in July 1939 that a rural purification program to bring stability to Zhenjiang was being planned, though famine the next spring made the region only that much more difficult to secure.[32] When rural pacification finally got going in the summer of 1941, Chinese soldiers were dispatched into the countryside to clear safe areas and construct bamboo palisades around the pacified zones, but partisans went out at night and burned the palisades down almost as fast as the soldiers erected them by day. By the time the soldiers had put up ninety-one kilometers worth of fencing, two-thirds of it was already gone.[33] A more thorough program was launched in March 1943, but the rural areas remained beyond control. Unable to afford the costs of creating vertical integration with their rural collaborators, the Japanese could not incorporate rural Zhenjiang into the occupation state, nor derive benefits for themselves. Only urban Zhenjiang had a place in the new order, and then only at great cost to collaborators and resisters alike. We cannot say whether collaboration paid, but occupation did not.

— 5 —

Complicities / Nanjing

Nanjing is, among all the sites of occupation on the Yangtze Delta, the special case: a site of memory, to use Pierre Nora's term, where many thoughts and dreams converge. For Chinese, Nanjing is the site of an exceptional massacre that serves to confirm their historical victimization at the hands of foreign powers. For Japanese, Nanking has come to be seen as a test of the legitimacy of Japan's wartime claim that it was the liberator of Asia, and a challenge to Japan's right to respect in the postwar world. The politics of memory are so powerful at this site that what actually happened in December 1937 almost doesn't matter to the kind of record either side chooses to create.

One component that is absent from all declared memories of Nanjing is a memory of collaboration. Nanjing was no exception to the history of occupation, which must expect collaboration. This feature of Nanjing's experience of occupation is what this chapter reconstructs. But there is an even more interesting story to tell about the Japanese takeover of Nanjing, for what emerges from the documents is not only the stark theme of collaboration but the more nuanced theme of complicity, a willingness to go along with the way things were, to accommodate and cohabit, because no other course seemed possible. The documents that allow us to glimpse the crossovers among collaborators and noncollaborators are the diaries and letters of the two dozen Westerners who remained in the city during the Japanese takeover. Their presence in fact doubled those complicities, for while they were opposed to what Japan was doing, they ended up working closely with the collaborators. Occupation thus entangled occupiers, collaborators, and noncollaborators alike in the common project of finding a way back to normal. Robert Gildea has noted that "Franco-German accommodation was an art that had to be learned in the interest of all parties, and most parties managed it extremely well."[1] It is hard to say of Nanjing that most parties managed this accommodation well, at least at the outset, but even here they learned that survival depended on the art of working together.

On the morning of Monday, 13 December 1937, Japanese soldiers poured through several gates in the old city wall surrounding Nanjing (Nanking). Chinese soldiers had resisted for four days while Japanese artillery pounded the city's defenses, but at dusk on Sunday evening, when they learned that their commanding officers were abandoning the city, morale broke. They threw down their weapons, shed their uniforms, and fled through the northwest gate to the river port of Xiaguan in a desperate rush to cross the Yangtze River. The Japanese army continued to shell the city through the night, rattling windows and starting fires, unaware that the rout was already under way. When morning dawned and no one challenged them at the gates, the first Japanese units marched in. The occupation of Nanjing had begun.[2]

Despite its reputation for atrocity, the Japanese takeover of Nanjing proceeded much as it had in other locations on the Yangtze Delta through November and December. Here as elsewhere, Japanese soldiers arrived in force and mounted a full-scale attack on a center of civilian population, resulting in a large number of casualties and extensive destruction of property. Here, as Chinese had done elsewhere, the Red Swastika Society mobilized its members to bury the corpses that lay strewn about the city streets. Here, as elsewhere, a team of Special Service agents showed up in the army's wake to begin the work of creating a civil administration. And here, too, a small number of local residents came forward to work with the Japanese team and constitute themselves as a civil administration. For even in Nanjing, occupation elicited collaboration. Even here, occupied and occupier wove themselves into a web of complicities.

Nanjing was the largest city that the Central China Area Army occupied after Shanghai. Although its prewar population of a million had shrunk to half that by November, at least a quarter of a million were still in the city on the morning of 13 December. The size of the civilian population meant that Special Service agents would have to administer something on a scale far beyond anything the SSD had previously dealt with. Second, Nanjing was a national capital. During the eponymous decade leading up to 1937

when the city had enjoyed this status, Nanjing had been partially trans-
formed into something that was beginning to look like a national capital,
with new street layouts, handsome buildings, and an extensive planting of
trees. It had also gained enormously in symbolic stature in the previous
four months with the refusal of Chiang Kaishek and his National Government to negotiate with Japan. In 1927, at the beginning of the Nanjing Decade, Chiang had declared that his new government would "live or die"
with Nanjing,[3] and through the autumn of 1937 it seemed that he was
honoring that pledge. Chiang's refusal to capitulate made the capital even
more an obsessive focus of Japanese ambition: if he would not compromise with Japanese interests, then his regime had to be overthrown, and
that, it was clear by the time the CCAA received the order on 1 December
to advance on the city, could only be achieved by submitting Nanjing to
military conquest.

Matsui Iwane, the CCAA commander-in-chief, understood the importance of capturing Nanjing so decisively that the Chinese people would
know that continuing resistance to Japan was futile. This would not be just
another capture of just another city. Prior to the attack, Matsui reminded
his officer corps that their conduct would be a demonstration of the
"honor and glory of Japan" and a chance to win the "trust of the Chinese
people."[4] The commander wanted a prompt victory, though not, if we can
reconstruct his intentions from his own evasive statements later, an atro-
cious one. The soldiers who fought their way across the Yangtze Delta and
up to the walls of Nanjing also sensed the glory of taking the capital. When
the prize fell easily into their grasp, they shook it for everything they could
get. Their commander's logic, differently arranged, was theirs as well. They
would show the Chinese who was boss. As Japanese soldiers entered the
city that morning, a thirteen-year-old girl, whom the American surgeon
Dr. Robert Wilson later treated, "with her father and mother were standing
outside the entrance of their dugout watching them approach. A soldier
stepped up, bayonetted the father, shot the mother and slashed open the elbow of the little girl giving her a compound fracture. She has no relatives
and was not brought to the hospital for a week."[5] The city was not in resistance, but it would be punished.

One factor that made Nanjing a different place to occupy was the presence of some two dozen foreigners—mostly Americans and Germans, plus
two Russians and an Austrian. They were all that remained of the Western
community that had come to live in the Chinese capital through the 1920s

Japanese soldiers approaching Nanjing outside Guanghua Gate, 9 December 1937. From *Shina jihen gahō* (27 January 1938), p. 8.

and 1930s, offering their services as businessmen, educators, technicians, doctors, and missionaries. Most had left toward the end of November. Those who elected to stay behind constituted themselves as the International Committee for the Nanking Safety Zone. As the Japanese army approached, the committee marked out roughly an eighth of the city as a neutral zone from which combatants on both sides were barred and to which city residents were invited to withdraw for protection. Untouchable by the Japanese army for diplomatic reasons, the Westerners were in a unique position to act, and also to record what the occupying force did to those among whom they had lived and worked. Their status as "third-country" nationals, to use the Japanese expression of the time, meant that their reports of what quickly came to be known as "the Rape of Nanking" created a public chronicle that was credible.

What the Western observers saw was beyond the worst they could imagine. As John Rabe, the German businessman who chaired the International Committee (IC), declared in a letter to the Japanese embassy on 17 December, "All 27 Westerners in the city at that time and our Chinese population were totally surprised by the reign of robbery, rapine and killing initiated by your soldiers on the 14th." The records the Westerners kept of those terrible weeks from mid-December to mid-February have made this city the centerpiece of Chinese accounts of the Japanese occupation of central China, and the major bone of contention between Chinese and Japanese as to what the occupation was about and what the extent of Japanese moral and legal responsibility for Chinese suffering should be. This "incident," as Japanese historiography likes to call it—this "massacre," as Chinese prefer to denote it—has come to define the entire history of Japan's occupation of China. General Matsui had declared the capture of Nanjing to be a test. Steadfastly oblivious that the conduct of his soldiers had ensured that Japan had failed to win the "trust of the Chinese people," Matsui wrote a poem on the occasion of entering the city in which he praised his troops for "coming to drive out the sickening miasma and turning the landscape to spring."[6] For this failure, the postwar military tribunal in Tokyo would judge him personally responsible for the massive mistreatment of Chinese civilians and sentence him to death by hanging.

The presence of the International Committee also altered how the Special Service would go about organizing the work of pacification. The SSD did not dispatch just another pacification team, as it had elsewhere. It established a higher-ranking entity that went by the grander title of Special Service Agency (SSA). A military officer, Major Sakata Shigeki, brought two civilians, Matsuoka Tsutomu and Mabuchi Seigō, both Mantetsu employees, into the city the day it fell to begin the SSA's work. The scale of what they faced was overwhelming. Sakata appealed to Shanghai for more personnel with strong China experience. The first to arrive, on 28 December, was Maruyama Susumu. Satō Tsukito, Kojima Tomō, and Kawano Masanao followed in the second week of January. Kawano came with the experience of having headed the Songjiang team, though as noted in the preceding chapter, he came after being replaced by Zhenjiang team leader Nakayama Yojirō. Was it his expertise or his incompetence that got him posted to Nanjing? The latter, it seems, for within two weeks Kawano disappeared from the organization. Major Sakata was transferred away at the same time, though he was only ever on temporary assignment to see the SSA properly installed. When the SSA held the second of its two meetings with the International Committee, on 28 January, it was Matsuoka Tsutomu who was running the agency.

The Nanjing SSA was not the only Japanese organ sent in right at the start to begin the hard work of rebuilding what the takeover had destroyed. Other SSD personnel were also dispatched. One who later wrote about his experience as a military advisor to the occupation regime was Okada Yōji. He too arrived on the 13th, but with the staff of Prince Asaka, the emperor's uncle, for which reason his presence is not recorded in SSA records. An economic specialist, Okada had no connection to the pacification team. He was assigned the task of taking over the financial organs of the municipal government and implementing the policy of replacing Chinese money with Japanese military scrip. On the day he arrived, he went straight to the Bank of Communications to place it under Japanese supervision, only to find the bank abandoned. The staff had fled, taking with them all records and assets. Okada went on to the Bank of China to find the same situation, and so on from bank to bank.[7] Banks in some of the other cities on the Yangtze Delta yielded dividends; when Suzhou was captured, its banks were found to have deposits totaling half a million yuan in cash.[8] The Japanese gleaned nothing from the banks in Nanjing. Okada's presence in Nanjing shows that the SSA was not the only Special Service entity in Nanjing. The Nanjing SSA would limit its responsibilities to political and social matters; economic reconstruction was left to specialists such as Okada.

The records the SSA left behind do not make it easy to reconstruct its work. The agency sent monthly reports to Shanghai, as other pacification teams did, and the Mantetsu office produced a composite report in April, but compared with the reports for other teams, this one is oddly uninformative about process. It focuses on administrative structures and procedures, but it says very little about the negotiations and conflicts that occurred to get them in place, and reveals almost nothing about the people involved. The report runs to eighty-seven pages without opening many windows on the lived experience of pacification in Nanjing.

The best trove of sources are the documents that the Westerners in Nanjing kept: the records of the International Committee, published a year later and distributed internationally by the Chinese government, and the diaries and letters of the Germans and Americans on the committee, many of which have only recently been published. These sources are invaluable for making it possible to reconstruct the process of collaboration, which is otherwise lost beneath the opaque surface of the SSA's pacification report. Since the IC was not granted status as the SSA's counterpart agency but had to go through impotent consular officials to negotiate with the Japanese side, its members were little informed about the pacification process. But they do have intriguing observations regarding the operations of the Nanjing Self-Government Committee. These observations make it possible to reconstruct the politics surrounding this committee in greater detail than is the case for most other SGCs.

The SSA was allergic to the International Committee, in the first instance because it consisted of Europeans and Americans, the very imperialists from whom Japan was proposing to rescue China by invading it. More to the point, the SSA was disturbed by the IC's insistence that it remain independent of Japanese desires. The IC was not some hastily assembled peace maintenance committee, after all, staffed by shoddy opportunists who could be cajoled into obedience or pushed aside. Its foreign status meant that it could afford to be self-governing in a way no Chinese self-government committee could dream of. Equally importantly, it was competent, free from corruption, and in command of popular respect. The future administration of Nanjing could not proceed without taking it into account. Nanjing thus was not an emptied space waiting for Japanese agents to fill it with compliant Chinese politicians. Japan would have to delegitimize what was there before it could field a substitute that might win at least the submission of city residents, though not their enthusiastic support.

The members of the International Committee, while conscious of their advantage as non-Japanese foreigners, did not presume to interfere in the conflict between China and Japan. They took their role to be one of protecting Chinese people on a temporary basis. They could not block the Japanese army from taking possession of Nanjing or installing whatever sort of local regime it wanted. The Westerners saw themselves as buffering the city's residents from the dislocations of military takeover. In so doing, they in fact eased the transition from Nationalist to Japanese rule. Unlike Shanghai, foreigners in Nanjing had no concessions or legally constituted administrative bodies through which they could exercise legitimate authority. Their posture vis-à-vis the Japanese had to be one of accommodation. They hoped to keep Japanese soldiers from running riot over the city, but they could not otherwise interfere in Japan's victory.

On the evening of the first day of occupation, John Rabe drafted the first of roughly twenty official letters he would write to the Japanese side over the next seven weeks, seeking to improve the conditions of occupation for those within the Safety Zone. In it, Rabe makes clear that the committee members accepted their own authority in the city as temporary and declared that they were eager to "cooperate in any way we can" with the Japanese army "in caring for the civilian population of the city." There was no response. In that silence a reign of terror began to unfold. Three days later, under mounting frustration, Rabe wrote again to reassure the Japanese embassy that the committee understood that its "authority did not extend outside of the Safety Zone itself, and involved no rights of sovereignty within the Zone." He expressed puzzlement that order was not being restored, and requested that a competent administration be put in place as quickly as possible. Sakata, Matsuoka, and Mabuchi were on site by this time, but no pacification work was in evidence during the first days of the occupation, nor were any visible steps being made toward setting up a civilian administration. As Rabe wrote in his letter to the Japanese embassy on 17 December, "The stage was all set for you to take over that area peacefully and let the normal life [in the Safety Zone] continue undisturbed until the rest of the city could be put in order. Then the full normal life of the city could go forward." Sensing nothing but a vacuum, he went so far as to suggest in the politest terms that the Japanese "kindly bring an expert in Municipal Administration to Nanking to manage the life of the civilian population until a new city government can be formed."

The offer to cooperate as equals was politically intolerable to the SSA. The very existence of the IC confounded Japan's aim, which was to appear as China's savior rescuing the Chinese people from the contagions of nationalism and Communism that they had contracted from the West. Yet here were "white" foreigners showing just the sort of leadership that the Japanese felt was now their prerogative as "yellow" foreigners in China, and doing it with greater effect and to popular acclaim. They were the imperialists against whom the Japanese were raising the flag of anticolonial resistance. The presence of a popular Western organization only cast their own efforts in a negative light and underscored that their presence was unwanted and illegal.

The Westerners' activism thus entailed a huge cost to the legitimacy of Japan's presence and Japan's actions. It also cast doubt on the legitimacy of any Chinese collaborating agency that came forward to take over what the Westerners had started so well. The Japanese demanded collaboration of the Chinese, but could not be seen to collaborate with EuroAmericans. The Japanese tactic was in fact to reverse the image and to claim, as Major-General Amaya Naojirō did before the assembled Western diplomatic corps on 5 February, that "without foreign interference, the Sino-Japanese relationship in Nanking would have developed harmoniously!"[9]

It took only a day or two for the CCAA to demonstrate that it was not prepared to conduct its occupation according to the laws of war to which Japan was a signatory nation. By the third day, Robert Wilson was noting in a letter home that "the slaughter of civilians is appalling."[10] Under such circumstances, the IC judged it unwise to turn over its resources and authority, either to the invading army or to its Chinese delegate, until basic conditions for the peaceful occupation of the city were in place. That would take almost two months. Those two months would unfold in a mix of resistance and collaboration between the International Committee and the various Japanese authorities and Chinese collaborators with whom it had to deal. The mix was awkward, but it moved everyone toward collaboration.

The members of the IC were initially in the dark about the SSA and did not know with what arm of the Japanese military they were supposed to deal. The Japanese embassy was their official channel of contact with the Japanese side, but after a meeting with consular officials on 19 December, it was clear to the four IC members present that the consular arm had "no control over the military," as Wilson phrased it.[11] The embassy was powerless to do anything but forward the foreigners' complaints to its ministry in Tokyo and the army command in Nanjing—though exactly to whom it was not clear. Rabe and others attempted to make contact in the first two days of occupation by approaching officers in the street and seeking communication with their commander. At last, on the morning of the third day, a junior consular official and a junior naval officer called at the IC offices. They were handed Rabe's first letter, in which he promised that the members of the IC would "cooperate in any way we can." This time the response from the Japanese side was immediate. At noon that day, the IC was summoned to a former Chinese government building to receive instructions from the "Chief of the Special Service Corps," as he is referred to in an IC aide-mémoire of the meeting.

The Special Service report for this period makes no mention of Major Sakata's meeting with the IC. This is not an exceptional blank, however, for none of the work of the Nanjing SSA during its first ten days in Nanjing is recorded. The absence of any record creates something of a puzzle regarding the status of the SSA. Officially the SSA came into existence on 24 December, yet the Special Service agents had arrived on the 13th. The only explanation I can think of is that the SSA delayed its official start date so that whatever it did prior to the 24th would be off the record. Why would it want that grace period? There may be a glimpse of this logic in what one Japanese soldier wrote in his diary on 22 December, which was that soldiers attached to the SSA that day led defeated Chinese soldiers to the bank of the Yangtze River and shot them.[12] This is not the sort of activity normally associated with Special Service personnel. In other locations on the Yangtze Delta, however, there is evidence that Special Service personnel did get involved in counterinsurgency operations.[13] Did the SSA delay its official inception in order to play the trick of deniability: that if there were no paper trail, it would be impossible to discover that anything had ever happened?

When the Western representatives were ushered into Sakata's presence on the 15th, it was made clear to them that they were dealing with a military officer who issued instructions, not a civilian who would enter into discussion. The thrust of his short briefing was that the Japanese army's first priority was to find and remove all the Chinese soldiers in the city. He told his guests that they should trust the Japanese army's "humanitarian attitude" with regard to what he termed "care for disarmed Chinese soldiers." This at least is the language in which the American secretary of the IC, Nanjing University professor Lewis Smythe, recorded his comments. On this, the third day of the occupation, it was a trust the IC was still prepared to extend.

Rabe had already raised the issue of the Chinese soldiers earlier that day in a letter to the embassy, saying that "we told them that if they abandoned their arms and all resistance to the Japanese, we thought the Japanese would give them merciful treatment." A Red Cross branch was set up that same day expressly for the purpose of sheltering the soldiers left behind in the city. Inasmuch as the Chinese army had not in fact surrendered, strictly speaking the unidentified soldiers could still be regarded as combatants in active service. But there was a natural expectation that the occupying army, and the SSA in particular, would interpret the laws of war liberally and treat their captives as though they had surrendered. This expectation proved faulty. Japanese policy at that juncture was to execute captured soldiers, as officers in the street made plain to IC members on several occasions as they rounded up suspected Chinese soldiers during the first week.[14] Japan declined to extend to them the protections due to prisoners of war. It would appear that the SSA was directly involved in this practice of executing prisoners.

The rest of Sakata's instructions at the 15 December meeting consisted of permitting the IC to provide rice to refugees, allowing them to deploy unarmed police within the Safety Zone, and requesting help to recruit workers to do cleanup and reopen public utilities. The second concession was immediately compromised the following morning, when fifty policemen, including their captain, were removed from the Ministry of Justice building and shot. The utilities workers fared no better. The IC discovered a few days later that, in Wilson's words, "when they went to round up the workers in the electric light plant they found that 43 out of the 54 had been taken out and shot for no reason at all and now there is no one who can run the plant. They have also burned the telephone building."[15] Not quite "for no reason," according to IC member Searle Bates: the street cleaners had been taken to be government employees. The Japanese army judged them to be in the service of the enemy and, as such, legitimate targets of execution.

The SSA's concerns during the first few days of occupation were in any case elsewhere. High on Sakata's priorities was the formation of a Chinese collaborationist administration. Given the documentary silence before 24 December, the SSA's reports provide no information about the meeting of Chinese sympathizers it convened at the Japanese embassy on 21 December, where proposals for the formation of a municipal government were discussed.[16] The SSA decided, presumably on orders from Shanghai, to by-pass the usual peace maintenance stage and proceed swiftly to a self-government committee. There is no record of who took part in this meeting, though Wen Zongyao, a Cantonese businessman who emerged in March as the number two collaborator at the national level, made a comment at his war crimes trial that implied he was present at this meeting.[17]

The day of the meeting was not a good one, according to Robert Wilson:

Huge fires are set in every business section. Our bunch has actually seen them [the Japanese soldiers] set the fires in several instances . . . Several more stories of the slaughter keep coming in. One man came to [American missionary Rev. John] Magee today with the tale of what happened to one thousand men led away from a place of supposed safety within the zone. The bunch contained perhaps one hundred ex-soldiers that had given up their arms and donned civilian clothes. The thousand were marched to the banks of the Yangtze, lined up two deep and then machine-gunned.[18]

The SSA called a second meeting two days later when "things seem to be calming down slightly," in Wilson's words, though he suggests this was because "there are no more houses to burn and the people have nothing more to be stolen and there are only a few able bodied men left to lead out and kill."[19] At this meeting, an SGC preparatory committee was struck. The political "pacification" of Nanjing was about to begin.

To recruit people for the SGC, the Special Service Agency used the only available and willing Chinese organization, the Red Swastika Society.[20] Nanjing had two Red Swastika branches, both founded in 1922, one inside the city and the other in Xiaguan, the commercial suburb down by the Yangtze River outside the northwest city gate. Before 1927, when the city had nothing that could be called a municipal government, organizations such as the Red Swastika provided the destitute of Nanjing with aid in hard seasons. It also furnished traditional elites with positions and a purpose in the new urban sphere. Even after the Nationalists made Nanjing the national capital and created a full municipal administration, these benevolent societies and the elite gentlemen who led them continued their activities as dispensers of food and clothing in winter and buriers of abandoned corpses. The Red Swastika Society was once again involved in organizing relief during the winter of 1937–38, just as it had done in previous winters, especially now that the municipal government had decamped. Facing a crisis on a scale that dwarfed the worst years of the natural and man-made disasters of the 1930s, the organization enlarged its membership to about six hundred and mobilized its resources for emergency relief work of all sorts. It was this humanitarian impulse that brought Red Swastika activists, unfazed by the prospect of cooperating with anyone, even military invaders, into early contact with the occupation authorities.

The head of the Nanjing chapter of the Red Swastika was an elderly businessman, Tao Xisan. Tao had pursued a local political career in earlier times, but had been cut out of power with the arrival of the Nationalists in 1927. His philanthropic activism with the Red Swastika and other organizations during the 1920s and 1930s garnered him a public reputation outside government politics: elderly, respected, not in the pocket of the Nationalist Party, a "fine old man," in the words of Lewis Smythe. Tao was not the first choice of the Japanese. The embassy's second secretary, Fukui Kiyoshi, had attempted instead to woo Chen Rong. Chen was a graduate of Hokkaido Imperial University, head of the Department of Forestry at the University of Nanjing, and fluent in both Japanese and English. His good relations with the embassy made him a known and attractive candidate, but he resisted the invitation and chose instead to work informally as a liaison between the embassy and the IC. Fukui next approached Lou Xiaoxi. Lou was a Nanjing businessman who had studied in Japan, worked as an interpreter in Shanghai, and in the years prior to the invasion acted as an informal channel of communication between the Chinese government and the Japanese embassy. Lou proved willing, but the SSA blocked his candidacy on the grounds that he would look too much like a puppet.[21] They wanted someone who appeared to have some authority in his own right, not just an adjunct to the Japanese. Tao Xisan, with his elegant white beard and good connections into the old elite networks of Nanjing, better fit the bill. Allegedly Tao's condition for agreeing to serve was a commitment from the Japanese army to stop the killing. There is no evidence that his demand made any difference. Indeed, the army was not even able to guarantee the security of Tao's own house. A group of intoxicated Japanese soldiers barged in on the 19th and started rooting about for loot, only to be driven out by two members of the International Committee (Tao's home lay within the Safety Zone).[22] Tao at that point had not yet been approached to become the collaborationist mayor. The attacks were not enough to dissuade him from collaborating.

Organizing an SGC was a Special Service task, but the Japanese embassy had the local contacts needed to identify potential collaborators and at the start seemed to have the upper hand. George Fitch, the American head of the Nanjing YMCA, was even given to understand that the Nanjing SGC was the creation of Consul-General Tanaka Sueo.[23] The SGC's Muslim vice-chair, Sun Shurong, for instance, was an embassy employee—and his close relations with Japanese in Nanjing had placed him under early suspicion as a spy. The SSA did not care for some of the people the embassy put forward, however. Within a day or so, Rabe picked up a rumor that "the military command here does not want to recognize the Japanese-Chinese Committee that the Japanese legation has put together—one similar to our committee for the Safety Zone." The rumor carried some weight of truth. SSA agent Maruyama Susumu characterizes the SGC in his recent memoir as "rather opposed to the Japanese army," which suggests that the SSA found those the embassy had put forward to be not the sort of people it wanted in the local self-government organ.[24] Thwarted in their expectations, the SSA was in a position no different than that of pacification teams elsewhere on the delta in finding its would-be collaborators disappointing.

The six other members of the SGC were Zhao Weishu, Zhao Gongjin, Ma Xihou, Hu Qifa, Huang Yuexuan, and Wang Chunsheng. Huang was a Red Swastika activist whose name appears among those who had sat on the winter aid committee the previous year.[25] Wang had been a police officer before the Nationalists took over Nanjing in 1927, after which he ran a hotel and mingled with the city's underworld. This network would serve him in good stead when he took charge of the SGC's police force, which worked with both the SSA and the Military Police during January to root out Chinese soldiers hiding among the city's residents. Wang had a prior connection to Japan: he had received his police training there. So too did several other SGC members. Tao Xisan was a graduate of Hōsei University in Tokyo; Sun Shurong had spent two years in Japan and spoke good Japanese; Zhao Gongjin had trained as a medical doctor in Nagasaki. Zhao Weishu and committee secretary Wang Zhongtiao had also been students in Japan. For those who were seeing to the day-to-day administration of Nanjing, a prior involvement with Japan was a significant qualification.

Five other men were appointed to the SGC as advisors: Zhang Nanwu, Tao Juesan, Zhan Rongguang, Xu Chuanyin, and Wang Chengdian. At least three had ties to Tao Xisan: Tao Juesan was a kinsman, Xu Chuanyin was a Red Swastika associate, and Zhan Rongguang, who ran a patent medicine shop in the old commercial district around the Confucian Temple, was a personal friend. Zhan was also fluent in Japanese, for Minnie Vautrin, the American missionary who ran the refugee camp at Jinling Women's College, identifies him as "an interpreter" whom she approached on New Year's Day to see whether the Japanese might stop registering men on her campus.[26] From the reference in her diary, Vautrin seem to have been unaware of Zhan's role the previous day in promoting just such registration. According to a Chinese history of the occupation, an eyewitness heard him address the men who had sought refuge in Jinling College on 31 December, advising soldiers to identify themselves to the Japanese and promising that they would receive lenient treatment for doing so. Zhan could not have been ignorant that the consequence of turning oneself in was likelier execution than mercy, given what had gone on five days earlier in the refugee camp at the University of Nanjing. There, according to Searle Bates, "Chinese under the instructions of Japanese officers" encouraged Chinese soldiers to come forward voluntarily.[27] Those who complied were taken away and killed. Zhan Rongguang helped to repeat that history at Jinling College.

Xu Chuanyin presents a different figure. He had an engineering Ph.D. from the University of Illinois and was wealthy enough to have both a Dodge and a piano stolen by Japanese soldiers. Xu's command of English and his social connections with the foreign community made him the Red Swastika's natural choice to serve as its liaison with the IC. He occupied nodes in many networks: vice-chair of the Nanjing Red Swastika chapter, advisor to the SGC, housing commissioner for the Safety Zone, and IC liaison with the Japanese embassy. As a friend of Tao Xisan, Xu was a pivotal figure in the early weeks of the occupation, knitting together the many networks through which the occupation state was constructed.[28] He also knew how to cross from one to another when more than one network was needed to get something done. In mid-March, when Minnie Vautrin was trying to help women secure their husbands' release from Japanese incarceration, she sought out Xu Chuanyin for advice about whom to approach in the regime. Deeply implicated in the early work of shepherding in the new order, he soon withdrew. In 1946 he reemerged at the Tokyo trial as a prosecution witness against General Matsui.

Equally important among the SGC advisors—even more so when it came to gaining access to networks that led not laterally to other elites but downward into Nanjing society—was Wang Chengdian. Almost nothing was known of this man until the recent publication of journals and diaries previously unavailable. There he surfaces as the Westerners in Nanjing knew him, as Jimmy Wang the auctioneer.[29] Lewis Smythe first mentions him in a letter dated 24 December, where he notes that the IC had taken Wang on as its business manager. He also observes that Wang "has many connections with the underworld in Nanking," a point he repeats in an entry two days later. At the same time that he was working for the IC, Jimmy Wang was also taking part in the negotiations to form the SGC, and appeared on the inauguration podium with the other collaborators when the SGC was unveiled on New Year's Day. Jimmy Wang inspired a measure of good-humored cynicism among the Westerners, especially for his performance at the inauguration. Robert Wilson that day describes him as "one of the chief men [who] has been working in a rather subordinate capacity under the International Committee and has a long record with many connections with the city underworld, and other undesirable characteristics."[30] Charlie Riggs, an American working at the University of Nanjing, punned on Wang's profession as an auctioneer of used goods by observing that his role in the inauguration was "very fitting for a second-hand government." Lewis Smythe refers to him the same day in an affectionately amused tone as "the famous 'Jimmy.'"

When the members of the IC learned five days later that he was put in charge of SGC food supply operations, Searle Bates snorted and said, "Rice must be going to be the most paying proposition."

"Well," Smythe replied, "he is the one man in the outfit that may get some rice moving before March first."

Two days later, German legation secretary Georg Rosen acknowledged Wang's capacities in this regard when he labeled him as "the most active member of the new system." A fixer who made himself indispensable to all parties, Jimmy Wang was the sort of person who would never have found a place in the historical record of Republican China were it not for the calamity that struck his city, his willingness to act rather than flee, and his dealings with the foreigners who came to admire his forthrightness and his energy.

Wilson's uncharitable assessment of the others in the SGC was that they were "a second-hand crowd, but then there aren't any first classers in town." The judgment was harsh but not unfair. These men had no public stature and no experience in the management of urban affairs, as the SSA caustically pointed out in its confidential January report. The official narrative of the founding of the occupation state in a Japanese history of collaborative regimes in central China, published in 1940, could not afford to be so uncomplimentary. It characterizes them instead as "local capable men":[31] not "first-classers," perhaps, but the sort of elites who occupied responsible leadership niches in conservative entities such as the Red Swastika Society. To the extent that they were "capable," it was not so much their talents as their patron-client ties into Nanjing society that enabled them to be reasonably effective in getting things done without worrying overly about how they did it. These were not the new intellectuals of the Republican era, nor were they activists in the new Nationalist administration. Indeed, if anything qualified them for this job, it was the experience of having been driven out into the political cold by the Nationalist regime after it took power in 1927. They were old-style elites whose new-style education, in many cases acquired in Japan, supplemented their traditional resources of patronage networks, brokerage skills, and connections throughout local society that were effective to the extent that they remained local.

The reach of the SGC elite flashes into view in the foreigners' records. When Japanese officers entered Jinling Women's College to recruit women for brothel service on 26 December, Minnie Vautrin staunchly refused their demand. Rabe describes the scene:

She is not going to hand over even one of them willingly; but then something unexpected happens. A respectable member of the Red Swastika
Society, someone we all know, but would never have suspected had any
knowledge of the underworld, calls out a few friendly words into the
hall—and lo and behold! A considerable number of young refugee girls
step forward. Evidently former prostitutes, who are not at all sad to find
work in a new bordello. Minnie is speechless![32]

If Vautrin was taken aback by the connections that a "respectable member
of the Red Swastika Society" had with the sex trade, the worldly-wise Rabe
was more amused than surprised. The SGC in fact set up three brothels
and recruited the women to work in them, though arguably that was business as usual for men of this social stratum. The collaborators accepted
that the provision of sexual services was a concession they had to make to
please the Japanese, and an arrangement they could justify if it got sex-
starved soldiers away from other women.

Whether burying corpses or recruiting prostitutes, members of the Red
Swastika Society engaged in an activist program that proved to be a dou-
ble-edged sword that cut both ways. For being too visibly close to Japanese
authorities during the occupation, the society was dishonored and disbanded after the war. Yet the knowledge it thereby gained of Japanese actions and the records it kept would be used against Japan at the International Military Tribunal for the Far East in Tokyo. The Red Swastika kept a
record of these burials, which it submitted every day to the SGC. By early
March the total was up to 31,791, according to an SSA report, and that
number kept climbing. A Red Swastika petition to the SGC for financial
support stated that, as of the beginning of April, its members had disposed
of well over 30,000, mostly in the last three weeks of February after the
final wave of soldiers' violence against city residents had subsided. A later
report by the Nanjing branch put the total number of burials between December 1937 and April 1938 at 43,121. This is the figure that Red Swastika
member Xu Chuanyin would read into the record at the Tokyo war crimes
trial in 1946.[33]

Regime apologists who seek to minimize Japan's responsibility for the
atrocity at Nanjing now consistently invoke this number as incontrovert-
ible evidence that the scale of killing was not in the hundreds of thousands,
as Chinese claim. Special Service agent Maruyama Susumu, for instance,
repeats the Red Swastika number in his memoir. Elsewhere he charges Xu

with having submitted false evidence to the tribunal, so it is not clear what Maruyama thought. The Red Swastika number is a shockingly eye-catching fig leaf for the atrocity, offered almost as though 43,000 were both an understandable and an excusable figure. But this has become the standard final offer from those who desire to counter the popular Chinese estimates that run over 300,000. The high estimates may well be too high, yet 43,000 is too low. Whom the Red Swastika counted, and whom they didn't, is unclear. Most observers agree that the society's burials could not represent a complete record of how many died in the Rape of Nanking. Whether this figure excludes soldiers, for example, whether it excludes those who died beyond the immediate vicinity of the city walls, whether it excludes those whose corpses were burned or submerged: these are the sorts of questions that continue to provoke fierce dispute between those who desire to take the tarnish off Japan's reputation for military brutality and those wish to add another layer. The historian may contribute by bringing forward data that narrows the range, but not by cutting a deal between the two sides.

The Nanjing SGC made its first public appearance at the public inauguration ceremony at the Drum Tower in the early afternoon of 1 January 1938. Their audience was a thousand captive locals whom the SSA had recruited by informing every refugee camp two days earlier that it had to send an appropriate number of "representatives." George Fitch had called on the Japanese embassy just as preparations were getting started and caught them at it:

> They were busy giving instructions to about sixty Chinese, most of them our camp managers, on how New Year was to be celebrated. The old five-barred flag is to replace the Nationalist flag, and they were told to make a thousand of these and also a thousand Japanese flags for that event. Camps of over a thousand must have twenty representatives present, smaller camps ten. At one o'clock New Year's Day the five-barred flag is to be raised above the Drum Tower, there will be "suitable" speeches and "music" (according to the programme) and of course moving pictures will be taken of the happy people waving flags and welcoming the new regime.[34]

The flag of the old Republic had not been flown since the sun-and-sky iconography of Sun Yatsen's Nationalist Party replaced it a decade earlier.

Fitch notes that his fellow foreigners were less concerned about a regime

The inauguration of the Nanjing Self-Government Committee at the Drum Tower, 1 January 1938. From *Shina jihen gahō* (27 January 1938), pp. 10–11.

inauguration than about the two days' holiday that the Japanese army was granting in its honor, "for it means more drunken soldiers," and drunkenness meant rape. According to surviving Japanese soldiers' diaries, soldiers started the day with a morning ceremony in which they faced east and called out long life for the emperor. Then they had the rest of the day off to go drinking and "buy ass," to use their phrase for acquiring a prostitute's services. Those who wanted voluntary sex and were willing to line up could use a military brothel; one diarist mentions seeing Chinese people on the streets waving Japanese flags as he headed over to a brothel to join five hundred other soldiers sharing the services of seventy prostitutes.[35] Many others chose rape in their pursuit of this pleasure. (IC records identify two of the victims that day as fourteen-year-olds, and two of the perpetrators as military policemen.)[36] One gang of New Year's revelers even had the temerity to show up at Rabe's home that evening with a truck and ask him to fill it with girls, a request he declined. His foreign identity allowed him that luxury; many Chinese men were shot for doing the same.

Back at the Drum Tower, the audience was treated to speeches from the new Chinese politicians and their Japanese patrons (all the Special Service agents were on the podium). Tao Xisan recited the SGC's five-point manifesto. The first point committed the new regime to ending the Nationalist Party's dictatorship. The second and third vowed that the SGC would cooperate with Japan to fight Communism, and that it would correct "the concept of reliance on EuroAmerica," which it admitted was strong among the people of Nanjing. Fourth, Tao called for the revival of the economy and the improvement of the people's welfare, though he did so as the buildings on either side of the University Hospital behind him were burning.[37] Last, Tao committed the SGC to meritocracy at the center and self-government among the people—code words among 1930s conservatives for prying loose the Nationalists' grip on power. The Japanese newspaper *Asahi shinbun* carried an article on the inauguration two days later. It reported that the SGC had been able to "unite with all pro-Japanese organizations" in the city, though the historian is hard-pressed to guess what organizations the reporter had in mind.

Nanjing now had two administrative bodies with different jurisdictions: the SGC, with few resources and less reputation, and the IC, with fair stocks of both. The SSA hoped that the SGC would elbow aside the IC. The latter suspected as much, and got confirmation the day before the inauguration when it learned that the embassy had promised the SGC all the IC's money and grain stocks. The IC sought to preempt confiscation by issuing a statement, explaining that it was a private relief organization whose resources were held in trust and not transferable. The SGC's response the following day was to position itself as the legitimate alternative to the IC by announcing that it was assuming full care for the refugees in the Safety Zone. It turns out that this declaration was issued for a specific purpose. On the following day Japanese military authorities entered the zone to identify, remove, and execute soldiers and any other young males they regarded as "anti-Japanese elements." They exercised this prerogative by virtue of the declared SGC jurisdiction over the zone. Asserting control of refugees had nothing to do at this point with regularizing administration, and everything to do with exterminating Chinese males of military age. The SGC's declaration of responsibility on 4 January for refugees thus amounted to complicity in war crimes. That complicity blossomed into proxy management as, over the following weeks, the SGC's Investigation Subcommittee and Wang Chunsheng's police force helped the Military Police to round up ex-soldiers for execution.

IC members initially adopted a cool attitude toward the SGC, suspecting it of trying to engineer nothing more than a resource grab. As Rabe noted in his diary two days before the inauguration, "We have nothing against their taking over our work, but it looks to us as if they simply want to take over our money. I'll not voluntarily hand over anything." Within a day of the inauguration, vice-chair Sun Shurong approached Rabe for a meeting. Rabe was skeptical as to his intentions. As he wrote in his diary, Sun "condescendingly informs me that he must speak to me very soon about an important matter. Please do, I've been waiting for this. I have a very good idea of what your intentions are!" It quickly became apparent, though, that the real force was not the SGC but the SSA. When consular attaché Fukuda Tokuyasu called on Rabe on 6 January (a day so cold that the creeks froze over), it was to inform him that the "military authorities"—by which he presumably meant the SSA—had decided that the IC should dissolve and hand over its assets to the SGC.

The IC responded the following day by setting its own condition, which was that the Japanese lay out a concrete plan for restoring law and order

Sun Shurong, vice-chair of the Nanjing Self-Government Committee, 1938.
From *Chūka minkoku ishin seifu gaishi* (1940), p. 377.

prior to the IC's turning over anything. The Westerners were careful to make clear that they were not opposed to handing over Nanjing to a Chinese administration. As Rabe wrote in his reply, the IC was eager for the SGC to "assume as speedily as possible all the usual functions of a local civic administration: policing, fire protection, sanitation, *et cetera*. The International Committee has, I am quite certain, no desire whatsoever to carry on any of these administration duties which are normally assumed by competent local authorities." The issue for the IC was not administration in general, but the responsible and effective administration of relief. The problem was the virtual absence of "competent authorities." In his diary that day, Rabe wrote that the SGC "hasn't the vaguest idea how to tackle these problems, even though they are being advised by the Japanese. All that interests them are our assets."

One week into its existence, the SGC had not yet demonstrated much capacity to meet the challenge of housing 62,500 people (the camp's average population in January) and providing food aid to many more.[38] Rabe was really targeting the SSA, which he could not detect as having done anything to address the needs of the people in the city. He phrases his expectations of the SSA as graciously as possible in a letter, expressing his hope that "the Japanese military authorities will cooperate, even more liberally than they are now doing, with the Self-Government Association in the provision of food and fuel for the refugees." The point for Rabe, who had no interest in securing for any of the players the political legitimacy that so consumed SSA attention, was not to fight over scarce goods, but to ensure that they did not go to waste and to coordinate efforts to deliver them. "Even so," he pointed out, "the combined efforts of all agencies will scarcely overtake the need."[39]

A recent Chinese history of the occupation concludes from the evidence of tension between the two organizations that, in its particular jargon, "the bogus Self-Government Committee and the International Committee for the Nanjing Safety Zone were in opposition from beginning to end."[40] That was certainly how things might look from a distance, especially during the first week of SGC operations. In fact, though, all sorts of factors encouraged quiet complicity: cross-over appointments, friendships, common concerns, a distrust of the Japanese, and a recognition that resources were limited and had to be carefully managed.

The combining of efforts to meet extraordinary survival needs that winter pushed diverse actors into unexpected cooperation. A key player in this complicity was Wang Chengdian: Jimmy Wang. Wang visited Rabe on 10 January to inform him that the Japanese had decided not to force the closure of the International Committee, contrary to Fukuda's information four days earlier. The new Japanese condition was more modest: that the IC continue its relief work but let the SGC take over the sale of rice to refugees. The IC agreed and suspended rice sales the following morning. The SGC had not at that point organized a distribution system of its own, though by the afternoon Wang opened an SGC rice outlet inside the Safety Zone. The next move by the Japanese was to cut off the IC's supply of rice and coal at noon the following day and forbid it from hauling these goods. In the meantime, though, Jimmy Wang worked out an agreement with the IC to use its trucks to move rice for the SGC, which lacked its own transport. One move thus defeated another, and given that this rice was coming to the SGC from the Japanese, the irony of the blockade was all the greater. After a few days, however, the two committees were able to get food supplies moving with minimal interference from the Japanese. The sole Japanese condition was that the coolies the IC hired to lug the rice could not wear IC armbands but would have to display SGC insignia while doing the work. Where the IC was involved, it had to look as though it were not.[41]

The man who oversaw the food supply system on the IC side was an American, Charlie Riggs. Riggs was the IC's associate housing commissioner, working under Xu Chuanyin. He was responsible for organizing relief on the campus of the University of Nanjing, during the course of which he developed close ties with Chinese relief workers, including Jimmy Wang. Between them, Riggs and Wang set up the food supply system that would keep the Safety Zone refugees fed through January and early February. As Lewis Smythe put it in his 22 January report on relief work, the two "together are moving heaven and earth to get the Japanese to allow them to have more rice, flour and coal for the population and then to truck it in." Riggs had his status as a foreigner to protect their operations from Japanese interference, although he was physically assaulted on at least two occasions by Japanese soldiers. Wang for his part had the contacts throughout Nanjing society and a willingness to get what he wanted. The chancellor of the German legation in a report commended Wang by saying that he "has at least shown courage and told the Japanese: 'If you are against me, then you'd better shoot me here and now!'" Fixers like this are not the sort of paragon that Chinese historiography likes to celebrate. Were we to rely entirely on the Chinese and Japanese records of the event, we would now know Jimmy Wang only as Wang Chengdian, a name on an SGC roster. Only in the Western sources does something of his role leak through.

The SGC had no stocks of grain in its possession. Jimmy Wang in the committee's first week of operation asked the Japanese army for 200,000 piculs, suggesting half for free and half by sale (one picul of lower-middle-grade rice weighed 62 kg). This extravagant proposal the army turned down flat, but it came back a few days later with a delivery of 1,250 sacks for free distribution plus the promise of another 10,000 sacks to sell (one sack weighed 77.5 kg). The one condition was that the SGC distribute this rice outside the Safety Zone as an inducement for refugees to leave. As of the end of the month, 4,200 sacks of rice had been delivered—less than half of what had been promised, and barely 3 percent of Jimmy Wang's original request. The army also promised 1,000 sacks of flour (one sack weighed 22.8 kg), again for distribution outside the Safety Zone, though no flour was delivered until February. Using the IC calculation that one sack of rice could feed 125 adults for a day, and then reducing that level to subsistence rations, the Japanese army had given the SGC in January enough grain to feed the city's refugees for barely three days.

After being frozen out of food distribution, the IC petitioned the Japanese embassy several times that it arrange with the army for permission to recover 10,933 sacks of rice and 10,000 sacks of flour from a former government warehouse in Xiaguan where they sat embargoed. On 28 January it also filed a letter with the SGC proposing that, "if this rice is secured, we shall be glad to cooperate with you in making it available for free distribution to civilians both outside and inside the boundaries of the Safety Zone." When the Japanese embassy finally responded in the first week of February, it did so informally through the American consul, John Allison, who spoke Japanese. Counselor Hidaka Shinrokurō asked Allison whether the IC was willing to cooperate with the SGC to distribute this food. This assurance had already been made and put into practice several times, but the SSD was still anxious lest that food confer political legitimacy on the Westerners. Hidaka was concerned to make sure that if any symbolic capital accrued to the release of the precious grain stores, it would go to the SGC.

Starting in mid-January, the SGC was able to set up a network of rice shops around the city. Poor security hampered this process, however. On the 21st its newly opened rice shop on Shenzhou Road was held up by Japanese soldiers no fewer than three times in one day. The SGC decided to set up a somewhat complicated arrangement that involved the issuing of rice tickets at one office, the payment of money at another, and the delivery of rice at a third. On the following day the SGC tried to open another rice shop on Baotai Street, close by its headquarters, though it had difficulty maintaining security and organizing transport. The ability of the SGC to protect its operations from Japanese looters remained precarious until at least the end of January.[42]

As order improved in February, Tao Xisan proposed opening rice shops in the abandoned residential areas and selling rice at below-market prices in order to encourage people to return home. To supply these shops, he put together a plan to buy grain north of the Yangtze and ship it into Nanjing. Vice-chair Sun Shurong moved against him. He saw this as an expensive move and spoke out against what he regarded as Tao's wasteful liberality. He felt that all grain should be distributed from the shops the SGC had already set up, both to protect SGC revenue and to demonstrate the committee's importance to the Japanese. Sun even turned to the Japanese army to support his attempt to get Tao's initiative overruled. The dispute over food resources broke open the animosity between the chair and vice-chair that had been building all through January. The unity of the organization was falling apart.

The Japanese army was not interested in taking sides in the factional struggle between Tao and Sun. At the same time, Japanese patience with Tao was running out. SSA agent Maruyama remembers the early SGC as anti-Japanese, and Tao as unhappy: wanting to maintain an arm's-length relationship with the Japanese, yet unable to do so as long as the SGC had to rely on Japanese for funding: the classic dilemma of the collaborator. As Tao lost ground in the struggle to make the SGC independent of Japanese control, Sun Shurong was eager to move into his place by offering himself to the Japanese as the more cooperative leader. According to Maruyama, Jimmy Wang and Zhao Gongjin threw their support to Sun. Wang was nothing if not good at telling which way the wind was blowing. By the third week of January, Tao was complaining that he was SGC chair in name only. When the SGC gathered at the Japanese embassy to meet with General Matsui on the 23rd (Matsui observed that they made a poor impression), Tao presented a united front. The following morning he submitted his resignation, citing advanced age and ill health. The Japanese refused to accept it. Five days later, Tao's new residence was stripped of its contents and the SSA declined to investigate who was responsible.

Compounding Tao's conundra—how to avoid the appearance of being a

Japanese puppet while accepting Japanese money, how to assert leadership when his chief competitor was in cahoots with his patrons—was the realization that the Nanjing SGC would get financial support only in the short term. Fifty-eight percent of the committee's income for the month of January (17,895 of 31,085 yuan) came from the sale of confiscated grain and flour that the CCAA had given to the committee as a way of kick-starting its revenue flow. That amount roughly covered SGC salaries. Another third of the SGC's January income (10,000 yuan) was an outright gift from the CCAA. The committee was able to generate only 3,190 yuan (10 percent of its income) on its own through commercial levies and a rickshaw tax. After this first month, however, the revenue holiday was over. The committee was forced to become self-supporting in February. Direct Japanese support—in the form of a gift from the Japanese embassy—was cut back to a miserable 1,000 yuan (2 percent of total income of 51,257 yuan). A few other gifts from Japan's military followed: 2,000 yuan from the Fujita Unit, and 500 yuan from Major-General Harada Kumakichi, head of the Special Service Department in Shanghai. But these amounts were not sufficient to fund an urban administration. Nor would the proxy financing continue forever. Once in, the SGC had to find its own means of support.

On 28 January, it was announced that all who had taken refuge in the Safety Zone had to return to their homes within a week. The notice went out over the SGC's name, but it was the SSA that formulated the order and imposed the deadline. Many no longer had homes to which to return, however. The SSA confidentially admitted in its January report that over half of the housing had been destroyed when the city was occupied.[43] The survey of war damage that Lewis Smythe conducted in March estimated that one-quarter of the buildings in Nanjing were burned, and that they were "thoroughly, even systematically stripped of their contents before the burning." Another two-thirds were looted but not burned. "Practically without exception" the 11 percent neither looted nor burned had been "entered by soldiers who robbed to some degree, later followed by civilian thieves in unoccupied buildings." Returnees thus went home to find their homes stripped clean.

Concerned that the IC go along with this plan, the SSA called IC leaders to a meeting at SGC headquarters on the afternoon of 28 January. Matsuoka gave no indication of how the lack of housing would be resolved, other than to explain that the Japanese army would help to empty the camps by sending in soldiers to drive the refugees out. The popular reaction was hysteria. The IC responded the following day by petitioning the SSA to extend the deadline and suggesting that the SGC get involved by taking over the refugee operations in government buildings. The SSA's response the day after was to repeat what Matsuoka had announced on the 28th. The refugee camps were to close, and that was final. The SSA's direction of this process indicates that the return to residences was in effect not a transfer of authority from foreign to Chinese, with which the IC would have been happy to oblige, but from foreign to Japanese.[44]

The SGC dutifully put the SSA's resettlement plan into operation by posting notices informing residents of the 4 February deadline and warning them that the temporary structures in which they had been living would be torn down. Those who had something to return to were keen to do so in any case. What no one anticipated was the reaction of Japanese soldiers to this order, which was to fan out across the city in a renewed frenzy of rape, theft, and murder. This mayhem peaked during the first three days after the notices went up, but continued for a week.[45] Soldiers' expectations were so aroused with the thought of easy pickings, in fact, that a truckload of them pulled up to SGC headquarters on the morning of 2 February "and demanded at least 13 girls or as many more as they could find," as John Magee notes in a letter written that day. "The Chinese tried to stall them off but they surrounded the place and were still there this afternoon. The Committee did succeed in finding two prostitutes but these were not enough." Not even the SGC was safe from those it was supposed to serve.[46]

Only after a week of this riot was it at all feasible for refugees to live outside the camps without harassment. The procedure became more orderly toward the end of the second week of February. By the end of the month, by SSA count, 172,502 people had returned to their homes or other makeshift dwellings outside the Safety Zone. The exception was the devastated area of Xiaguan, home to Nanjing's poorest. Of the refugees who returned home, only 4 percent went back to Xiaguan. When the American biologist Albert Steward passed through Xiaguan the following December, a year after the occupation, most of it was still a flattened waste.[47]

By the end of March, several indicators were pointing to a modest stabilization of life in Nanjing. One was that the number of refugees who had been resettled was up to 235,056. Another was the renewed flow of commercial rice into the city from the regional wholesale market upriver in Wuhu, which was easing supply difficulties and giving the SGC something to tax (the SGC had to get SSA approval to levy sixty cents on each *dan*).[48] A third was the fall in the number of fire alarms to twenty-two from forty-eight the previous month. Despite these modest improvements, much of the city remained a shambles for a long time. On the afternoon of Sunday, 24 April, a visiting American consular official based in Tokyo, Cabot Coville, joined several other Westerners on a trip into the business section of the city. He was struck by the extent of the damage, and puzzled by its pattern: "There are few signs of bombardment; but individual shops and other buildings are gutted by pillage, looting, and fire. It is not that the entire area has been swept over by a conflagration. Places left here and there show such was not the case. One shop will be utterly barren of any contents; the next will be a charred wreck, set afire after the removal of most of its goods and equipment. Photographs taken now would be completely damning."[49]

Coville meant that the evidence would be damning to the Chinese, whom he assumed had done the looting. The burning, though, was the work of Japanese soldiers acting on their officers' orders. People at the time wondered why the Japanese army would choose to engage in what Lewis Smythe in his report identified as "the deliberate burning of extensive commercial and industrial sections" of the city,[50] though this was standard practice elsewhere on the Yangtze Delta. Some speculated that it was to hide the extent of Japanese looting, others that it was to punish the Chinese for resisting Japan's conquest. It did not make the task of restoring the capital to proper functioning any easier.

Coville's party then drove outside the city walls and saw other evidence of what Nanjing had been through.

> Leaving by one of the city gates we stop and walk into the official residence of the chairman of the executive yuan. It is a wreck. Huge shell holes pierce the brick walls, glass and brick is all over the place, one can walk in and out anywhere. In the center of the reception room is the carcass of a horse. There are trenches in the garden with exposed Chinese bodies. The Sun Yat Sen memorial seems unharmed. It is covered by bamboo scaffolding and straw mats. In the park below trenches run about without much plan. The Chinese bodies in them have not been covered.

The trenches had been part of the Chinese army's preparations for hampering the Japanese attack. The Japanese army found them useful as mass graves. The damage to Nanjing's cityscape was still visible when Albert

Steward arrived in December 1938. In the south part of Nanjing, he found that "the destruction which has been wrought is beyond calculation. The people are still few, and in most places houses of business are still scattered." Referring to Smythe's survey of war damage, Steward proposes that "if both sides had cooperated in giving such protection to civilian life and property as would not have interfered with military operations, not over one or two percent of the actual losses need to have occurred." This sort of rationality did not enter Japanese calculations a year earlier; the logic at work then was not profit and loss but victory and humiliation. If Steward's hypothetical is a reasonable supposition of what cooperation might have achieved, it is also retrospective testimony that the Nanjing SGC and the SSA between them failed to achieve what they were put in place to produce.

Petty trading between a Nanjing peddler and Japanese soldiers in the Nanjing Safety Zone. From *Shina jihen gahō* (27 January 1938), p. 16.

The people of the city paid the price for this failure well beyond the initial occupation. Small-scale peddling revived soon enough, but in 1939 unemployment was 73 percent and average earnings were 60 percent below what they had been before the occupation. Out in the surrounding countryside, the loss of tools was estimated at over five million yuan and the loss of crops and domestic animals in excess of fifteen million.[51] Searle Bates summarizes the situation in the final report on the work of the International Relief Committee, as the IC was retitled in February: "The living standard of the whole Chinese population of Nanking is very close to that of the poorer groups selected in various Chinese cities for surveys by social workers before the war. The events of the last two years have reduced the native population to that level, which means of course that many are on the margin of survival." Nanjing was locked into "a desperate poverty grossly abnormal for this region. No general economic improvement is in sight, while factors of a military and governmental nature continue to worsen the currency situation and potentially to endanger much else." In terms of what Bates called "the actual influences at work upon the people's livelihood," the collaboration experiment was a failure. "Prosperity and security seem pitifully remote from the local people," he concluded.[52]

The Sunday Coville toured the city and suburbs was also the day on which Tao Xisan's Self-Government Committee was disbanded. Its fate had become tied to politics at a higher level. A new "national" regime, the Reformed Government, had been installed several weeks earlier at a ceremony in the city on 30 March. The installation was a formality, since Nanjing was much too disorderly to house a government; the Reformed Government personnel returned to Shanghai and stayed there until October. Nonetheless, a new regime now existed, and it expected to rule over its capital city at the very least. Just as the Nationalists had done, the new center took municipal leadership out of the local hands in which it had briefly rested for four months and brought it back under its own control. The SGC was replaced by a centrally appointed entity dubbed the Nanjing Municipal Commission. The new mayor was Ren Yuandao, a prominent figure in the new Reformed Government and concurrent head of the Ministry of Pacification, the military ministry to which the Nanjing police now reported, as they had under the Nationalists. Ren would give up the mayoralty in a further reorganization of the municipal government five months later, handing it off to his vice-minister, Gao Guanwu. (Both mayors narrowly missed being assassinated, Ren in July 1938 and Gao that winter.) Not until mid-1940 would control of the city be separated from the Ministry of Pacification, part of the shake-up that accompanied the installation of a new national government under Wang Jingwei. Gao relinquished his vice-ministership and became full-time head of the once again renamed Nanjing Special Municipality.

Many of the collaborators who came forward to serve the SSA in its attempts to neutralize the IC were abandoned in these shuffles, but some were able to turn their opportunism to longer-term advantage.[53] Tao Xisan was promoted to sinecures in the Reformed Government, first as vice-chair of the Great People's Association, later as a member of the Legislative Yuan on the recommendation of its president, Wen Zongyao. When the Reformed Government was in turn dissolved in March 1940, Tao was given an "advisory" position in the Wang Jingwei regime. That December, however, he came under investigation for corruption and his political career ended. After the war, Tao was sentenced to two years' imprisonment for abetting the enemy. It was a modest punishment. The case must have struck the tribunal judges, so many years after Tao's SGC had briefly come and gone, as a minor bit of collaboration. Had he stepped from the political limelight when the SGC was disbanded, he might have gone unnoticed and unpunished. Tao Xisan died in Nanjing in June 1948, two months after his release from prison.

Of the other members of the original SGC, Zhao Gongjin made it into the new municipal administration, promoted from head of the Transportation Department to director of the Industrial Bureau under both the Municipal Commission and the Special Municipality. Tao Juesan also continued to hold positions within the municipal government into the 1940s. The only other leading SGC figure to survive politically was Jimmy Wang. He first served as the head of the Commercial and Industrial Department, and then under Gao Guanwu captured the powerful position of head of the Social Affairs Bureau, a post in which he was still active until at least the summer of 1939, according to a 2 July article in the *New Nanjing Daily* on the training of neighborhood watch organizers. I have found it impossible to track Jimmy Wang beyond that point. His name does come up, however, in a published interview with an elderly Christian conducted in the 1980s. The man recalled Wang, who happened to have bedded down beside him in a Safety Zone refugee camp in December 1937, telling him that this was "such a good opportunity to make a fortune" and trying to tempt him with a post as an SGC district head. Wang dismissed the man as a fool when he declined. That was all the man remembered of Jimmy Wang, other than that he "died long ago."[54]

The disappearance of the original SGC personnel from later municipal lineups indicates that new political elites had replaced them. But there is sufficient documentation about post-1938 Nanjing to show that their disappearance did not signal that they had fallen out of the city's elite entirely. They may have been pushed out of their municipal posts, but they continued to have a public presence, according to a list of the heads of public organizations in Nanjing published in 1940. Several SGC activists appear there: former vice-chair Sun Shurong as the manager of the Nanjing mosque, the hated Zhan Rongguang as head of the Jiangxi Provincial Guild, Huang Yuexuan running the Buddhist Charitable Orphanage and the Lodge of Universal Goodness (Tongshan tang), and policeman Wang Chunsheng heading a "charitable organization" called the Lodge for Stimulating Goodness (Xingshan tang). The list also names Mayor Gao Guanwu as the head of the Japan-China Buddhist League, and none other than Tao Xisan running the Guangfeng Granary. (Was managing the granary where the charge of corruption against him originated?) These were just the sorts of position in which one would expect to find "local capable men," but not politicians of national stature. The SGC elite was thus socially still in place, though it had lost its political traction. A sign of this loss is the diminished political clout of the Red Swastika Society. As of September 1942, Tao Xisan was still named as the leader of the Nanjing branch. This was the sole public post in his grasp after his corruption disgrace, but no longer enough to catapult him into leadership elsewhere. As for the other four members of the executive, all were political unknowns.[55] The Red Swastika was no longer the temporary bridge of convenience by which the Japanese could make contact with local elites, discarded now that better contacts had been found.

Conflicting pressures trapped the Nanjing Self-Government Committee in a narrow defile, just as they trapped the would-be politician Tao Xisan. The goals of the fledgling municipal administration were both modest and grand: modest in trying to get a ruined city back to some semblance of order, grand in hoping to build from that rubble the foundation of a healthy civic regime in their control. The assets on which it could pursue these goals were as contradictory as its political position. On one hand, the SGC had an army of occupation to turn to for financial and political support, though only for the short term. On the other, a well-organized group of Westerners was positioned both to compete and to cooperate, within limits. The Western presence did not so much disrupt the process of collaboration as complicate it by doubling the layers of complicity. The SGC's complicities ran in many directions: with the Japanese who brought it into being; with the Westerners who were providing essential support for city residents; and with the local organizations that furnished the original collaborators. Thus it was that collaboration could produce such odd figures as Jimmy Wang working all sides of the street and both ends as well: in one context defying Japanese interference over food supply, in another setting up SGC brothels and recruiting Chinese to work in them. For perhaps it was he who winkled the girls at Jinling College out from under Minnie Vautrin's nose—and then did the same at the University of Nanjing. Wang was not a man to entertain illusions about the position he or the SGC found itself in. As he told Lewis Smythe in March, " 'Self-government' means only this: 'When the Japanese say 'Yes,' we do it!' "

For doing what they said, Wang was put on the official list of "traitors" that Chiang's regime published in 1939 (so too was Tao Xisan). What he had done to feed and protect the population of Nanjing—of which officials in Chongqing (Chiang's capital) were completely unaware—might have been enough to cancel out the charge of collaboration, had he not gone on to hold an official post under the Special Municipality.[56] Because Jimmy Wang's service to the new order coincided with the war of resistance, his collaboration put him and the members of the International Committee on opposite sides of a moral fence. Casting Wang as a traitor and the Westerners as heroes is not the only perspective from which the events of this time and place have been arranged into moral meaning. From the point of view of Communist anti-imperialism in the 1950s, they were on the same wrong side of the fence. Wang had worked openly for the Japanese, but the Americans had ended up abandoning China's political interests in order to protect their own economic concerns. This jaded view of the IC as purely self-interested was even voiced at the time by a British businessman whose egg-packing plant fell outside the Safety Zone boundaries.[57] We might do better to put both the IC and Wang on both sides of the fence. Jimmy Wang served the interests of the occupier as well as of the people of Nanjing; so, in a way, did the Westerners to the extent that what they did helped restore a public order that could only strengthen the position of the Chinese collaborators and their new regime.

Searle Bates was not unaware of this complicity. He alludes to it in his report on the execution of suspected soldiers who had sought refuge in the Safety Zone: "To deal for a number of days with [Japanese] officers and soldiers who played varying parts in the drama, showing smiles and deference when necessary for the welfare of the tens of thousands brought to the University for registration, was torture." The deference was the only way to help the Chinese, even if it was what the Japanese wanted as well. Bate's burdened sense of complicity surfaces again at a lecture he gave in New York in June 1941. When asked whether relief work strengthened the collaborationist regime, his reply was: "The consensus is that the contribution to the Japanese is very slight; that the contribution to Chinese morale and character much more than overbalances anything we are doing for the Japanese."[58] This is a fair observation that was nonetheless able to acknowledge that their relief work had made a "slight" contribution to the making of the occupation state. Even when gains are felt to outweigh losses, complicity brings losses as well as gains. Appealing to the authority of consensus is his way of exonerating the complicity that, from a hostile perspective, might not so easily be excused.

Searle Bates and Jimmy Wang both understood that complicity denied them the heroism of resistance. They also understood complicity as something other than surrender: managing as best one can, under circumstances one did not seek and could not change, to achieve something, often at costs none ever wished to pay and with consequences none anticipated suffering. The appealing opposition that places agents and collaborators on one side and victims and resisters on the other can be imposed on the events in Nanjing as well as it can on other places. Indeed, the occupation state arose here as surely on the executed bodies of young Chinese men and the raped bodies of young Chinese women as it did anywhere else on the Yangtze Delta. But many other things happened as well, even as the carnage occurred. Were it not for the unusual range of records that have survived in Chinese, English, German, and Japanese, we would not be able to untangle the many strands of complicity that tie resistance and collaboration together. Complicity was painful to experience and hard to acknowledge in a situation where a nod was enough to condemn a man to death or a woman to prostitution, and a well-placed word might bring either reprieve. But it was as irreducible a feature of the occupation state as violent repression. Both conjured that state's presence in Nanjing.

— 6 —

Rivalries / Shanghai

Collaboration is never a simple relationship, as the previous chapter has shown. Viewed from a distance, collaboration looks like a straightforward agreement by compliant local administrators to work with an armed occupying authority. Up close, it reveals a resilient web of complicities running in many directions among many actors. The multiplicity of these lines of complicit engagement produces complicity's flip side, rivalry. For where there are many clients crowding the narrow corridor that military authority makes of occupation politics, these clients must compete with one another for recognition. An absence of rivalry would indicate that elites had declined to form relationships with the occupier; it would be evidence of an almost complete failure on the occupier's part to engage them in the necessary work of state building and regime legitimation. But rivalry was far from absent in China. Occupation politics makes rivalry likely; it also expects it.

Because occupation is sudden and disruptive of the ways of doing politics and the personnel involved in doing it, it invites opportunistic initiatives from a wide range of actors, from power holders anxious to preserve their privileges to nonelites now looking for higher status. Those whom we might identify as collaborators, and who were so identified at the time, were not the only ones to enter the politics of occupation. Noncollaborators ambitious to protect their own interests or take advantage of the suspension of the normal routines for getting things done also muscled their way onto the political terrain that occupation produced to compete with those who had grasped power early. They might even press their claims to the point of seeking to unseat reigning collaborators, exposing them as opportunists and themselves as upright citizens dedicated to the public good. Shanghai under the Japanese is an ideal site for exploring just such rivalries, in part because of its sheer size and complexity, and in part because of the rich archival documentation from the lowest levels of municipal administration where rivalries were played out. The effect of these rivalries was not just to make the process of collaboration more complex; it was also to erode the feasibility of producing a stable occupation regime.

Shanghai was not pacified as other places on the Yangtze Delta were. To other locations, as we have seen, the Pacification Department dispatched small teams of South Manchurian Railway Company personnel in small teams to reestablish administrative practices however they could. Shanghai was different. The creation of a collaborationist regime within this politically and socially more complicated urban space was not a Mantetsu project. It fell instead directly under the supervision of the army's Special Service Department. Lower-level Mantetsu people were considered adequate for the counties, but the work of pacifying Shanghai was kept in the hands of agents who had a longer record of promoting Japanese political and military interests in China. For a task this important, hastily recruited amateurs could not be trusted.

Although more studied than other sites of occupation, Shanghai under the Japanese remains a difficult and elusive subject. In part the difficulty is a matter of scale: the city is simply too large, too complex, too densely populated, and too divided among its multiple foreign and Chinese jurisdictions to permit easy summary. The International Settlement and the French Concession, which formed the heart of the trading city, were exempt from Japanese control until 8 December 1941. The Japanese ruled their own piece of the International Settlement north of Soochow Creek, which is the part of the city where the Special Service ran its operations. As of November 1937, the rest of Shanghai outside the concessions was theirs as well. South of the French Concession lay the old walled Ming city, known as Nanshi or the South City, which was the center of indigenous business trading. To the west of the International Settlement lay the Extra-Settlement Roads Area, which the Chinese administrators referred to as Huxi, the Western District, and Westerners liked to call the Badlands. To the north lay the newly laid out municipal offices of Jiangwan (known in English as the Central District). In addition there were the districts of Zhabei and Zhenru to the north of the International Settlement, and Pudong, the area east of the foreigners' Shanghai across the Huangpu River. What went on in any one of these places was not necessarily what went on in any of the others, even when they were under the same jurisdiction.

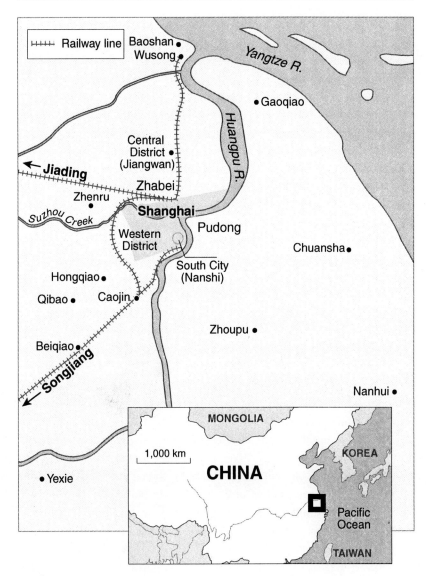

Map 3. The Shanghai region.

Even if those who lived there imagined their subdivided city as a single place, "Shanghai" was not a unified entity.

There are, to my knowledge, no surviving Special Service or Mantetsu reports on Japanese administrative operations in Shanghai. Nor are there any memoirs by Japanese agents or observers who were close to the process of building a municipal regime. This means that the story of local collaboration in Shanghai has to be reconstructed almost entirely from the unevenly preserved documents the Chinese side has archived.[1] The Chinese documentary perspective reveals relatively little about the occupiers, though a great deal about the situations in which collaborators found themselves. The collaborators navigated between competing claims from above and below, dealing both with the Japanese, who remained the final arbiters of all disputes, and with the many contenders who popped up at every turn to transmute the disruptions of occupation into opportunities for themselves. The picture is made only more complicated by the common practice of dragging as many ideological red herrings across one's tracks as possible, so that this was made to look as though it were that, and that recostumed to look like this. The rough consistencies of pacification practice found in other cities are not as evident in Shanghai. What will become visible instead is a fascinating tangle of rivalries that made ruling occupied Shanghai a headache for everyone involved, Chinese and Japanese alike.

The history of the pacification of Shanghai begins with the inauguration of an improbable entity called the Great Way Government on 5 December 1937. The opening ceremony took place in the South City. There, before a small and motley gathering, the head of this new entity, Su Xiwen, read aloud the obligatory manifesto. The party then ferried itself across the Huangpu River to take up the business of ruling Shanghai from its makeshift headquarters in Pudong. The new regime's first act that day was to distribute a set of documents communicating the regime's legitimacy and authority to the greater public of Shanghai: a formal declaration that Su had assumed mayoral authority, a provisional organizational outline, a telegram to other governmental bodies announcing the changeover of administration, and a similar announcement to the powerful Bankers' Guild and the Chamber of Commerce. The Great Way Government also put out a notice to former municipal employees informing them that they had seven days within which to declare whether they planned to return to work. Copies of the manifesto, telegram, and reemployment notice were sent to all Shanghai newspapers with a cover letter demanding immediate publication. The dilatory received a follow-up letter the next day repeating this order in curter terms.[2]

In these founding documents the identity of the Great Way as merely a

Su Xiwen inaugurating the Great Way Government, Shanghai, 5 December 1937.
From Mōgi Kikuo, *Shanhai shi daidō seifu shisaku hōkoku* (1938).

municipal government gets tucked out of sight behind a phantom nation
on whose behalf the regime seems to speak. The Nationalist Party created a
"hell on earth," states the manifesto, damaging the viability of genuine political life by making it "impossible to select the wise and capable." Its
"Party dictatorship" also created a negative atmosphere in which "internationally it has not been possible to speak of trust or cultivate closeness"—
here is the only oblique reference to Japan. The Great Way Government
was to remedy the sickness that the Nationalists had inflicted on China,
and would do so as Chinese curing Chinese. The manifesto weaves the
goal of peace—the occupation's code word for Japanese hegemony in East
Asia—with an appeal to the traditional notion of a seamless cosmic order,
expressed through the image of the Great Way. To quote its phrasing,
"Only when people as well as nations carry out the Great Way in their relations with each other can they achieve true peace. Otherwise, regardless of
what laws restrain them, if they do not act in accordance with the Great
Way, then certainly one cannot speak of true peace." The term "Great Way"
has been taken from the ancient Chinese text known as *The Classic of Rites.*

When the Great Way was pursued, in James Legge's translation of the passage, "a public and common spirit ruled all under the sky; they chose men of talent, virtue, and ability; their words were sincere and what they cultivated was harmony. Thus men did not love their parents only, nor treat as children only their sons."[3] The new Shanghai regime hoped to recycle this Great Way as a conservative Chinese vision that rose above familistic particularity to produce an ideology of public service and public good. Choosing the yin-yang circle as its symbol, the regime used this and other markers to self-identify as a thoroughly Chinese undertaking dedicated to restoring ancient Chinese values and rescuing coastal Chinese from their recently acquired foreign ways.

Japan's role in creating this local regime crosses these documents as only a vague shadow. The telegram to government bodies acknowledges that Japan played a role in shepherding the transformation when it states: "Fortunately the Japanese Imperial Army has brought its presence to the Central Region and has cut out the evil and obstinate on our behalf." Otherwise, the documents that the Great Way issued on 5 December are utterly silent on the work the Japanese side did to bring the regime into existence. Not a word of a pacification team is breathed, or even of Japanese advisors. Japanese accounts of the Great Way Government share this discretion. A brief comment in an internal Japanese report, dated 31 January 1938, notes that the regime was formed "with the help of the Imperial Army." A propaganda booklet on the regime published the following month in Tokyo identifies Nishimura Tenzō as the chief Japanese advisor to the Great Way Government, but insists that "there are only two Japanese officials in this government." It is hard to pick out the thread of literalism by which this claim is supposed to hang, given that the internal report names no fewer than thirty-four pacification agents working as full-time advisors to the regime. Clearly both sides decided that the Great Way Government had to have the outward appearance of complete autonomy from Japanese control. The pantomime of political autonomy and popular legitimacy that the inauguration ceremony acted out was a piece of theater that every political actor in the Republican era had to perform in the search for something better than mere warlord status. For collaborators, the pressure to appear legitimate was that much harder to assert, particularly when the patron was as visibly present as Japan was.

So we have the names of the thirty-four Japanese who, as of late January, were pulling the strings of the Great Way Government from behind the scenes; beyond that, however, we have almost nothing to show what these people did or how the core of the new municipal administration functioned. The entire process of regime formation is almost a blank. The only surviving fragment is a comment that appears in a short book that a Tokyo official published in 1938 on the basis of a fifty-day tour he made of occupied China. In his book he reveals that the head of the regime, Su Xiwen, and the head of the Special Service team, Nishimura Tenzō, were not collaborating for the first time. He reveals that sometime after 1931, Su and Nishimura had worked together in Shandong province to organize a "peasants' self-government movement"—in other words, to set up rural networks that could extend Japan's economic and political influence into that province.[4] In October 1937 the two men sailed to Shanghai, where they resurfaced as the leaders of the new regime. The surprise inauguration of the Great Way Government on 5 December was as bold a gesture as Mussolini's occupation of Rome, the author of the report declared. This rhetorical alignment of Su Xiwen with the international fascist movement was a tendentious move to cast him as a leader of Mussolini's stature.

Given his utter obscurity, Su attracted rumors as well as official fictions. According to a Hong Kong newspaper, his original name was Su Junying, but he changed it to Su Songzhi, and later to Su Youxiang. He had other identities as well, for a Japanese magazine in January 1938 refers to him as Su Jixiao.[5] When he emerged as the mayor of Shanghai at the age of forty-five, he was a political unknown. He came from an Amoy trading family on the south coast of Fujian and spoke Japanese, encouraging many at the time to assume he was a Taiwanese in the service of the Japanese empire. In his early twenties Su studied political economy at Waseda University in Tokyo, then returned to China about 1916 to hold a series of mid-level posts in Guangdong and Fujian provinces, rising to the position of finance bureau chief in the Fujian government. He joined the Nationalist Party faction around Hu Hanmin, but broke with the party as Hu's group shifted to the left. Factional struggle finally pushed him out of government service after a decade, at which point he moved to Shanghai and got a teaching position at Chizhi College.

Su's shift from active politics to an academic career provides his official biography with the opportunity to cast him as an intellectual and the thinker responsible for the concept of the "Great Way." In Shanghai, we are told, Su began to draw on Daoist and Buddhist ideas to develop a religious philosophy that he called the "Great Way spirit." This philosophy advocated the unity of all peoples and the common origin of all creeds ("the realm is one family, all doctrines revert to a unity"). His Buddhist inclination apparently caused him to change his name yet again, this time to Su Xiwen, though I remain unable to detect the term's alleged Buddhist significance.[6] According to this same biography, his allusively heterodox Buddhist philosophy drew him back into politics, where moral principle, rather than factional allegiances, led him to agitate for transparency in government. His commitment to resist the corruption of the Nationalist regime and seek an alternative induced the government to issue a warrant for his arrest. More likely, he was suspected of spying for the Japanese. The most we can conclude is that the leader of Japan's first sponsored municipal government in Shanghai was a lesser figure at the bottom end of the Republican political profession, someone who had regional, business, and educational ties to Japan, and who drew on those connections once he lost his foothold in the Nationalist Party.

An article in the English-language *Eastern Times* on 22 July 1938 reveals a few more intriguing facets of Su Xiwen. The article is a report on the assassination of Su's nominee for chief prosecutor. It reveals, first of all, that both Su and the candidate were natives of Fujian. The Fujian connection was important, for it tied Su not only to this man but potentially to many within the leadership of the Reformed Government, where Fujian natives predominated. Fujian ties within and beyond China may have done more than political defeat or collaborationist ideology to recruit the new leaders of 1938. Equally salient for understanding the particular elite group that took control of the city under the Japanese is that the assassinated candidate was "a devout Buddhist as well as a zealous Daoist." He and Su were members of the same religious group, something called the China Mutual Aid Association, a Daoist "spirit sand-writing altar" (apparently an automatic-writing cult) on Weihaiwei Road. According to the article in the *Eastern Times*, the association's headquarters was the site of much coming and going among the city's politicians, and had facilities to house its members in times of "political difficulty."[7] The article does not specify what political difficulties China Mutual Aid members found themselves in, though it implies that the association sheltered politically reactionary elements who used the association as a cover to attack the Nationalists: a sort of Chinese freemasonry. This network appears to have provided Su Xiwen with a network of contacts through which he could establish links with like-minded elements and recruit supporters for his regime. As a Shanghai outsider, he needed a network of this sort in order to assemble a pro-Japanese administration that could compete with the networks of power through which the former Nationalist administration had functioned. These men came from a completely different sector of the city's lesser elite, one that had been unsuccessful previously in gaining access to political office. Collaboration gave them the break they needed to move into power.

There is even less to know about Su's Special Service counterpart, Nishimura Tenzō. Su did play a public role, vestiges of which appeared in the Shanghai press, whereas Nishimura was expected to remain largely out of sight, which he did. As I have already noted, Nishimura and Su arrived in Shanghai as a team, and they appear as such in a photograph printed in a propaganda booklet published in Tokyo early in February. Opposite the first page of the text, a photograph shows Nishimura and Su standing on either side of a large calligraphic scroll that reads "the man of benevolence

Shanghai mayor Su Xiwen and Special Service officer Nishimura Tenzō, December 1937. From Mōgi Kikuo, *Shanhai shi daidō seifu shisaku hōkoku* (1938), opposite p. 1.

has no enemies." (The text opposite repeats this theme with the phrase "no enemies under heaven" to describe the military power of the Japanese army in China, in a conscious echo of a famous pronouncement by the revered Meiji emperor.) This picture places the two men on equal footing as partners in the creation of the new order in Shanghai; no other pacification agent got such billing with his handler.

Even more revealing, though, is an advertisement on the inside of the back cover for two short books by Nishimura. One is a newly published set of two essays, "On the Fundamental Unity of Religions" and "The China Affair and Japan's Mission." The former sounds suspiciously like the sort of philosophical interest that Japanese biographies allege Su Xiwen to have held—and which accordingly he may not have. More significantly, the other advertised book is the eighth edition of Nishimura's *Sekai kensetsu no daidō, The Great Way of World Reconstruction.* In other words, it was Nishimura who borrowed the term from the *Classic of Rites* as an ideology that could be used to organize the nations of East Asia under a "public and common spirit" over which Japan should preside. Nishimura, not Su Xiwen, wove the fabric that draped this regime with a purely Chinese cover, and had already done so seven editions before Su and his cronies appeared at the South City inauguration. Ironically, this easy-to-grasp phrase stuck. People continued to refer to the Shanghai municipal government as the Great Way for many years beyond its formal dissolution in May 1938.

Su and Nishimira could hardly have put their regime together on their own, but the process by which this pair managed to surface in Shanghai cannot be reconstructed. The one thing that can be determined is that the inauguration date of 5 December had nothing to do with either man, and everything to do with internal politics within the Japanese military. The Central China Area Army was based in Shanghai and the North China Area Army in Beijing. Since November at the very latest, each had been waiting for a go-ahead from Tokyo to shift from invasion to occupation, from the military supervision of conquered territory to the installation of a civilian government. As noted in Chapter 2, Tokyo was reluctant to endorse this shift, but late in November the mood in the cabinet shifted toward the idea of a comprehensive solution involving the removal of Chiang's regime. The turning point came on the first of December. On that day, the Supreme Command in Tokyo separately authorized the CCAA to capture Nanjing and the NCAA to form a Chinese provisional government in Beijing. That provisional regime came into being two weeks later. The power to control Nanjing would be a huge advantage for the CCAA in terms of dominating the formation of a new regime in China, but without similar permission to form its own, the CCAA feared that the NCAA would use its Beijing client to undercut its advantage by claiming prior founding. Every day that the NCAA gained for a Beijing regime, however provisional, was potentially a day of legitimacy lost for whatever regime the CCAA might sponsor. The two armies were in a race to control China's future, and time was now on the NCAA's side. The CCAA had to do something to stake its claim on controlling occupied China, and that something was to set up an administration in Shanghai before the provisional government was inaugurated Beijing. The Great Way Government was only municipal in scope, but it was conspicuously declared to be a "government," not just a peace maintenance or self-government committee. This was the CCAA's bid to outflank its northern rival.

The entity that the CCAA created on 5 December had little at first to administer. It had no claim over any part of the foreign concessions, even the section of the International Settlement that Japan controlled. Its jurisdiction extended only to those Chinese parts of Shanghai that Japan occupied when the three-month defense of the city finally collapsed on 12 November. Its home base was in Pudong, across the river from the downtown area. It claimed the South City, but as we shall see, that was a claim that South City residents challenged. The bombed-out Central District was its to control, but there was not much there once the dust of invasion settled. As late as May 1938, the Central District had only 7,050 residents. Far worse hit was the industrial suburb of Zhabei, where in May only 365 people were said to be living.[8] Occupied Shanghai had another Chinese district well north of the International Settlement, Wusong, but that had been made a Japanese military zone and remained outside Great Way jurisdiction. The Great Way declared that it had jurisdiction over the outlying counties of Shanghai (renamed Beiqiao), Baoshan, Fengxian, Nanhui, Chuansha, and Chongming, as well as Jiading county—the case study county in Chapter 3. Only gradually over the first year would some of these counties actually come within the control of the municipal government.

Unlike collaborators elsewhere on the Yangtze Delta, the Great Way leaders were not locals. This was not a grassroots Shanghai regime. Zhu Yuzhen, appointed as chief of police on 3 December, was, like most career policemen in the Republican period, a native of Shandong province and a graduate of the prestigious Baoding Military Academy. For the preceding fifteen years, Zhu had pursued a policing career in Fujian, which is where he appears to have made the connections that drew him into this regime. The head of accounting, also appointed on 3 December, was similarly an outsider. These two were the only officials appointed prior to the inauguration, suggesting that not much was in place by the founding date and that the regime was rushed into being. The other early police appointment, dated to inauguration day, was the head of the police administrative section, a man whose education and prior career had been entirely in Manchuria and who accordingly had a long career of working under Japanese direction. Ten days later, two other section heads were appointed, and again both were outsiders to Shanghai.

Only as office staff and secretaries at lower levels were appointed starting on the 18th did the regime draw from the pool of former Shanghai police and civic personnel whom the previous administration on 31 August had ordered to remain in their posts without salary. A sense of who was motivated to answer the Great Way Government's notice to report back to work within seven days can be gleaned from a file of applications for reemployment that has survived in the Shanghai Municipal Archives.[9] The first in the file is a letter residential surveyor He Yi wrote on 9 December, the day after he saw the reemployment notice in the newspaper; here was a man eager to get his job back. The next letters in the file date to early January. In one dated the 5th, Li Gengsheng refers to the same notice when asking for his tax-collecting job back, even though the notice had imposed a week's deadline for reapplication. Li concedes that he had held his job for only a few months before the "Incident," but to fortify his application he states his admiration for Su Xiwen's having organized an administration "that takes morality as its guiding principle, that is committed to saving the country and succoring the people, and for which the common people of Jiangsu and Zhejiang have thirsted." Li is responding not simply to the moral claims of the regime, but to the as yet undefined nature of its jurisdiction, as though it might become the core of a new regime extending over the two adjacent provinces. Li's name, Gengsheng, "rebirth," was a popular regime catchword in the first year of the occupation, when some spoke of New China and others of Reborn China.[10] Did Li Gengsheng rename himself in the hope of getting his prospective employer's attention? If he did, he was successful, for his application was approved five days later.

Li Gengsheng's willingness to mouth the ideals of the new regime is unique among the applicants, both former employees and job-seekers. The

Office of the Great Way Government in Pudong, Shanghai, December 1937.
From *Shina jihen kahō* (1938).

others, if they explain their motivation for submitting an application at all, simply say that unemployment has reduced them to financial desperation. Sun Dongliang candidly wrote on 4 January that he had lost everything when he fled with his parents, wife, and child to the International Settlement at the outbreak of hostilities. When he went back to his home, he found it "temporarily occupied" by Japanese soldiers. "Facing a severe crisis of livelihood," he asked for a position appropriate to his five years' experience as an accountant for an import-export firm trading with Japan. Ding Zhiming makes the same declaration of desperate circumstances on 26 February. For two decades starting in 1911, Ding held a series of minor government posts north of the Yangtze, the last of which was in the Yangzhou Opium Suppression Bureau. In 1931 he decided to join a lay Buddhist community, but the collapse of the community's finances drove him to Shanghai in the spring of 1937 to look up old friends and find work. At that point Japan invaded and he found himself unable to return home to his native Hanyang. Hearing that the new regime needed qualified personnel, he hoped that there might be a job for him. A reply was immediately sent asking Ding to bring his documents to the personnel office to discuss suitable employment. The other letters in this file of applications are mostly in this vein: desperate for income, not for collaboration.

Of the people who were given jobs with the Great Way Government, it is difficult at first glance to distinguish them from those who served under the Nationalists. In fact, many held positions under both. The five senior staff members in the administration's secretariat, for instance, look much like any other group of mid-level officials of the Nanjing Decade. Zhou Zhicai, a forty-eight-year-old from Shanghai, had been a county magistrate in Jiangxi and the general administrator of the Shanghai Chamber of Commerce. Zhang Da, a forty-seven-year-old from Zhenjiang, had served as the chief of the Grand Canal bureau of the salt administration and the general manager for Jiangsu province of the Nanyang Tobacco Company. Zhou Jianxun, a forty-eight-year-old Cantonese, had worked as a police officer and as head of the Shanghai Fourth District Longshoremen's Union. Police experience is an element common to the backgrounds of lesser Great Way employees. The fourth-ranking member of the secretariat, forty-three-year-old Zhou Yuesan of Shanghai, was a policeman, having worked as a detective for the Shanghai Municipal Police in the International Settlement before moving over to the Great Way.[11]

A few of this cohort of mid-level officials had some sort of connection to Japan. This is most visible with the fifth-ranking member of the secretariat, a businessman named Xu Zhiping who graduated from the Imperial University in Tokyo. Still only in his thirties, this distinction, and presumably the ability to speak Japanese, must have leapfrogged Xu over men lower down the list whose greater age and work experience could not match Xu's knowledge of Japan. Japanese connections also emerge in the curricula vitae for Zhou Zhicai and Zhuo Jianxun. Both held positions in the East Asian Anti-Communist League, a Japanese-backed organization designed to mobilize public support for Japan's policies in China. Whether Zhou and Zhuo got into the organization simply to improve their chances of getting jobs, or were there on the basis of other commitments, is impossible to know. The coincidence suggests at the very least that associational networks outside the administration linked to Japan shaped recruitment and advancement within it—hardly a surprising discovery, but one for which there is evidence.

The documentation that survives in the Shanghai Municipal Archives keeps the Japanese in the background and highlights the actions Su Xiwen and his administration took in the early days of the Great Way Government, notably to assert police and fiscal jurisdiction over the city and its suburbs. Being an unknown entity over in Pudong, the South City's poor and disreputable junior cousin, the Great Way Government faced as its first task the challenge of establishing authority where none existed, and where none could be expected to exist without the coercion Japan's military presence supplied. It was a situation that put the Great Way Government in the position of appearing both opportunistic and powerless at the same time. The heads of the many PMCs and SGCs within the nominal boundaries of Great Way jurisdiction freely used this situation to their advantage by playing Great Way and Japanese personnel and policies against each other whenever doing so would strengthen their hand in local affairs. The Japanese were not averse to playing the same sort of game when it worked to their benefit in striking local deals. Asserting regional authority thus became the Great Way Government's particular nightmare.

Little PMCs and SGCs proliferated, apparently without plan, in the first month after Shanghai's fall. They appeared sometimes on their own account, but more often when the Japanese army unit garrisoning a town needed to sort out cohabitation arrangements with the local people, particularly local merchants. This happened at the level of the six districts directly beneath Su's administration, and it happened as well further down, in the market towns and rural districts scattered around suburban Shanghai. Not surprisingly, the local elites who created these committees were not keen to hand away the power that had come to them, and *were* keen to secure a place in the new order. They could either fight to withstand the imposition of municipal control, or, when that became impossible, maneuver themselves into getting recognized as subunits of the Great Way Government. The Great Way preferred to dissolve the entities that were there and replace them with its own appointees, but sometimes, as we shall see, they had to live with the other arrangement. And so lengthy rivalries were played out between the new center demanding obedience from below and local entities clamoring for autonomy and for recognition from above.

A common tactic of local collaborationist organs to win such recognition was to profess full conformity to Great Way ideology and protocols. As it turns out, not all such professions have even a discounted value. For example, the men who organized the PMC in Shanghai county (which lay upriver from the city of the same name and was reorganized as a municipal district called Beiqiao) appear to have followed the municipal regime's lead by echoing its language in their charter, declaring that "the Great Way of humankind" was best put into practice by "organizing as one family to establish a politics of self-government and condemning Party-state politics and Communistic thinking."[12] This formula was not exactly what *The Classic of Rites* had in mind, but it was as good an attempt as any to lend substance to a vague term. But what looks to be an instance of local collaborators parroting a born-again Confucianism to their superiors may not be that at all, when one examines stylistic ticks in the language of the charter. The text makes extensive use of the copula *shi*, repeatedly uses the pronoun *ci* ("this"), and tends to position verbs at the end of sentences—all of which hint at Japanese diction. Occasionally awkward language in this PMC's manifesto, notably the extensive use of pronouns and copulas as well as the adverb *dai* (J. *hotondo*), further strengthens the suspicion that Japanese wrote the PMC's documents. In other words, what we have here is not the Shanghai PMC harmonizing with Su Xiwen so much as its Special Service agents singing Nishimura's tune back to him in order to protect their local clients.

The draft organizational charter of another PMC, in Gaoqiao, appears to be a genuine attempt by lower-level collaborators to align themselves with higher. The three governing principles with which the text opens suggest an astute reading of the politics emanating from Pudong. The first was "to promote the Kingly Way of Great Japan." The polite second was "to function under the direction of the Great Way Government." The third principle—to deem every resident of Gaoqiao to be a member of the PMC—was unique among PMCs, though to this open constitution the Gaoqiao PMC attached the qualifying pledge that every member was bound to identify Communist sympathizers who would then be handed over to the Great Way Government. The Gaoqiao PMC seems to have done all it could think of doing to make itself attractive to the new regime in Shanghai. The bid was successful, for the PMC was recognized and later converted into a district office of the municipal government. The people who ran the Gaoqiao PMC were careful to keep the Japanese commander of the local Military Police unit abreast of developments by sending him a

copy of the regulations, at his request. Su Xiwen may not have been entirely happy with having these would-be subordinates present him with a
fait accompli, if we may read his ill temper into a comment scrawled on a
28 January letter from Gaoqiao. To "Mayor Su," the chair and vice-chair
had added the suffix *dian,* which might loosely translate as "Your Excellency." Someone in Su's office, possibly Su himself, has circled the suffix
and written: "Let them know hereafter not to use this word again." "Your
Excellency" went beyond the appropriately sycophantic, it seems. The implication of rhetorical excess, as Su was astute enough to realize, was that
the Gaoqiao PMC's integration into his government was all language and
no substance.

Local SGCs were similarly careful to position themselves within the jurisdictional wake of the Great Way Government, while at the same time
picturing themselves as essential to the restoration of order and therefore
indispensable as building blocks of that regime. The founding manifesto of
the Pudong SGC makes all these moves:

> In the aftermath of the military devastation, the area has been chaotic,
> bandits have arisen in a swarm, and residents have seen their homes de-
> stroyed and have fled. They have been left uprooted with nothing on
> which to depend. This disaster is entirely the responsibility of the Party
> Army, which has driven the people to this suffering. Troubled by what we
> have seen, we have set up a self-government committee to stabilize the
> area and encourage businesses to return in order that the markets may
> flourish again. By so doing, we are laying the foundation for the Great
> Way Government and affirming our close friendship with Great Japan.
> As a result, loyal subjects can live in peace, take pleasure in their work,
> and be permitted to enjoy happiness.

The Great Way Government was not uniformly cheerful at the prospect
of opening its arms to already constituted and entrenched local entities. It
reserved the right to ratify or annul these quasi-independent bodies, which
meant that the road to its authority had to be laid over the wreckage, or at
least the subordination, of the PMCs and SGCs dominating the smaller
communities around Shanghai. Su's first move along this road was to issue
Great Way Government Announcement No. 8 in early January. There Su
concedes that the PMCs that have sprung up around the city did play a
valuable role in managing local affairs as the fighting moved west and left

chaos in its wake. Now that central authority had been reconstituted, however, their usefulness was at an end:

> The PMCs emerged at an appropriate moment, but not all on these committees were good people. Some members used them to expand their own power, coming up with ingenious excuses to collect taxes, making outrageous assertions, and allowing corrupt practices to flourish. Not only were they unable to restrain themselves and work for the public good and extend benefits through the countryside; quite the contrary, they used the occasion to profit from and harm their local areas. What started out as well-meaning has ended up as evil. If they are not dissolved right away, who knows how deep the damage these committees are doing to their local areas will go? Now that the various organs of this government are being established and police authority has already been restored, the tasks [of administration are being met by] those responsible for them and there is no need for parallel organs. In addition to ordering the bureau of police to have its stations determine whether [the committees] within their areas are speedily dissolved, this order is promulgated so that merchants and people alike all know of this.[13]

Within a paragraph, Su Xiwen goes from praising the local committees to damning them. He makes a particular effort to delegitimize their attempts to raise operating funds, a source of independence that had to be blocked. The police received many more such orders over the next twelve months. Local resistance to takeover, not surprisingly, was strong.

Su Xiwen began a concerted campaign to bring these autonomous bodies under his control by ordering the police on 21 January to submit a list of the names of elected leaders in every town, village, and neighborhood in the region within ten days. The task might have been a good way to start, but it was impossible to carry out. Zhu Yuzhen, Su's chief of police, told him ten days later that local police had reported to him that, "given the difficulties in holding elections," they needed another week to complete the assignment. Even that postponement was optimistic. Two months later, police in both the South City and the Central District were still reporting that "local circumstances"—meaning the power of these committees to refuse giving information about their memberships—made it impossible to forward the names as requested. Three days later both the Baoshan and the Gaoqiao police filed similar excuses. All that Zhu Yuzhen could counsel was patience: "Local administration will hereafter gradually be carried out," he assured Su. "When it is, matters will eventually improve."[14] The Great Way grip over these areas was next to nil, and no alternative procedure presented itself. All the regime could do was to continue pressing for regularization by demanding that when a local SGC was formed, it, or the district SGC to which it reported, provide updated lists of committee members and service personnel.

The Great Way's last move to control local SGCs, announced on 26 April, just two days prior to being disbanded and reconstituted as the Shanghai Municipal Commission, was to rectify names. Lower-level entities would no longer be called PMCs or SGCs. These terms were appropriate to a period of transition but not to a normalized administration. District and town committees were henceforth to be called Administrative Affairs Offices and Town Affairs Committees.[15] Some districts, such as coastal Chuansha where the Japanese army maintained an active presence, complied immediately. Many did not. The Municipal Commission re-initiated the process by striking an SGC Incorporation Committee. On 29 June, it ordered the SGCs in the South City, the Western District, and Zhabei to wind up operations immediately. This was followed by a general announcement on 11 July that SGCs were to be converted into district offices.[16] One SGC wrote back complaining that since order had not been restored and the residents had not yet returned, normal administrative functioning was simply not possible. Local bodies were told that the change was only in name, but many local collaborators suspected rightly that a change in name would mean the extinction of their careers, as those higher up the hierarchy moved to insert their own clients into positions further down. The 11 July order was explicit in acknowledging that the municipal government reserved the right to appoint district heads: it was not about to confirm as district head whoever had managed to gain the leadership of the SGC. The contest could be tough. The South City SGC dutifully reported the following day that it was going ahead with the appropriate steps preparatory to handover, but this was a stalling tactic. Only when the municipal government sent in a team of five on 26 July to dissolve the SGC was a proper Administrative Affairs Office put in place. Other local SGCs continued to resist until as late as the following January, when the municipal government was finally able to enforce its oversight.

Despite its clear policy of closing down these bodies, the Great Way Government continued to receive requests from local bodies for recognition. Two representatives of the fishing population on the coastal islands, previously split between the former counties of Baoshan and Chuansha, petitioned the Great Way for permission to form a PMC. They phrased their request in language that was emphatic in its denunciation of the Nationalists' "Party military government," which "never once sent an official to direct an organization for us, but only knew how to levy the fish tax, which was a heavy burden on the people." The petitioners claimed that the islanders were ecstatic about the founding of the new regime, which will "rescue the people from disaster," and felt that the appropriate local response was for local people to organize a provisional PMC.[17] The Great Way Government appears to have ignored the petition.

The last such request to reach the Great Way arrived on 4 April. The prospective chair and vice-chair of a new PMC in Tanziwan town in Zhabei wrote to be confirmed in what they were doing. This PMC had only just been organized, they explained, because Tanziwan had been devastated during the invasion and was only just now beginning to be restored. Tanziwan was the last place in Shanghai to be revived, and the timing was urgent because of the importance of guaranteeing spring planting. The bid failed. The wordiness of the letter and its annoyingly ingratiating language may have done something to excite suspicions. The head of the Social Affairs Bureau, who reviewed the file, pasted a note to the front the following day observing that most PMCs were flawed and had been shut down, and that Zhabei had in any case been completely reopened with a functioning police station where returning refugees could register. He suspected that these men were up to no good. What their letter produced was yet another Great Way directive to subordinate agencies reminding them of the order to dissolve all PMCs.

The Japanese role in the process of unifying the administration of Shanghai is ambiguous. An early striking example came out of a meeting at the Kung Dah Cotton Mill in the Western District on 13 December, to which the Japanese Military Police called Chinese shop owners and Japanese residents to discuss measures for maintaining law and order. Under Military Police guidance, the body passed a resolution to set up a police bureau in the Western District. It was to be headed by a Chinese who had the strong support of Japanese mill owners, without reference to Great Way police authority. Not only that, but its office was 94 Jessfield Road, which was also the headquarters of the local pacification team and the Military Police. This police bureau operated there under close Japanese direction for seven weeks. On February 5 police authority in the Western District was finally transferred to the Great Way Government.[18] (Something of the same struggle would recur eleven months later, when Fu Xiaoan, Su's successor as mayor, discovered that the Military Police had set up a para-military force in the Western District to protect the drug trade. This time, however, the Chinese side was successful in getting the force suspended and obliging the Military Police to discuss the rules under which it could operate.)[19]

There is no record of Su Xiwen's reaction to Japanese control of police authority in the Western District. Su received reports from his chief of police regarding the activities of local committees that appeared to infringe on the rights of his administration, but when a Japanese garrison commander or Special Service agent was involved, he could do no more than ask for information. When he learned, for example, that the Tangqiao SGC was operating without Great Way authorization and ordered the Pudong police to investigate, he was told that the SGC was working closely with the army unit there, and that the PMC it replaced had been formed by the local garrison commander. The garrison had reported this arrangement to the North Pudong Garrison Command, and that agency had approved the body and provided passes to assist its members in their work. When the PMC was made over into an SGC on 16 January, provisional regulations were drawn up that are explicit regarding the SGC's primary dependence on the Japanese army. The first regulation notes that this body was set up by the local army unit; the second, that it was charged with working to resolve misunderstandings between Japanese soldiers and the local people; the fifth, that all important issues be reported to the army; the eleventh, that all SGC decisions be ratified by the army; and the thirteenth, that the regulations themselves had to have army approval (they were in fact duly submitted to the local army unit). These regulations reveal that the Tangqiao SGC was entirely indifferent to the existence of the Great Way Government and related exclusively to the authority of the Japanese army. Su Xiwen might order an investigation, but he could do nothing more.[20]

Su was somewhat more aggressive two months later with the Zhoupu SGC. The town of Zhoupu, in southeastern Pudong, had set up a PMC before the Great Way Government was founded. In the third week of January, its members dissolved the PMC in accordance with the dissolution order and then replaced it with a Chamber of Commerce. The chamber's existence came to Su Xiwen's attention because its head, Zhang Xuezhou, was the same man who had headed it under the Nationalists. Su was concerned that pre-occupation interests were regrouping to the potential detriment of his own authority, and authorized his chief of police to mount surveillance on the forty members of this organization. Less than two months later, his chief passed on a report from the Zhoupu police station that a pacification team had set up an SGC at the City God Temple on 12 March, with none other than local boss Zhang Xuezhou in charge.[21] If Su Xiwen was hoping to centralize control over the Shanghai region, this must have been a frustrating development. He was in no position to challenge the pacification team's action. What he could question were the powers that the Zhoupu SGC seemed to have claimed for itself, particularly the licensing of boats and the collecting of taxes. SGCs existed to help revive the infrastructure and economy of damaged areas, but anything with revenue consequences was within the purview of the municipality. Su Xiwen therefore directed the head of the Pudong district office to get Zhang to revise his program immediately, adding the annoyed comment, "He cannot just act as he likes."

Zhang Xuezhou could not just act as he liked, perhaps, but the Special Service could. The Japanese controlled the process in the field. If a local commander or SSD agent perceived a need to have an SGC in operation, he did so regardless of the jurisdictional claims of the Great Way Government. Both, after all, existed at the pleasure of the Japanese army. No direct objection from Su Xiwen appears in the documents I have seen in the Shanghai Municipal Archives. He might chafe at the independence of local elites, but he had no freedom to maneuver against his patrons when they were also his rivals'. Whether because of his Japanese backing or his entrenched local authority, Zhang Xuezhou managed to resist further encroachments from the municipality, for he survived the reorganization later that year that turned Zhoupu into a town within Nanhui district and became town head.

The process of deciding which local entity might become an arm of municipal administration, and which local businessman might be recognized as its head, could thus pit the Great Way Government against competing Japanese interests. Local elites who wanted to force a concession from the Great Way Government could best do so if they got the local garrison on their side. This factor appears to have counted against the heads of three businesses in Chuansha, who wrote in January 1938 asking to upgrade the Chuansha PMC into an SGC and nominating the man who would head the committee. Su Xiwen's response was to inform them that they had no authority to assemble such an organization and that their nominee could not assume any authority beyond serving as acting head of his own town. The Chuansha petitioners sought to make their case more persuasive by noting that they were seeking permission as well from the local Japanese military commander. The situation was, however, more complicated than it appears, for a document in the national archives in Nanjing indicates that the Japanese garrison in Chuansha had already appointed someone to run local affairs, and that person had already negotiated recognition from Su Xiwen.[22] It is possible that the petitioners were unaware of this; more likely, they were aware of what was in play and were using their proposal for an SGC as an attempt to do an end run around the Japanese army's candidate.

The struggle for central jurisdiction over local rivals was not purely a matter of face: it had revenue consequences, as everyone involved in this game understood. The initial expenses of the Great Way Government were covered, according to a Japanese source published at the time, by a contribution of a million yen that an unnamed "friend" in Tianjin had given to Su Xiwen.[23] The regime was therefore able to afford a brief tax holiday for war-damaged areas between mid-December and January.[24] The tax holiday was intended to relieve local businesses as well as to lure others across the Huangpu River to Pudong. The city's need for revenue meant that the exemption could be only temporary. At the end of December, Su issued Directive No. 6 to his police and finance bureaus, stating that as businesses were reopening all over the city, they should be expected to assist the regime in meeting the heavy expenses of rebuilding Shanghai. Agents of the finance bureau would be sent out in the company of policemen to Pudong, the Western District, the South City, and Zhabei to begin collecting business taxes starting on the first day of the new lunar year, which fell on 31 January 1938.[25]

The more immediate source of revenue was traffic—of goods in transit and of people on ferries. The earliest such levy appears to have been on the eight ferries crossing the Wusong River. The Great Way Government began collecting a ferry tax cooperatively with the Wusong SGC on January 2. This was followed by a levy on vegetables brought into the Western District starting on the 11th. In both cases, Special Service personnel were involved, which could put them in some conflict with the Great Way police. In fact, two days before the new tax regime was to begin on the 31st, police chief

Zhu Yuzhen warned Su Xiwen that the Japanese appeared not to have understood that as of that date, all taxes would be collected by agents of the municipal government and not by themselves.

One of the toughest and most successful rivals for revenue was the South City SGC.[26] The South City was the core of the old Chinese city and economically the most vibrant part of the occupied parts of Shanghai. The self-government committee that a Japanese pacification agent established there in mid-January was remarkably resistant to municipal pressure. The Great Way Government placed the South City SGC under police surveillance and discovered that it was doing a great deal to stimulate the revival of the South City economy and assist the masses of refugees who collected there or just across the boundary with the French Concession. The committee's ability to control rice, which both fed the refugees and generated revenue, was the key to its success. By late February, the South City SGC controlled the rice market by placing the dozen rice shops within the refugee zone under the supervision of its Office to Sell Confiscated Materials. This office had seven or eight outlets in Jiumudi and two or three in Dongjiadu. An official in the Great Way Social Affairs Bureau thought they were charging monopolistic prices (second-class *yangxian* rice was being sold by the picul for 13.2 yuan, more than 3 yuan higher than the price in Pudong, and at an even higher rate when sold in smaller amounts) and accused them of driving up food prices by excessive taxing. Such policies ran counter to the "benevolent administration" of the Great Way Government, he judged.

The South City SGC Finance Bureau also raised revenue by taxing vegetable stalls in the markets at Jiumudi and Xiaopudu, both of which flourished under the stimulus of demand. To gain access to the world of wealthier merchants, it managed to co-opt the South City Chamber of Commerce. The chamber, which predated the occupation, was particularly prosperous because of an agreement with the French authorities allowing its members to operate in the Concession freely. When the SGC replaced the chamber with its own Commercial and Industrial Bureau, most members registered, though the chamber seems to have continued a shadow existence, carrying out its liturgical functions and levying the fees necessary to keep the markets running. Despite the complaints of some merchants that the new bureau was exacting excessive taxes (a situation that obliged Japanese pacification agents to step in and negotiate between the merchants and the SGC), the SGC was able to run South City affairs with im-

Rice distribution center, Shanghai, December 1937. From Mōgi Kikuo, *Shanhai shi daidō seifu shisaku hōkoku* (1938).

punity. As a police report on South City commercial affairs that spring makes plain, it "has arrogated all power in this area and taken over every aspect of its administration, taxing at will. The South City is under the formal aegis of the city government, yet it has set up its own banner and has placed all manner of obstacles in the way of the administrative powers of the Great Way Government." The Great Way Government reported this situation to its pacification office but was unsuccessful in ousting this local body and replacing it with its own officials. I suspect that the key factor in keeping the South City SGC independent was the support it enjoyed from its own pacification team. Had the Special Service wanted the South City placed under Nishimura's team, it would have done this. That it did not had to do with the financial viability of the South City SGC. As it was meeting its administrative commitments and operating at a profit, why change the arrangement simply to please Su Xiwen's desire to centralize power?

The man who headed the South City SGC was a lawyer named Chen Yun. He appears to have enjoyed considerable local authority. In late April,

he represented his committee at the major reorganization meeting preparatory to reestablishing county administrations (see Chapter 8).[27] More
tellingly, he was powerful enough to carry on as the head of the South City
district affairs office when the SGC was disbanded at the end of June along
with most other SGCs on the delta. Chen did not live to enjoy his success as
the boss of the South City for long, though. On 30 August, he was stabbed
to death. The assassination did not just remove him from the ranks of the
collaborators. It had a chilling effect on others, which was the intention: to
show current and prospective collaborators what would happen to them
should they continue to throw in their lot with the new regime.

Shanghai newspapers were understandably full of the story when it first
broke, which kept newspaper censors busy. Censor Wu Hongkai was careful to check all the morning papers on 3 September for any subversive sentiments, but ended up reporting to his superiors that none of the articles
he read "furnished information prejudicial to the public office" in the
South City, so he had to let them through. The one article on Chen's assassination that he did interfere with was set to appear in the evening edition
of *The Times (Shibao)* on the 7th. It closed with the comment that since
Chen's assassination, no one was willing to come forward to take over the
administration of the South City. Censor Wu judged the final observation
to be "inappropriate" and cut it, though he let the rest of the story go to
press. When the same newspaper submitted an article six days later to report that Ling Qihong, the newly appointed head of the municipal Bureau
of Social Affairs, "did not dare" *(bugan)* take up his appointment, implying
that Chen's assassination had intimidated him, Wu changed the expression
to "as yet had not" *(shangwei)*. The intimidation was short-lived and failed
to end collaboration in the South City. Chen Yun's second-in-command
on the SGC, Ling Jitan, continued in office while a new man, Shen Shijing,
took over in Chen Yun's stead. Ling Qihong eventually showed up for
work.[28]

Chen's death was part of a wave of assassinations targeting Shanghai
collaborators through the spring and summer of 1938.[29] That wave subsided later that autumn. Thereafter, it seems, simply being an official of the
occupation state was not enough to get yourself killed. You had to do
something proactively treasonable, such as betray a Nationalist agent. This
was the mistake that Fu Xiaoan, Su Xiwen's successor as mayor, would
make. When Nationalist agents sounded him out about conspiring in a
plot to assassinate the future collaborationist leader Wang Jingwei early in

1939, Fu leaked the plan to Wang, from which followed the arrest and execution of several Nationalist operatives. This act marked Fu as a legitimate target, and on 11 October 1940, after two years in office, he was assassinated by an old family servant whom the Nationalist underground recruited.[30]

Su Xiwen was an early target, but he managed to escape several attempts to kill him. Maintaining security around Su was an unrelieved burden for Great Way police chief Zhu Yuzhen. Zhu could try to protect him, and succeeded every time an attempt was made, but he could not guarantee that there would be no more attempts. Su eventually lost patience with having to face assassins after someone bombed a meeting he walked into on the morning of 15 April. Su escaped unscathed, but when Zhu submitted the conventional letter of resignation for breach of security with his report three days later, Su surprised him by accepting it. The attack did not deter Su from carrying on, but others quailed. He Jiayou, who had been running the city's Finance Bureau for only six weeks and was present at the bombed meeting, submitted his resignation the same day Zhu Yuzhen did. He pleaded "a weak constitution and old illnesses" to get free of his entanglement.[31]

Some regimes might have wanted to hide the fact that their personnel were being killed. The Reformed Government took a different tack. Its approach was to turn their deaths to advantage by publicizing them. The martyrs got their names entered on a published honor roll, and their families received compensation.[32] Collaborationist officials were almost as useful dead as they were alive, for they were the evidence that people were willing to die for the new order.[33]

The financial health of occupied Shanghai demanded that more be done than fight over the right to collect taxes. The shattered economy had to be stimulated to a level such that goods were once again being moved publicly and so could be taxed. The inhibitor here was the Japanese military ban on boat traffic. Unless the functioning of the inland waterways was restored, goods could not go in and out of the city, to the detriment of both urban and rural commerce. As a group of petitioners from Tangqiao wailed, "If we do not speedily find a way to allow commerce to flourish, we won't have the means to maintain our locality."[34]

The implied consequences of economic recovery were more than economic, "maintain" being a code word for Japan's program of "peace maintenance." The Tangqiao SGC attached its name to the petition out of concern that schools in Tangqiao needed police protection, which had to be paid for. The petitioners asked for assistance to allow commercial boats to move without hindrance on the inland waterways. One petitioner asked that the route between Tangqiao and Zhangjiabang be opened to allow supplies of rice and firewood to come in from the villages in Songjiang further west. Two other merchants asked that the route from Tangqiao into the concessions be opened so that they could transport dyed cloth and liquor. One farmer needed to get to his source of supply for lime down in Yexie. Another wanted permission to transport vegetables to the South City. Requests to reopen waterways gave the Great Way Government a point of fiscal leverage, for a local committee asking to resume traffic would have to allow that traffic to be taxed. Each side saw this differently, and the first step in any negotiation over changing conditions could only generate conflict.

Despite these standoffs and the general difficulty of restoring the economy of the region, some SGCs had the organizational capacity to collect substantial revenue. Financial records for the first half-year of the occupation are scattered and unreliable, yet one set of summary fiscal data survives for an otherwise undocumented entity in Shanghai called the North District United Self-Government Committee. The committee prepared and submitted this data in response to the Reformed Government's demand that all SGCs compile a statement of accounts prior to dissolution in the summer of 1938. The figures are presented in their entirety in Table 6.1.

The most striking item of information in this account summary appears in the bottom line: income (over four months) exceeded expenditures (over five months) by a factor of four to one. The Northern District United SGC ran a hugely profitable operation, at least on paper. It was helped in June by a one-time-only grant of 15,000 yuan from the Reformed Government as part of the package encouraging the SGCs to carry through the conversion to the new public offices. Remove the grant from the calculations and the balance tilts back. Even with that gift factored out, however, the Northern District SGC still collected half as much again as what it paid out. Given what we have seen of the fiscal insolvency dogging the SGC in Zhenjiang (and we will note the same in the next chapter on Chongming), the profitability of this SGC comes as a surprise. Another striking feature of the accounts is the variability on both sides of the balance sheet from month to month. This fluctuation reflects the instability of the occupation

Table 6.1 Accounts of the North District United SGC, Shanghai, March–July 1938

		Amount			Amount	
Month	Source of income	Yuan	Yen	Expenditures	Yuan	Yen
March	Factory shipping fees	2,450		Patrolmen uniforms	158	
	Ferry fares	961		Patrolmen salaries	40	
				SGC expenses	69	
	Subtotal	3,411			267	
April	Shipping fines	3,500		SGC salaries	666	48
	Ferry fees	949		Patrolmen salaries	625	
	Gift for SGC move	80		Cargo recovery	472	
	Other	64		Gift of car to army	308	
	Confiscations		452	Gift to Sakuraniwa	54	
	Subtotal	4,593	452		2,125	48
May	Certificate sales	344		Road repairs	59	
	License sales	34		Gift for team leader	47	
				SGC expenses	12	
				Car repairs		27
	Subtotal	378			118	27
June	Ref. Govt. gift	15,000		Patrolmen salaries	730	
	2 factories' gifts	1,800		Branch SGC expenses	550	
	Confiscated guns	10		SGC expenses	412	61
				SGC salaries	340	
				Other	293	
	Subtotal	16,810			2,325	61
July	None reported			Branch SGC expenses	550	
				SGC salaries	504	38
				Electric installation	218	
				Building repairs	185	
				Patrolmen salaries	179	
				Other	95	
	Subtotal	0			1,731	38
	Total income	25,192 yuan	452 yen	Total expenditures	6,566 yuan	174 yen

Source: SMA, File R1–2–1637.

Note: These figures are rounded to the nearest Chinese yuan, except where Japanese yen are indicated.

situation, and must have pushed many an SGC to favor collection over disbursement. After all, who knew where next month's collection might come from or what it might amount to?

This one example cannot be cited to prove the financial viability of the entire regime; every place was different. Nor can reported figures, even those submitted for internal inspection, be assumed to reveal the entire truth: who can say what was on the books but never actually paid out or received, or how much revenue was kept off budget? Nonetheless, these figures show that this SGC was able to extract enough from its local economy that it had funds left over after covering its costs. They also suggest, however, that the committee was not integrated with local economic processes in a way that could provide it with a long-term foundation for stable fiscal administration. This was closer to tax farming than financial planning. Local officials could not hope to keep feeding off these sources indefinitely; indeed, this SGC's feeding appears to have entirely ceased in July. The lack of integration arose from, and perhaps compensated for, the disruption that the occupation had forced on the economy, but it also testified to the inability of this committee to function except by relying on the local Japanese garrison: its parasitic relationship to the economy was both imposed and made possible by its parasitic relationship with occupation power. To be fair to the SGC's mode of operation, fiscal stability was not initially the top Special Service priority in the opening months of the occupation. Its prime goal was to put some kind of Chinese authority in place and get it to share in the tasks of establishing the new order. Regular administration and fiscal accountability would follow once that was done. Indeed, given that the SGC system was temporary, it almost did not matter whether any particular committee was financially successful or not. Success did not win reprieve from dissolution. The most that turning a profit could do was to line the pockets of those involved (recall Jimmy Wang allegedly telling his floormate in a Nanjing refugee camp that the invasion was "such a good opportunity to make a fortune") and provide their superiors with evidence of worthiness to be kept on under the new dispensation.

The Great Way Government lasted less than five months. It was replaced on 28 April by an entity more purely municipal in its ambitions, the Shanghai Municipal Commission, which in turn was replaced in October by the Shanghai Special Municipality. Su Xiwen kept his leadership position in the first changeover (with Nishimura carrying on as his handler), but lost it in the second, when he became the second-in-command to the much more eminent Fu Xiaoan, the former chair of the Shanghai Chamber of Commerce. Su regained his position on a temporary basis following Fu's assassination in 1940, then lost it again six weeks later when Chen Gongbo stepped in from the political center and took the post of mayor.

These shifts were part of the occupation regime's attempts to regularize municipal administration. The rivalries between above and below in 1938 did not simply disappear, though. The battles from 1939 onward were not over recognition or upgrading, nor even over revenue, which the municipal government became more successful in controlling, but over the control of local political resources. This is the context in which a self-styled "representative of the people" wrote a letter to the Western District office of the municipality on 14 January 1939, from which I have already quoted briefly in Chapter 1. The man claimed to write on behalf of the 118 members of the Huangpu West Residents' Association. Careful to reflect the posture of the current administration, he declares that the Western District prior to the arrival of the Nationalists in 1927 had been well governed by locally respected administrators. The arrival of the Nationalists had plunged the area into disorder by moving the district out of Shanghai county and into the municipality, but people had more or less managed to weather the storm. When the war of resistance moved west, however, competent administrators disappeared. The consequences were disastrous:

> Hoodlums *(liumang)* living here and there [in the district] rushed forward to take over, wielding power and running an administration under the guise of "maintenance." They treated the locality as though it were a profit-making business, imposing levies and accumulating wealth. There was nothing they would not do and no evil they would not commit, with the result that good people vanished without a trace and bandits arose in great number, committing murders and rapes every day. The exactions they imposed on small businesses, the names for which constantly changed, were too numerous to count.[35]

Calling the new opportunists "hoodlums" tallies with a report filed by the International Settlement police stating that the Chinese who worked with the Japanese agencies in the Western District were from the "loafer class" (which is how the term *liumang* is usually translated into English in Shanghai Municipal Police documents). The author says that the local elite of merchants and teachers, of which he was a member, refused to have anything to do with such disreputable types. They met at the time to draw up their own program of action but, not being a legally constituted administrative organ, realized they had to wait until a thorough municipal reorganization got rid of the "monstrous maintenance committees and all other illegal organizations" that had come into existence in the early days. The disdain may camouflage the possibility that the established local elite had fled to the International Settlement during the invasion and returned to find themselves shut out of power.

Did good people vanish without a trace? And were good people now trying to come forward to cleanse the occupation state of its more venal collaborators and make it a political space in which the virtuous could come forward to serve? The politics at work behind such claims are always difficult to tease out of surviving documents. The one thing that can be determined, though in the case of the Huangpu West Residents' Association, we know that the object of attack was a young lawyer and former government office worker named Chen Xishun. In January 1939, Chen headed the Western District suboffice in the town of Longcao. There is no evidence that Chen was one of the "hoodlums" the association felt had grabbed power. He may have been, but it is equally possible that the association's reconstruction of the history of the early occupation of the Western District was concocted to cast aspersions on someone who was blocking the interests of the association's members, whether for good or ill. The municipal government was not persuaded that Chen Xishan should be removed. Chen must have come under other pressure, however, for on 8 March he sent in his resignation, claiming that his youth and inexperience made him unequal to the task of postwar reconstruction. Intriguingly, he also asked the municipal government to return the curriculum vitae and photograph of him that it had on file. It was as though he wanted to remove all traces of his role as a minor official in the occupation state, which could signal that he was coming under pressure from a different quarter. The municipality turned down this request, claiming that no precedent existed for returning employment documents. It did accept his resignation, unwillingly.

Up to this point, the exchange of documents that the residents' association and Chen Xishun had with the municipal government could lull us into assuming that these matters were in the hands of the Chinese who appeared to handle them. Chinese may have originated the accusation that resulted in Chen's leaving office, but the handling of the affair, it turns out, was in Japanese hands. The decision came not from the municipality but from Kitaoka Takeo, the Special Service officer appointed to the Western District office. It was he who allowed Chen Xishun to step down in March, and he who appointed his replacement. Kitaoka's new appointee in Longcao had served as the head of the secretariat of the former South City SGC, and most recently had run the Caojin PMC: a man with a solid record of reliable cooperation with the SSD. Who knows whether the Huangpu West residents got what they wanted in this shuffle?

Kitaoka's control of the Western District is demonstrated by another appointment conflict in the town of Beixinjing that same month. On 15 March 1939, eleven merchant representatives petitioned the head of the Western District office, Li Zidong, to allow them to open a district suboffice and appoint a local person to run it.[36] Beixinjing, they noted, had had an SGC office which functioned until February, when it was closed down in response to the municipality's order to dissolve all such local bodies. The members of the SGC withdrew from public life, including its thirty-seven-year-old chair, Wang Ao, and its thirty-three-year-old vice-chair, Hou Shunmin. The cancellation of the Beixinjing SGC left the town without any administrative body whatsoever. Given the town's importance as a transportation nexus, the petitioners asked that a public office be set up in the town. They nominated SGC vice-chair Hou Shunmin to head it. Hou, a local merchant, was willing. The petitioners asked Li Zidong to ratify their choice. Someone in the Western District Office attached a memo the following day, noting that Beixinjing had in the meantime been amalgamated with neighboring Huacao to create a new administrative town, Xinhua, with only one public office and one town head to administer both areas. The appointee, a primary school graduate who had been a clerk in the former municipal finance bureau, had recently "retired," just as Chen Xishun had, though both were only thirty-three years old at the time. ("Retirement" was a euphemism often used by those who feared for their lives for collaborating.)

Li Zidong was naturally cautious about approving a request that came in cold. He was undoubtedly aware that local factions could use administrative restructuring to manipulate dubious candidates into positions of power. He would have to consult Kitaoka Takeo. There is no information on the nature of Li's relationship with Kitaoka, or with the Japanese occupation more broadly. Li was a northerner (as were three of the other six top figures in the Western District office) and a graduate of the Beiyang Police Academy. His name does not appear on the list of leading SGC organizers that the Western District submitted to the municipal government in July 1938. He was, it appears, an outsider to Shanghai politics who had been parachuted into the Western District in the autumn of 1938 to take control away from local interests. Nor was he alone: all six of his immediate subordinates were also new to the Western District. Whatever the grounds on which he chose to collude with the Special Service and work with a collaborationist municipal government, Li Zidong appears to have been committed at least to propagating the conservative vision of the Great Way in which Nishimura and Su Xiwen wrapped their enterprise. When a *Great Way Annual* for 1938 was being planned, Li wrote the preface, extolling "Confucius, the Jade Sage of Great Completion," for having the wisdom to refuse to "use policies to lead the people and punishments to keep them in order." Policies and punishments only showed the people how to get around policies and punishments. What they needed to develop was a true sense of shame, and that is what Confucius did by "using morality to lead the people and ritual to keep them in order."[37] The keenly committed at the time may have been able to conceptually manage the violent reversal here of reality and dream, in which occupied Shanghai was approaching a realm of morality and ritual and shunning the use of policies and punishments. It is difficult for us to do the same.

When the two men met two days later, Kitaoka decided that he needed more information before he could make a decision, so he asked the local Japanese army unit to check on Hou. The Military Police responded two days later by arresting Hou along with former SGC chair Wang Ao. Four days later Hou and Wang still had not been released. The original eleven petitioners wrote in a panic to Li, pleading that he intercede on their behalf. Wang, they insisted, had been a reliable public figure who had not overstepped his jurisdiction while running the SGC. They could only speculate that the two men must have offended someone while serving on the SGC, and that that someone was now manipulating the Japanese army to get back at them. Li Zidong this time asked his appointee as head of the Zhoujiaqiao suboffice, a former SGC chair, to investigate. He reported back to Li that Hou Shunmin had the genuine support of the merchants who put his name forward. A businessman who had no prewar administrative experience, Hou had done neither great good nor great harm as SGC vicechair. Li's appointee could learn nothing more, as Hou at the time of writing on 1 April was still in detention. The next item in the file in the Shanghai Municipal Archives is a third letter from the eleven merchants, dated 28 April, responding to Li Zidong's order that they elect representatives for the Xinhua town office. Hou and Wang had been released in the meantime, for they again put Hou forward to be town head and Wang to be his second. A note dated 5 May, probably by Li Zidong, ends the paper trail with the simple observation that Kitaoka would have to approve. Apparently he did so, for when Li filed a memo on local personnel on 7 June 1940, he listed Hou Shunmin as the head of Xinhua town.

These two struggles over minor appointments in the Western District illustrate the sorts of conflicts that could arise in the face of reorganization from above and competition from below. More important, thanks to the survival of office correspondence from the Western District, they indicate that final control in these matters remained in Special Service hands. Japanese control of the occupation state did not always go all the way down to the bottom of the administration, even though they hoped it might. At lower levels, local elites had leeway to work the opportunities the occupation state provided to their advantage, regardless of what the SSD thought it was doing. The resilience of those at the bottom of the system is suggested by the success with which SGC personnel from the opening months of the occupation were able to hang on to their posts through subsequent reorganizations. They were helped by Fu Xiaoan's announcement on 1 November 1938 that Great Way personnel could continue in their posts under his administration, though that guaranteed little when patronage practices ensured that they could as easily be pushed aside.[38]

The ability of collaborationist officials to survive politically can be gauged by scanning the curricula vitae of local officials under the Western District office, the files of which remain largely intact in the Shanghai Municipal Archive.[39] Looking at only the new heads of the local organs, continuity appears slight. As of January 1939, only one of the six heads of town offices in the Western District had been the chair of the earlier SGC, though another had been a vice-chair elsewhere. The other four came from outside the Great Way. At the level below them, however, continuity comes into view. The staff at three of the six offices as of 1940 were the same men who had worked for the original SGCs three years earlier. At the Xinhua town office, three of the four staff members had worked for the earlier SGC. Of the three staffers at the Hongqiao town office, two had been employees of the Hongqiao SGC and the third had been with the SGC in nearby Qibao. Finally, of the four staff members in Longcao, two had been in the Caojin SGC, one as an interpreter, and two had come from the South City SGC. Down at this level of the occupation state, reorganization did not bring about a huge turnover in personnel. The Japanese indeed hoped that something of this sort would happen, bringing administrative stability and a quick recovery.

Continuity is not always an asset when the people who hold on to positions at the bottom of the system lack the skills or intelligence to manage the tasks set before them. The Great Way Government might advise its police to rely on "gentry of the local area" when looking for people to take charge of local affairs, but it could only work with those who came forward.[40] As we have found in the case studies, those who volunteered were not usually the people who commanded the authority or resources to make occupied China a better place for those who had to live there. Their resilience was a fact of the occupation, but it could also be a liability for the occupation state, and even more for the occupier. Administrators such as Li Zidong could only do what they could to control local factional conflicts while keeping up a stream of ideology that claimed, as he does in his preface for the 1939 *Great Way Annual,* that occupied Shanghai was "tending in the direction of accepting Confucius as its guide."

Great Way ideology is hard to accept as representative of much of the spectrum of opinion in Li's time, given the widespread cynicism about government by morality in 1930s Shanghai. When for instance a Shanghai bureaucrat circulated a new set of slogans about "ancient morality" and "moral concepts" for comment two months after the Great Way had been dissolved, an official higher up the hierarchy pasted a note to the file objecting to "government by slogans" as "the detestable technique of the Communist and Nationalist parties, which there is really no need to imitate."[41] We do not know whether Li Zidong cared for slogans, but we might at least suppose that he did care to instill a moral purpose in the world he was trying to administer. That purpose had nothing to do with serving the Japanese, as he saw it; their presence simply provided the opening to suspend the false modernism of the Nationalists and Communists and get China back to what it should be. If it seemed to him that such a return was possible, most reform-minded intellectuals would have dismissed his Confucian ramblings as vacant of any moral legitimacy, and made more vacant by the Japanese patronage on which it relied.

This account of local politics in occupied Shanghai signals the vulnerability of the occupation state to fracture where politics was most resilient, at the bottom. The Japanese plan for Central China was to construct the occupation state at both the local and the national level of the political structure simultaneously, but the case of Shanghai shows, among other things, that there was no one local level. Every political instantiation of the local takes place above the networks and organizations from which individuals emerge to engage in a politics of interests. This emergence can hap-

pen in the village, in the market town, in the county seat, and in any number of nodes interstitial to these locations. Each time politics happens, it
does so at a level above the actual operation of the interests that are proj-
ecting their presence into local politics; which means that each time politics takes place, it does so with the possibility of being undercut from below. For every local arrangement, many other more local arrangements are
already poised to act. On the scale of local, the Great Way Government sat
well above the politics of everyday life. It claimed partial administrative authority over the largest and most modern city in China, and it did so with
the organized support of at least three dozen military officers assigned by
the Japanese army to make Shanghai a place that was both secure and
profitable for Japan's colonial enterprise in China. In one way, Shanghai
was not greatly different than any other county seat on the Yangtze Delta: a
node in what Japan hoped would be an emerging network of control operating in its interests. And yet the dense complexity of the local, as would-
be regime leader Su Xiwen discovered to his ongoing frustration, turned
Shanghai into something quite different: a realm of complicities even less
easy to untangle than Nanjing, and a field of rivalries that scale made more
unstable and intransigent than any other place in occupied China.

Rivalry is not resistance, however much it might dislodge certain collaborators, unsettle their handlers, or thwart the plans and desires of either.
The rivalries in this chapter did not undo Shanghai's contribution to the
making of the occupation state. They may in fact have reinforced it by un-
derscoring the dependence of local competitors for political power on the
Japanese military, whose presence served to exclude many of the more
powerful rivals that had been active in local settings up until 1937. Local
political actors might play games with the Great Way Government, but
success became an investment in its continuation and the perpetuation of
the occupation state.

It has been suggested (mostly by themselves) that participants in collaborationist regimes in occupied France turned their access to knowledge
and power into resources for resistance, thereby acting to weaken German
control more than aid it. Nothing in the surviving documentation suggests that any player in the Shanghai administration understood or inten-
tionally produced this kind of effect. Local rivalries stalled and may well
have ruined some Japanese plans, but the documents I have seen from
the first two years of the occupation yield no evidence of it. The argument is entirely retrospective. As long as Japan had the final say in all im-

portant administrative decisions in occupied Shanghai, anything deserving the name of resistance could only take place outside the operations of the occupation state. Real resistance, when it happened, did so elsewhere; but even then, as we are about to see, what was real is hard to distinguish from what was not.

— 7 —

Resistance / Chongming

Although the existing history of the Japanese occupation of China is built around the ideal of resistance, this theme has not loomed large in this book. My purpose in delaying resistance until this final case study has not been to save the best for last, withholding the capstone of the edifice for its final placing here. Quite the opposite; the theme has been put off because resistance does not appear to have had much influence over whether certain elites chose to collaborate. This, plus the weakness of the documentary base for reconstructing something other than a romantic history of resistance in the occupied areas, is why this chapter is shorter than the other case studies. I do not mean by this brevity to suggest that collaborators were entirely indifferent to resistance; we have already encountered cases of sabotage and assassination that were threatening to collaborators. Delaying the theme is meant to suggest, rather, that the intellectual structure in which we are accustomed to situate resistance as the opposite of collaboration—celebrating resistance as social imperative and moral high ground and denigrating collaboration as empty sign and redoubt of corruption—caricatures the reality of politics under occupation and overstates the capacity of individuals to alter the circumstances in which they find themselves. The reality framing the politics of collaboration was that many accommodated and few resisted. And the reality of resistance, at least as I have been able to reconstruct it in the following case study, is that the movement spent most of its energy preying on the local population rather than battling the Japanese. When guerillas did launch offensives, these brought consequences on the local people that were disastrous. This is, of course, the calculus of clandestine resistance, that it strike the enemy without direct engagement and then let the counterstrike fall where it will. The question is whether the imposition of such hardships on the local population succeeded in doing anything else. Resistance was ineffective in denying Japan a steady supply of collaborators. And yet it did raise the physical and moral costs of collaboration to a level that the occupation state could not always fund, pushing collaborators into a closer alliance with the occupier whose protection they could not do without. Resistance may not have defeated the Japanese, but it did eliminate any viability for a regime that posed as an alternative to Chiang Kaishek the moment Japan surrendered.

Chongming county was peripheral to Japanese military concerns, as it was peripheral to the political and economic goals of the occupation state. This meant that it was a place where a resistance movement could remain active during the war and drive the local collaboration bargain harder here than elsewhere. Chongming also yields an interesting example of a member of the lesser rural elite who weathered the occupation by remaining in the middle, resisting the resistance almost as strongly as he resisted collaboration—which is why it took half a century for his story to break through the intolerance of a nationalist historiography that has only resistance tales to tell.

On 21 December 1937, the newly formed Great Way Government sent a letter to the Chongming county magistrate informing him that it was taking over the county. It claimed two grounds for doing so. The first was that, having abandoned its capital, the National Government had extinguished its jurisdiction over the counties in Jiangsu province. The second was popular feeling. Representatives of the Chongming people had supposedly sent appeals to Shanghai asking to be taken over—a claim for which there is no documentary evidence. Su Xiwen gave the magistrate five days to reply, dangling as an inducement the possibility that he could continue in office if he responded quickly and favorably.[1] The magistrate ignored the request. Three months would pass before the Japanese military got around to sending two warships across the Yangtze Estuary to bring Chongming into the occupation state.

The county of Chongming is an island, a long alluvial deposit stretching seventy-five kilometers along the north shore of the Yangtze River. Despite its northerly position in the Yangtze Estuary, Chongming was tied socially and economically to the area south of the Yangtze. Still, the island was far enough from the areas of first concern for the invader that Japan could ignore the county. Only as Japan was able to build up its military strength north of the Yangtze did the presence of a Nationalist county administration and a Chinese army unit on the island inspire action.

Rumors that the Japanese were about to invade Chongming swirled for several days before two warships carried out the attack on the morning of 18 March 1938. One approached the island at Xinkaihe, the other farther down the shore at Shouan Monastery. From these positions, machine gunners on both ships fired on the defense posts on the shore while half a dozen planes flew in low to bomb the defenders. Badly outgunned, the Chinese soldiers were forced back. A brief gun battle with Japanese marines outside the East Gate of the city wall left a dozen Japanese dead, including a platoon commander, but the Chinese soldiers could not hold back a thousand attackers. They withdrew with their commander and the county magistrate into the countryside, leaving the town to the invaders. The magistrate had to abandon the island not long after and lead guerrilla operations, rather unsuccessfully, from Haimen along the north shore of the Yangtze.

The following day, the invading force fanned out across the entire island. Its purpose was to dig out soldiers in hiding and to confiscate cached weapons. The raid also included looting property and rounding up women for sexual service. Those unfortunate enough to get caught were dragged to makeshift brothels, though some were raped in the open air. Wealthy women slipped into hiding along unpatrolled stretches of the shoreline and were taken off in boats heading to Shanghai. Poor women disfigured themselves or kept out of sight until the orgy of invasion was over. The youngest, who was bayoneted by the soldier who penetrated her, was an eleven-year-old girl in the town of Changxing, the granddaughter of a prominent gentry family. The eldest to be raped, and who then committed suicide by drowning, was a grandmother on Jiangyuan Lane in Chongming city. After the occupation was secure, the Japanese army commandeered three houses in the city and set up "comfort stations" to which the soldiers were supposed to direct their sexual urges. Chongming Island later gained a reputation among Japanese soldiers as the place where you were sent for quarantine if you were found to be suffering from venereal disease.

None of this information appears in any of the surviving materials of the occupation regime. It comes instead from a detailed memoir that Li Helu, a well-educated resident of rural Chongming, wrote and published locally after the war.[2] Given that no Japanese report on the occupation of

Chongming Island survives, Li's memoir is particularly precious for pre-serving some knowledge of what occurred during the occupation. It gives a perspective rather different from the report on Chongming that appeared a year and a half later in the *New Nanjing Daily*, which described the Japa-nese arrival on the island simply as "reimposing order." The two perspec-tives produce two different narratives. The collaborationist press narrates the occupation as a story of a chaotic world into which the "friend-coun-try," left unnamed, brought order. The Japanese invasion thus marks the beginning of a long-delayed and long-awaited transformation of China out of backwardness and disorder: the making of a New China that looked toward a prosperous future. Li Helu tells a different story. His story begins in a morally and physically ordered world that then collapses into chaos when the Japanese invade and remains chaotic throughout the duration of the occupation. Li's narrative comes to a resolution when the Japanese withdraw in 1945. For the collaborationist narrative, of course, that defeat is the disaster that turns their epic of glory into a tragedy.

It is not clear from any of these accounts of the occupation how much damage the invasion caused. The only evidence regarding physical damage that I have found appears in the report that two inspectors filed with the provincial Relief Bureau the following December. Even though ten months had elapsed since the invasion, the inspectors found that most of the houses in the area of Miaozhen, which they inspected on their first day out, had been burned out. Over a hundred and fifty households there were still homeless and having to make do with small grass huts. As the inspec-tors prepared the next morning to set off for Baozhen, the head of the Chongming SGC, later its magistrate, Huang Zhiqing, blocked them from going on the grounds that guerrilla units were active in the area and that the Japanese army had "taken the opportunity to go on the offensive." The death toll in the preceding days had climbed to eighty or ninety, he said. For this part of the county, the inspectors had to rely on what they could learn from the county gentry. They estimated from the information they collected that sixty square kilometers of the county should be classed as a war-disaster zone. Add the areas damaged by flood and wind the previous summer and that estimate could be pushed up by half as much again.[3]

Ten months after this inspection, Magistrate Huang, in an officially pub-lished essay, looked back at the early phase of Chongming's occupation and recalled that "the residents of the city fled and left the place empty, leaving only the elderly and the weak behind as caretakers. The desolation of the markets, the flight of the women and children, the emptiness of the houses, the fear in the alleyways: these are all so hard to describe." He qualifies this chilling sketch with the qualifying observation that, "compared to most occupied areas, our Chongming was able to get by without much damage, leaving houses and buildings intact."[4] The provincial inspectors' report attests that Chongming did not get off quite as lightly as Huang implies.

It is difficult to see the occupation of Chongming from the Japanese side, given the lack of a pacification team work diary of the sort available for other counties. Of the team and its leader we know nothing. A Mantetsu summary of pacification work reports that the team consisted of three agents, none of whom was its employee.[5] SGC chair Huang Zhiqing gives the team leader's surname as Kawanōbito and praises him as having the safety of the area at heart, but otherwise says nothing about the work he did. Sixteen months after the occupation, on 10 July 1939, the *New Nanjing Daily* gives the team leader's surname as Miya. Li Helu mentions the team leader, but gives the name of Kurami Sadakichi. All may have held the post of pacification team leader, though in what order and to what effect is now impossible to say. The only source in which it is possible to catch glimpses of the team's work is a dossier of notes, minutes, and work reports that the Chongming SGC compiled and submitted to the Reformed Government at the end of May 1938, two months after the SGC was inaugurated on 1 April. This trove of materials constitutes the other main source, besides Li Helu's memoir, for reconstructing the history of the first two months of the occupation of Chongming.

Chongming Island was not an important prize for the Japanese army. The north shore of the Yangtze River, to which it was adjacent, was a swampy stretch without economic or strategic value, and the south shore was too far for the island to pose a military threat beyond weak harassment of the coastal area. Its agricultural economy had only modest commercial value. The island had a high population at the start of the war of between 400,000 and 450,000, but that was a function of sheer size (1,088 square kilometers at that time) rather than evidence of an intensive economy. Agriculture on this low-lying island was vulnerable to disruption, as it relied on a network of canals, dikes, and seawalls that summer typhoons destroyed with some regularity. Typhoons swept over the island in August 1938, in late July 1939, and again in mid-August 1943, each time causing extensive damage. (In the summer of 1942, disaster took the opposite form of a drought when no rain fell for forty-eight days straight.) A quarter of the island's cultivated land was devoted to cotton, which supplied Chongming's only modern industrial sector, consisting of the two cotton-spinning mills of Datong and Fuan (with a total of 38,000 spindles). The other was wheat, which made a profit when shipped off the island. Other grains tended to remain on the island for local consumption. The Japanese responded to these assets after the invasion by taking over the cotton mills (taxing these factories would be the county's main source of revenue) and confirming the embargo on whatever could contribute to the Chinese war effort, especially grain. The collapse of regional trading in any case induced cultivators to hold back their wheat for local consumption, knowing that grain would be difficult and expensive to buy on the open market. Not until July 1939 did the Japanese authorities allow any wheat to leave the island, which they did only in the hope of alleviating the poverty into which their policies were driving the rural population.

The impact of the armed takeover was as disastrous to the livelihoods of the island residents as it was to their dignity and physical safety. Farmers who owned their own land were able to continue working, but as landlords fled and crops were stolen, tenants found themselves deprived of the security that in normal times guaranteed they could harvest what they planted. Fortunately the spring harvest in 1938 was relatively good, which meant that the invasion did not throw the island into an immediate food shortage. The invasion did, however, shut down the urban economy. Anyone with any means fled to Shanghai, taking his capital with him, and anyone who was away at the time refused to return. Ordinary urban residents who worked in the factories and retail shops in the county seat found themselves unemployed. Even after the Japanese garrison and the SGC police reimposed a measure of security in and around the city, obstacles stood in the way of the urban economy's achieving a quick recovery. The larger ships that carried commercial cargo before the invasion had either been destroyed or confiscated, leaving only a small Portuguese vessel and a boat owned by the Nikkei Company to handle traffic. The Portuguese vessel soon quit the scene, reducing Chongming natives to travel on the Nikkei ferry, which eventually settled into a daily run down to Shanghai. The ferry was always jammed, and tickets were often only to be had from scalpers.

The lack of commercial shipping was almost beside the point in any case, for what was there for merchants to ship? Anything that could contribute to the war effort was embargoed. And how could goods be imported when the only legal tender on Chongming was Japanese military scrip, which suppliers elsewhere would not accept but which local merchants had to use on pain of arrest? Financial institutions had shut down, currency had dried up, and even small retailers could do nothing but close their shops. The SGC, which was inaugurated on 1 April, was concerned to reopen the main urban market, but two months passed and still it remained closed. The direct effect on the SGC was that it claimed it had nothing to tax (a bit of an exaggeration, though liabilities were running 40 percent above assets as of the end of May) and nothing with which to pay its employees.

These complaints are packed into the brief summary of the current situation at the front of the dossier of documents the Chongming SGC sent to Nanjing at the end of May. The author is concise in tallying the challenges facing occupied Chongming. At the end of his account of the economy, he departs from his official rhetoric to say that he regrets he lacks the literary skill needed to describe the poverty of the unemployed. (The problem of unemployment would only grow as Chongming natives working in low-wage jobs in Shanghai were thrown out of work and ended up returning home.) Other than one mention of the "visiting army" and a few references to the navy garrison, the opening summary of the SGC report blankets the dominating Japanese presence and the Japanese army's responsibility for the difficult conditions with silence. There are occasional exceptions to this silence in the other documents in the dossier. In its work report, the SGC General Affairs Department lists the provisioning of the Japanese army and the pacification team as one of its tasks for April and May. The report of the People's Livelihood Department notes that the team head lectured the department on the neighborhood watch system on 2 May. The SGC's Neighborhood Watch Section in a separate report mentions receiving the pacification team's help in setting it up. The Education Department reports that it passed on its survey of monasteries and churches to the pacification team, and that one of its employees accompanied the team on its inspection of urban schools. The Land Department report declares that it plans to consult the team on the breakdown of currency circulation. Lastly, the minutes of the SGC's bimonthly meeting on 25 May record the committee's resolution to consult with the pacification team head about arranging for the Military Police to arm the militia. These seven references are the sum total of evidence in the sixty-five pages of SGC documents regarding the reestablishment of local administration. Chongming's pacification team remains for us a shadowy organization.

Li Helu presents a different impression, though not a fuller one. He chiefly associates the pacification team with the initial security operation designed to isolate the resistance: the issuing of loyal subject certificates. Every resident was required to obtain one as proof that he or she had accepted the authority of the new regime. Most resistance accounts of the occupation highlight census and certification as pacification team operations, since this was one of the few occasions when the team was visible to ordinary people, and this is what Li does. He does not object to registration itself so much as to the fact that people were obliged to pay for the certificates. This he identifies as the team's first act of "coerced extraction." It also created the first opportunity for the Japanese army to legally discipline ordinary people, since refusing to get a certificate was considered the equivalent of banditry. The team thus instituted what Li calls Japan's "white terror" in Chongming.[6] To call these certificates the thin edge of white terror may be more a speech act than a fair description, but this is how Li and others felt about their imposition.

The work of issuing the certificates and collecting the money was done not by Japanese agents, though, but by Chinese employees of the SGC's People's Livelihood Department. Interests diverged between them. Both were concerned to reestablish security, but the Chinese administrators were even more concerned with acquiring revenue in order to pay for their operations. For them the quality of the registration was not the issue that it was for the Japanese: they just wanted the fees. In April, the People's Livelihood Department had 116,000 loyal subject certificates printed up. It retained 28,000 certificates for the main SGC to sell to urban residents, and sent 11,000 out to each of the SGC's eight branch committees, which were to distribute them downward to the heads of the rural quarters, towns, and neighborhood watch units within their jurisdictions for sale to rural residents. In Chongming, registration functioned as nothing more than an illegal tax, and it was universally understood as such. As of 26 May, the main SGC had sold only 15,000 of its consignment, from which it collected 1,230 yuan. The branch committees also failed to sell their quotas, though still they were able to forward 3,977 yuan back to the Department, which it then passed on to the Finance Department for accounting. Given that Finance's overall income for April and May was 24,898 yuan, the proceeds from the sale of loyal subject certificates amounted to over 20 percent of what the SGC was bringing in. This levy was a one-time-only income item, but it certainly helped the cash-starved SGC get on its feet. It fell as a heavy extraction on some people, Li Helu insisted. Even the People's Livelihood

Department's own report acknowledged that some rural people had to borrow cash to pay for theirs. The internal record indicates, however, that the receipts went entirely to the SGC, not to the Japanese, as Li Helu thought.

The People's Livelihood Department also took it upon itself to register transport: 544 boats, 22 bicycles, and 2 motor vehicles. The boat number seems reasonable, but not the other two. With ninety kilometers of public roads, Chongming before the occupation had considerably more cars and bicycles than this. One can only assume that the Japanese army expropriated what it did not destroy. The Commerce and Industry Department got into the business of issuing certificates as well by registering 621 shops and factories in the city and suburbs, and having the branch committees register another 2,039 rural businesses. The proceeds from this effort, 733 yuan, were transferred to the Finance Department.[7] Though it was a modest amount, it was enough to cover three months' salary for the SGC chair.

Although the pacification team was not the authority issuing these certificates, Li Helu was correct in crediting the entire operation to the team. He mentions team leader Kurami Sadakichi in one other context, a public rally, at which Kurami and garrison commander Tanigawa shared the platform. As Li recounts the event, which is undated, Kurami got up to deliver a lecture in which he pontificated on the value of practicing the ancient Confucian duties of self-cultivation, family discipline, and education. Li was not impressed with what he took to be a fraudulent claim to Chinese cultural values. "To hear him talk," he declares with passion, "he was more benevolent than Confucius, but examine his conduct and he was more cruel than Robber Zhi," the Confucian epitome of evil. "When a Japanese preaches morality, how is that any different than a tiger talking about benevolence? As for actually believing any of this stuff, who would?"[8] Unlike the accounts of public education in the work reports of other pacification teams, which liked to record how many people showed up for mass gatherings and how earnestly they took in the content, this is one case in which we have someone in the audience talking back at the propagandists.

What propaganda work the team did besides public lecturing can only be guessed from the work report of the SGC's Education Department. As I have already noted, that report includes two references to the team. One was to note that it received the department's survey of temples and churches, which the Japanese tried to use as sites for building Sino-Japanese contacts and cooperation. The other was to report that the team went out to inspect all schools in Chongming city, accompanied by a department staffer. Getting the primary education system up and running was a propaganda priority of pacification teams eager to show that life had returned to normal. Progress would be slow, however. A year and a half later, Chongming could report only sixty-four schools serving ten thousand students, a third the scale of the county's educational system before the invasion.

In addition to getting primary schools back in operation, the team was also keen to set up a Japanese language school. This project did not go smoothly. The school was initially started in the East City Primary School and a Chinese teacher appointed to run it, but then it was decided that it should be converted into a Japanese Language Normal School to teach Japanese to teachers.[9] This plan was then abandoned sometime in the first half of May in favor of going back to the original idea. The school principal surfaces in the minutes of the SGC meeting on 18 May, asking for salaries for his teachers while the school was still in the planning stage (turned down) and seeking additional funding beyond what had been ear-marked for the normal school (also refused). It is in this context that the SGC notes that the normal school was abandoned for lack of any good students. It is not clear when formal language education actually got established in Chongming. In May, the only Japanese language instruction was the obligatory hour-long class given every day at lunch to employees in the People's Livelihood Department. The Education Department's solution to the problem of Chongming residents' ignorance of Japanese was to circulate a mimeographed "Japanese Made Easy" to other departments for their comments.

One other undertaking the Education Department lists in its report that points to the invisible hand of the pacification team is the plan to publish the *New Chongming Daily*. The idea that every county should have its "new daily" came from the Special Service Department in Shanghai, and these newspapers sprang up wherever a pacification team went to work, as noted earlier in the chapters on Jiading and Zhenjiang. These publications were not simply offered to local residents as a source of news, but given a monopoly. No other newspaper was allowed to be read. Elsewhere, in Taicang county across the river, an elderly woman was discovered bringing several non-Japanese Shanghai newspapers into the county city on 26 January. Suspected of being a political agent, she was interrogated about her activities. What happened to her is not recorded, but a similar case in Chongming is. Newspaper vendor Zhou Hairong was discovered selling a newspaper printed by the resistance. For challenging the *New Chongming Daily*'s monopoly on information, Zhou was disemboweled and his corpse thrown in the river.[10] This story comes from Li Helu's memoir. Almost nothing of the dark side of the occupation ever surfaces in the SGC work reports.

Yet the work reports are all we have to decipher the SGC's activities. While they are informative as to what the SGC was up to, they make everything appear to happen as a result of what the SGC did, leaving the role of the pacification team obscured. The SGC reports thus produce the illusion that, as of inauguration day on 1 April, county affairs were in the hands of the Chinese collaborators rather than under the thumb of the Japanese agents. Despite their partiality, the reports are valuable in revealing more about this SGC than can be learned about any other SGC that operated in the region.

Of the head of the SGC, Huang Zhiqing, little can be learned. In an account he wrote in 1939, Huang explains that his motivation for taking office was to "make things a little better for the masses."[11] It is a pleasant sentiment, but where Huang came from, and what motives and forces pushed him to the fore, are impossible to determine. His power, though, was considerable. The SGC's provisional charter invested him with final authority in all decisions concerning the committee's business and its appointments, and he wielded it effectively. As we shall see, he was able to hang on to power under the occupation state longer than any other member of the collaborationist camp.

The first hurdle was the regularization of administration imposed from Nanjing in the summer of 1938, which dissolved the SGC. Of the six department heads who worked under the SGC, only two survived the dissolution. One was Huang Dounan, who headed first the General Affairs Department and later the Civil Administration Bureau; the other was Tao Zhiju, who ran the Land Department and subsequently the Enterprise Bureau. According to Li Helu, both were major landlords. They were able to exploit the unregulated environment of the occupation by joining with four other landlords, one of whom joined the Chongming administration, to build illegal polder walls along the shore. By diking coastal land and bringing it under cultivation, the six were encroaching on what had been public land, and there was no power to stop them. Tao additionally was the patron of a Chongming boatman-turned-pirate who later became a commander in the collaborationist army and shared the command of the island garrison from March 1940 to February 1943 with Tao's younger brother. Political unknowns before 1938, Li Helu calls them "infamous bullies and careerless literati."[12]

A few collaborators were able to turn local appointments to political advantage. Wang Zenglu had been at the edge of power as a Nationalist Party activist before the occupation and was brought into the new administration to head the Finance Bureau. His political background may have helped him make connections off the island, for he managed to get promoted up out of Chongming, passing through a series of posts in the Nanjing municipal government and the Jiangsu and Anhui provincial governments to become a county magistrate in Anhui. The occupation state thus offered career opportunities to Chongming natives whose ambitions were stymied under the Nationalist regime. Lu Mengxiong did even better than Wang Zenglu. Lu had had a career in the government of the early Republic and was able to parlay that experience into a position on the administrative committee of the municipal government of Qingdao. Qian Yingqing, whose record of public service included a post in the Yuan Shikai regime in the early 1910s, was called back by the Reformed Government to head the bond section of the Finance Ministry—for which he was assassinated in his bed in Shanghai on the morning of 29 November 1938. By far the most successful Chongming collaborator, though, was Gao Guanwu, an ambitious military officer whom the Nationalists pushed out of power but who came back, as we have seen in the preceding chapter, to become the vice-minister of the army and the collaborationist mayor of Nanjing. He too died a violent death.

An account in the *New Nanjing Daily* presents the inauguration of the county administration as evidence that the management of Chongming was getting back to normal—thanks to "the direction of the organ of the friend-country and the zeal of the local gentry." The "organ of the friend-country" was the elusive pacification team. Presumably Wang Zenglu, Huang Dounan, Tao Zhiju, and the rest were among this zealous local gentry. When Chongming county was slated to get reorganized as a district of Shanghai later in 1938, at least some of this local gentry were opposed. An article in the *New Nanjing Daily* at the end of November reports that "the masses" of Chongming objected to the restructuring and submitted a petition to Nanjing asking that the plan be reconsidered.[13] Chongming was much closer to the north shore of the Yangtze Estuary than it was to the south, the petitioners argued, and historically had always been oriented northward rather than southward. The argument was specious, for the extraordinary rise of Shanghai over the preceding century had fundamentally recast the economic networks around the mouth of the Yangtze, drawing Chongming into its orbit. Interests that benefited from keeping Chongming out of the administrative reach of Shanghai were eager to resist the shift.

The issue was not history but revenue. The real source of dissent emerged later that winter when Shanghai officials went to the provincial capital in Suzhou to negotiate the hand-over. Jiangsu provincial governor Chen Zemin stalled by claiming that he had received no such instruction from the Reformed Government. Asking for a postponement of discussions, he then appealed to the Executive Yuan in Nanjing to cancel the move. His reasoning was simple. When Nanhui, Chuansha, Fengxian, and Baoshan counties had been moved into Shanghai municipality earlier that year, the province lost over a million yuan in annual revenue. The governor was not keen to take another loss on this scale. The Executive Yuan claimed that it lacked the authority to overturn a decision of the government's Political Affairs Commission and proposed a compromise: for the fiscal year 1939, the province and the municipality would split the revenue from all six counties. This was the best the province could hope for. Shanghai officials returned victorious to Suzhou to negotiate the transfer, and the newly empowered "local gentry" of Chongming had to go along.

These reorganizations look too far ahead from where the first collaborators on Chongming found themselves in the late spring of 1938. The minutes of the SGC's twice-monthly meeting allow us to go back to that spring and examine more closely what tasks the occupation imposed on the collaborators. The issues on the agenda of the first meeting on 15 April all had to do with determining the administration's internal organization, its boundaries, and the salaries that its personnel would draw. These could not be resolved in one afternoon and had to be taken up again the following day. The crux of the problem at the outset was money. The simple sign of this problem is a handwritten emendation to the list of salary levels, reducing some, including the committee chair's, by 10 yuan.[14]

To extend its reach into the countryside, the SGC set up eight branch committees, one in the suburbs and seven in the main rural towns. These branch committees were permitted to have between five and eleven members, though none in practice had more than nine. Within their own jurisdictions they had the power to appoint neighborhood watch heads and to remove town or village leaders whose work was "weak," but they were under the direction of the central SGC. They were also funded by the central SGC. The final item of business on 15 April set the monthly support of committee expenses in the range of 300 to 400 yuan. This amount was raised to 500 yuan in early May when it became clear how much work they were expected to do in the face of rural insurgency.

The organization of branch committees was the first item on the agenda for 5 May, followed by tax deliberations. The SGC was well aware that it needed to start collecting the land tax as soon as possible, hence the need for committed branch committees at the next level down, but it put off the decision as to when the collection of 1938 taxes would be done. One decision the SGC did make was to forgive all back taxes. What looks like a concession to the troubles people were going through was more likely the result of having found the tax records to be in a mess, for once the Finance Department was ready to collect the land tax in 1938, it ordered collectors to demand payment of the next two years' tax as well. These measures were not sufficient to get Chongming's finances back on their prewar footing of relying principally on land taxes; the two cotton factories and a tax on goods coming in and out of the island would be the mainstays. The May meeting anticipated this reliance by deciding that the old traveler's tax of one-tenth of a yuan and the boat passenger's tax of two-tenths would be reinstated as of 11 May.[15]

The last item of business on 5 May was to clear the financial liabilities following the closing of the orphans' crèche. At the time of the invasion, the crèche cared for twenty-four infants. It was closed and the infants were farmed out to wet nurses. These women received 3 yuan for their labor that year, but this payment would not continue beyond 1938. Prewar Chongming also had an orphanage, which housed ten older children. This too was closed down. Three children were sent out to "serve society," as the People's Livelihood Department phrases putting them out to work. The other seven were moved to the Japanese language school with the idea of grooming them as the next generation of translators. For Li Helu, the career of translator was not an honorable one. He names four translators in his memoir who worked for the police, the garrison, and the Military Police, and is vicious in denouncing them for "giving their bodies as prostitutes to the enemy" and using their connections to the Japanese for their own benefit. "Dying once would not be sufficient to pay for their sins."[16]

An interesting item on the agenda of the 18 May meeting is a request from two men surnamed Zhou for permission to ship textiles through Wan'an Harbor. This is exactly what the island economy needed, but the SGC had to turn them down with the reminder that the Japanese naval embargo was still in place. The only boats that could leave the harbor were fishing boats, and those boats were expressly forbidden from carrying commercial cargo. The occupation's security came before its economy. The SGC also discussed the imposition of a cotton tax, though no decision was reached, and could not be until such time as shipping was permitted to revive and cotton could actually be sold again.[17]

The last SGC meeting for which minutes survive was held on 25 May. The agenda is divided between financial and security matters. On the financial side, the committee passed a proposal to tax coastal fishermen at a rate of 3 yuan per boat, although it was noted that the catches were small and intended primarily for home consumption. It also approved a suggestion to lift the ban on egg exports, while putting a tax of 0.7 yuan on each basket. The tax would prove modest, for once the egg trade revived, a basket of eggs could sell for 50 yuan. The committee also considered proposals to reduce the number of SGC staff in order to cut down its expenses, and to shut down the boat inspection station as an unnecessary burden on its resources. The SGC was getting desperate. It had already trimmed its employees' salaries three times in order to stay afloat, and even shut down the city's one public hospital for lack of funds, telling the sick to go seek treatment at the Japanese army clinic.[18] The occupation was not making financial sense on Chongming Island.

When the Chinese garrison commander abandoned the city on 18 March, the soldiers dispersed into the countryside, many of them to continue to engage in acts of resistance on a guerrilla basis. The Japanese army was unenthusiastic about having to penetrate the rural areas, which left the countryside for some time to a mixed reign of guerrillas and bandits. The SGC was in no position to act. It recruited thirty police initially, but they were too few and generally inexperienced, only ten having held police jobs before the invasion. There had been a water police unit before the invasion, but this force the SGC was slow to reconstitute as their motorboats had been taken. The most immediate limitation, however, was the Japanese army's refusal to let any Chinese have weapons, including the police. Only Japanese soldiers could go about armed. All the Chinese police got were new uniforms. The SGC thus made little headway in putting its police forces back into operation. Only after it was reorganized as a county government was a new Police Affairs Bureau created—and a Japanese surnamed Hashimoto appointed to run it.

The global solution to which the Japanese security officers in Chongming looked to provide security against armed resistance, as Special Service agents did throughout occupied China, was a neighborhood watch system. The first sign of SGC activity in this regard was when it set up a Neighborhood Watch Section on 22 April to plan and oversee this work, probably at the insistence of the pacification team. The minutes of the SGC meeting on 18 May note that branch committees were not getting residents registered fast enough, which was invariably the first step toward putting the system into operation. A week later, the section brought forward comprehensive proposals to implement the watch system and use it as the framework for creating a Self-Defense Corps. The SGC referred these proposals to a subcommittee of the heads of the departments concerned. In the meantime it authorized branch committees to receive funds to pay for two extra staffers to implement the system in their areas, though only until the end of June. Concerned to know how this militia was to be trained if it had no guns, the SGC resolved that the Neighborhood Watch Section should give the problem to the pacification team leader and ask him to approach the Military Police for guns.

The Self-Defense Corps that the Neighborhood Watch Section proposed to create was to be composed of both standing and reserve militia, plus a mobile unit that could go into quick action against guerrillas. The plan was ambitious in its aspiration to use local people to combat guerrilla resistance, at the same time providing a web of links that extended from the SGC downward through its branch committees and the rural district and town heads to fifty-household units and ten-household units, right on down to the individual household at the bottom of the pyramid. Except in some of its modernized terminology, it perfectly transcribes the system of census and levy that the imperial state had used for centuries to hold the people in place. As a model it enthralled the Japanese colonialists, who hoped that this vast agrarian realm could somehow administer itself, at no cost to themselves. It had had the same appeal for Republican reformers earlier in the 1930s, and would again for Communist bureaucrats in the 1950s, though each implementation engendered its own problems.

The Chongming plan was ambitious. According to a mimeographed handwritten supplement to the SGC's first set of printed regulations drafted in May, the system would guard against bandits, carry out surveillance against other members, report crimes, capture criminals, investigate arrivals and sojourners, control travel, prohibit gambling, provide fire and flood relief, protect transportation and communication, ensure that no land was left fallow, provide credit to cultivators, promote public health, improve sanitation, check the outbreak of infectious diseases, get drug users to give up their habit, spread "moral transformation" (an old and by 1938 rather empty term), encourage the people to be filial, loyal, and mutually respectful, organize mutual assistance and relief, instill in the people "the spirit of the neighborhood watch," nurture "a religious mindset," register households, and collect taxes. Not surprisingly, it was beyond the capacity of the SGC to organize something this comprehensive. All watch system work was shifted to the police bureau in August 1939, stripping it of any community function.[19]

A curious element in this grand plan is the notion of cultivating a "religious mindset." A key strain of ideological modernization during the Republic—persuasive in large part because it was analogous with an older Confucian critique of sectarianism and superstition—argued against the hold that religion had over the people. Religion was superstition and, along with the two other chief debilitations of the period, gambling and opium addiction, needed to be curbed to make China modern. If Chinese, even Chinese of the conservative stripe who threw their lot in with the Japanese in a desperate attempt to fend off Nationalist modernism, were going to yoke the system to a spiritual project, it would be to promote a mindset that rejected religious superstition, even religion altogether. It is difficult to imagine a Chinese adding a religious mindset to the proposed list of neighborhood watch objectives. It strikes me rather as a Japanese construction of what they thought would be good for keeping Chinese in order. Karl Marx was not the only one to think that religion could be the opiate of the people, apparently. No other neighborhood watch document from Chongming includes this item, so it must not have gone beyond the proposal stage.

The system cannot therefore be held responsible for promoting what the occupation did in fact excite among the people of Chongming, just as the author of the document hoped: an intensification of popular religious devotion. The rise in religious activity caught the censorious attention of Li Helu. As a member of the modernizing generation of the Republic, Li was dismayed at the revival of pious practices among people who, he knew, could not easily devise other responses to what they felt was a hopeless situation. He names six devotional societies—the Buddhist Laymen's Lodge, the Pure Yang Altar, the Benevolent Society, the Lotus Society, the Association to Aid Living Things, and the Orthodox Transmission Sect—as deplorable examples of the devotional turn among the majority of Chongming people during the later years of the occupation.[20]

The neighborhood watch system may not have done much to push the islanders to religion, but it was successful in extracting wealth and redistributing it upward—though too often into the hands of its own officers, not into the coffers of the county government. At every level, particularly among the sixty-nine town and rural district heads, the system created wonderful opportunities for self-enrichment. (Li takes pleasure in discrediting these sixty-nine by pointing out that all but one were opium addicts—a moralistic charge that cannot be substantiated, although two officially licensed opium retailers did open in Chongming city in the autumn of 1939.)[21] The higher up in the system, the larger the catchment area for payoffs. As a children's song that was making the rounds put the situation:

> District heads—build houses of brick,
> Watch system heads—eat meat till they're sick;
> Neighborhood heads—drink wind and sip gruel,
> The ordinary person—just weeps like a fool.[22]

Collaborators working at the middle levels of the control network were vulnerable to more than satire, and those who resisted their rule did more than compose rhymes. The most potent gesture that resistance could take under these conditions was assassination. The first prominent target of the island's Communist assassination team was the head of the branch committee at Xinkaihe, which is where the Japanese had landed in March. Early that first summer, guerrillas attacked his office, burned the building, and shot him. Fearful of receiving the same treatment, other collaborators hired bodyguards. The protection was good enough that the resistance switched from assassination to other forms of disruption and intimidation. Assassination got a brief reprise in Chongming after the war, when three rural district heads were executed for what they had done during the occupation.

It is not always clear—nor was it at the time—whether disturbances in the countryside were acts of resistance or the working through of other conflicts. Magistrate Huang Zhiqing complained that the island was much troubled by banditry, and while that label obscured the failure of the occupation regime to extend its authority into the countryside, it was probably a fair assessment of the disarray under which rural Chongming suffered through much of the occupation. Some armed bands were operating as guerrilla units, but others were simply parading under the banner of resistance in order to feed off an intimidated rural populace. Li Helu personally experienced what appears to have been an attack by the latter. The incident occurred early in the summer of 1939, when a gang of over sixty armed men burst into the family compound. His wife and small children looked on, terrified, as two men frogmarched Li to the main hall of the compound "as though I were a criminal awaiting execution." This was a particularly chaotic period on the island. Armed groups—Communists, Nationalists, bodyguards for the rich, village militia, and plain bandits—were proliferating at a bewildering rate.

The leader of the group, whose political allegiance Li Helu never ascertained, sat in a chair at the head of the hall and addressed his victim.

"What have you done for the Anti-Japanese Movement?" he barked. Li made the risky decision to take the high road by turning the accusation back at his accuser.

"Protecting the country and preserving the local district are duties that heaven has bestowed on the people of the nation," Li replied. "As long as the conscience of our citizens is not exhausted, we should regard those who help each other as friends, and treat those who invade us as foes."

The leader flushed with anger at the sly insinuation that he was the invader and leveled his gun at Li's chest.

"Who's the boss around here?" he demanded, but Li went right on with his lecture.

"When the emergence of the patriotic movement is inspired naturally by what is around us, even the powerful cannot resist it," Li declared. "But if the environment offers no inspiration, then even the most powerful cannot make it happen."

Suddenly, surprisingly, the gang leader laughed. The situation could have ended with Li Helu's death. Instead, the man conceded that he had lost the resistance argument. It seems that he was also amused that Li had the nerve to stand up to him.

"Well, this bookworm is no skin off my nose," he called out to his gang. "Let's go." They left Li and his family, unharmed and unlooted.[23]

Others were not so lucky. People who find themselves under a resisted

occupation can be in an intolerable situation, when the forces of occupation and collaboration are insufficient to guarantee security, and the forces
of resistance demand support but cannot protect those who give it. Somehow Li managed to stay apart from both sides without being harmed by either. Although he expresses sympathy for both Nationalist and Communist activists who went underground during the war, he took for himself
and his family the posture of withdrawal, which was probably the only
choice available to someone who had a family to support and lacked the
means to flee into the interior. He regarded his best choice as enduring the
occupation without succumbing to collaboration. Regardless of whether
the sixty armed men were actually a guerrilla unit or not, their challenge to
Li Helu—what had he done for the resistance?—was one that could be leveled at anyone in occupied China who was not engaged in armed struggle.
People like Li were in the majority, but that did not make the challenge of
maneuvering between the combatants any easier.

Longer-term motives besides resistance or parasitism may have fueled
some of the violence in the countryside. There is no specific evidence of
this for Chongming, but there is from Taicang county, on the south side of
the Yangtze Estuary. The pacification team there learned in late January of
disturbances along the western edge of the county. Japanese agents and
soldiers went out on an operation to surround and search a village close to
the border where their intelligence told them "criminals" were hiding,
though the work diary confesses that "there was no evidence and it was extremely difficult to tell loyal subjects from criminals."[24] Failing to make
contact, they spent the night in the home of a neighborhood watch head-
man listening to a fire fight between "armed bandits" and the local militia.
The militia failed to capture anyone, and by dawn the "bandits" had melted
away. This area continued to be disturbed by raids, robberies, and shoot-
ings over the next two months, and the pacification team went out many
times to make arrests, conduct searches, and carry out inconclusive investi-
gations. It took that long for the team to realize that this violence had
nothing to do with resistance. It arose instead from community feuds.
Over the preceding decades, famine refugees had moved into this part of
Taicang from Henan, Anhui, and Hubei provinces in the interior. Every
winter, tension between these outsiders and the local communities broke
into open violence as each side turned to raiding the other. The Japanese
team in Taicang realized that local PMC members had been using the new
structures of the occupation state to pursue their own subethnic conflicts,

all the while representing them as "bandit" suppression. This discovery that subethnic feuding was a regular winter distraction was comforting to the pacification team, since it could dismiss this violence as having nothing to do with Japan's presence. In fact, the disruption caused by the invasion only intensified the arming and fighting of the feuding communities. The loss of authority in the rural areas encouraged the recourse to violence when the competitors were confident that the state would not interfere. The team leader ordered the head of the local PMC to stop local organizing along subethnic lines. The two communities should put this dissension behind them and cooperate in building the new order, he stressed. Seven weeks later, the PMC head was found beaten to death.

The Chongming SGC fondly hoped that the neighborhood watches would weave a net of surveillance and defense so tight that the resistance would have no place to strike, yet the real bulwark against the threat of violence was the Japanese military. Magistrate Huang Zhiqing made this point at a banquet he hosted for a visiting Japanese commander on 30 January 1939. In his after-dinner remarks, Huang candidly admitted that "the security of this county is deeply reliant on the heartfelt protection that the Chongming team of the friend-country gives us."[25] Huang had good reason to highlight his debt to the Japanese military. The previous fall, guerrillas had destroyed roads, burned bridges, and cut down telegraph poles in a combined Nationalist-Communist offensive targeting several towns.[26] The first response from the Japanese side came from the pacification team, which called a meeting of all rural district and town heads, not to expatiate on the virtues of the neighborhood watch system this time, but to make clear to them that they were responsible for repairing the damage. Replacing telegraph poles on an island lacking trees proved to be an impossible burden, and communications remained out for many months. The second response came a month later, when the Japanese army launched a series of raids. That did not stop the insurgency, though, for the guerrillas returned with a further round of activity the following spring. Yet another guerrilla campaign in September 1939 disrupted communications by destroying bridges and telegraph poles across the island.[27] The cost of replacing the poles was too great and flimsier bamboo had to be substituted. The repairs kept the Japanese army busy for many months.

An extravagant second wave of sabotage swept the island the following spring. One of the mines planted on either side of the main highway running the length of the island succeeded in blowing up a Japanese troop truck near Shuhe, killing twenty-six soldiers. The Japanese garrison commander responded by calling in several dozen warships to seal off Chongming and then sending in a combined force of Japanese marines and some seven thousand Chinese troops to sweep the island. At the town of Shuhe, an army unit ordered the local collaborationist leadership to gather local residents at the City God Temple on 29 July 1940. Close to two hundred people dutifully assembled. The soldiers then went around to each of the people there and demanded at bayonet point to know where the guerrillas were hiding. Those who would or could not tell were stabbed. About thirty people who were carrying their Loyal Subject Certificates were allowed to leave. The rest were strafed with machine gun fire, burned, and left to rot inside the temple, which was locked and sealed. The summer heat reduced the bodies to a stench so terrible that no one could approach the place for several weeks. To ensure that another such bombing could not be repeated, the soldiers went on to raze every building within three hundred meters of the highway. Estimates of the casualties of the summer pacification program run as high as three thousand dead and ten thousand burned out of their homes.[28]

Magistrate Huang was not dismayed and would call for the same response a year later when yet another tide of insurrection swept the island. On 6 August 1940, he telegraphed Shanghai mayor Fu Xiaoan to plead that more Japanese troops be sent. "Ever since the 18 March incident [1938], most of the bad elements have revealed themselves as being anti-Japanese in order to gain power in the localities and organize guerrillas bands to pillage wherever they go. Over the last two years, all that came of the campaigns of the friend-army to root them out is that they have scattered and regrouped in other spots, popping up and disappearing at will." The effort to suppress them was destroying the lives, property, and homes of "loyal citizens," he declared. Huang was not keen to suggest that his island was so ill-governed that it had become a hotbed of anti-Japanese resistance, but he does report that mines had been detonated along the roads, that an explosion had destroyed part of the Datong Cotton Mill, and that guns had been found cached in the factory when it was searched.[29] He did not wish to send up too much evidence that he was failing to keep order and should be replaced, yet he had to convince his superiors to send more support by showing evidence of organized resistance.

Other Chongming natives were not keen to see more Japanese troops on the island. Two days later, three leading members of the Chongming Native

Place Association in Shanghai sent a telegram to Mayor Fu revealing a different perspective on the problems besetting Chongming. According to this report, the latest campaign that the Japanese army had carried out against the guerrillas had been wantonly violent. Since "jade and stone at the moment cannot be distinguished"—who could tell who was with the occupation state and who was against it?—the Japanese army did not discriminate in selecting its targets. "The killing almost turned Chongming city into an abattoir," they complained. "Send off a telegram at once to the military units of the friend-country to strictly distinguish the good and the bad, so that our rural elders, youngsters, and women will escape terrible unfortunate cruelty at their hands."[30]

The mayor responded by ordering Huang Zhiqing to pass the complaint from the native place association to his pacification agent and urge him to persuade the Japanese garrison to conduct their suppression work with greater discrimination. Together they had to prevent "military affairs and the people's livelihood from interfering with each other." Mayor Fu covered his back by sending a telegram to the Special Service Agency in Shanghai, reporting on what he had suggested Huang should do. He would not have wanted them to learn from the pacification agent in Chongming that he had been meddling in military matters. The SSD responded two weeks later by noting that the army's operations on Chongming had basically been wound up, and that the mayor should not worry. "Although loyal subjects suffered great harm because of this," the head of the SSD conceded, "yet the masses had been made to understand that the harm came because of what the guerrilla bandits were doing."[31] He then seeks to trump Huang's prediction by assuring the mayor that it will be difficult for guerrillas to start operating again on the island. He ends his telegram, though, with a mild apology for what the people of Chongming had suffered. But Huang Zhiqing still had a guerrilla insurgency to deal with. In his last communication on this issue in early September, Fu Xiaoan could offer no better advice from Shanghai than that Huang work more closely with the Japanese army to ensure that the innocent not suffer along with the guilty. The Chongming businessmen in Shanghai knew—and Fu must have known as well—that the line between the two was impossible to draw. As long as resistance continued to invite a counter-response, the debt of the occupation state to the Japanese army could only deepen, and the popular perception that that debt would eventually have to be repaid, only strengthen.

Huang Zhiqing was shuffled out of his magistracy in 1943 in a reorganization that made another a sweep of administrative personnel. Only one rural head managed to hold on to his post. The purge even landed some people in jail. One of the most conspicuous arrests was the head of the Chongming Chamber of Commerce, who allegedly had been using his post to line his pockets for five years. The new magistrate was replaced in March the following year by yet another outsider, Liu Shengwu. Liu rode out the next reorganization five months later, which removed Chongming from Shanghai's supervision and restored it to the jurisdiction of Jiangsu province. At the ceremony investing him with the county magistracy on 5 August 1944, Liu called on Chinese to mobilize their resources to the utmost to help Japan achieve its inevitable victory in the Greater East Asian War. The failure of Liu's prediction caught up with him a year later, when Japan surrendered to the United States and the Nanjing regime announced over the radio its decision to dissolve itself. Chongming residents last saw Magistrate Liu on 17 August 1945, sailing away in a rented motorboat. Liu did not depart empty-handed: he was followed by a small flotilla of junks carrying off whatever grain and cash he had been able to cart out of the county treasury.[32] So ended Chongming's occupation regime.

Liu Shengwu's administration did not collapse because of the resistance that simmered on Chongming Island or anywhere else on the Yangtze Delta. Local resistance was an irritant to the occupation state and entailed expenses and distractions that the Special Service would rather not have wasted its resources on. A few collaborators were assassinated, telegraph poles were burned, and bridges were destroyed, but these gestures could not destroy the occupation state. Defeat came about because the Japanese military could no longer provide the support it needed once it had overreached itself in the Pacific. What the resistance did accomplish was to keep alive the perception that the occupation state did not have the acquiescence of the people, that somewhere beyond its reach existed an alternative authority that, on the strength of the concept of national sovereignty if on no other, trumped every proposal and every argument that the collaborators could make to justify their authority. Regardless of the security they worked to reestablish or the services they rendered, the local administrators of the occupation state could not climb to higher moral ground in so brief a time. In that regard, resistance accomplished its goal of undermining the occupation state, though not of undermining the occupier.

— 8 —

Assembling the Occupation State

And so, one by one through the winter of 1937 and spring of 1938, little collaborationist administrations came into being in all urban centers across the Yangtze Delta. As they did, the larger edifice of the occupation state came into view, as intended, from the ground up. This, at least, is how the process was meant to look: regime building moving upward from peace maintenance committees in villages and town, to self-government committees in county seats and cities, to a new central regime in Nanjing. The pacification agents sent out that winter to restore civil administration appeared to have done their job.

And then, one by one, though much more quickly this time, these little collaborationist regimes all disappeared during the spring and summer of 1938. With the new central state, the Reformed Government, having been brought into being from the top at the end of March, the process of regime building now reversed course and turned back down to the local areas, canceling all the local committees and replacing them with central appointees. The bottom had been brought into existence to open the way for the top; the top, once installed, promptly removed all self-governing capacities from the bottom. The arrangements that pacification agents had worked out with difficulty that winter and spring were in effect overridden. What had been counties became counties again; where centrally appointed magistrates had served, they served again. The open arc of centralization that had been implied all through the winter and spring of 1938 was turned into a closed circle of recentralization that swallowed its own tail. It was in fact a perfect top-down model of bottom-up mobilization, bringing local elites into the political process as the grassroots of a unifying state and then encasing them in the structures of that state. The idealism of building from below had been overtaken by the necessity of imposing control from above. If we were to name that necessity, we would call it occupation.

Occupation is the imposition by military force of control by a state over a territory originally subject to another sovereignty; an occupation state is the political regime installed to administer that territory. I prefer to designate it an "occupation state" rather than a "collaboration state" to stress the prior condition of occupation from which all arrangements under collaboration must follow. Occupation may create collaboration, as I observed in the opening chapter, but the reverse is not true. Collaboration is a parasitic political engagement produced by a cancellation of sovereignty. The state emerges principally because the occupier wants it to emerge and takes steps to make that emergence happen, not because the collaborator takes steps to make it happen.

If we view the relationship from the side of the occupied, collaboration is the countercondition for the formation of the occupation state. Without collaborators, the occupier can only set up a purely colonial administration, as the British did in Hong Kong in the 1840s or as the Japanese did in Taiwan in 1895. Collaborators would in due course come forward in both those situations, but collaboration was not a precondition that the occupier had to produce before going on to create a political administration. The Yangtze Delta was not another Taiwan: Japan would not appoint Japanese to govern. It was closer to being another Manchuria, where the Japanese set up a Manchu as head of state in order to assert that this displaced sovereignty was a real one. And yet that was not really supposed to be what happened in Central China. There the project was to find people who were genuine alternatives to Chiang Kaishek and the Nationalist Party and lend these people the support they needed to dislodge the Nationalists and get China back on a prenationalist, prerevolutionary path that it could walk with Japan.

The CCAA's Special Service Department aspired to put such a regime into place with the hope that Japan could step back and watch China move naturally into line with Japanese desires. It was an unrealistic idea, made so by the problem of vacated sovereignty. However constructed or construed, the occupation state that the Special Service built from above and below was an artifice produced by military intervention in the absence of genuine political process. The only internal link was the one that Special Service personnel imagined, and that the new central regime in Nanjing deemed by fiat to exist. The occupation state, insofar as it could be conceived as a coherent whole, was an imagined state that could be assembled only in the presence of the Japanese army. There were attempts by the SSD to give the Reformed Government freer reign, to treat it as a legitimate government, in the hope that it might become one, but these efforts were viewed with suspicion by the Japanese army and cabinet. In a bid by the army to get a tighter grip over its collaborators, the cabinet dissolved the SSD in June 1939 and replaced it with the Kōain, the Asia Development Board, under its own tighter control.

However imaginary the regime the SSD built—first the Reformed Government of Liang Hongzhi, later the Reorganized National Government of Wang Jingwei—this does not mean that the state did not exist. At the local level especially, taxes continued to be collected, jails filled, streets patrolled, courts convened, schools run. This is why the collaborationist entities we have tracked at several sites on the Yangtze Delta were important, despite their transience. They were where the occupation state was first organized and experienced.

Legitimacy was another matter. This is where the imaginary quality of what the Japanese created becomes visible, for whatever Japanese agents or Chinese elites did to build the new order, they were unable to craft anything but the appearance of a regime. Their cooperation could not supplant the ever-self-renewing contradiction between national sovereignty and foreign occupation. There is no need to argue that national sovereignty is not naturally endowed, or that ideology creates political legitimacy, to observe that military occupation polarizes the occupied and the occupier into those deemed to have the right to be where they are, and those who do not. The collaborator is faced with the challenge of bridging this unbridgeable gap. The propaganda organs of the occupation state must work overtime to weave a veil of regime plausibility, to obscure the fact that its sole source of legitimacy is the presence of an occupying military and that its sole source of authority is its ability to call up the use of violence. From this perspective, the occupation state looks utterly artificial. It also, though, neglects what willing and energetic local elites actually produced by way of benefits or losses that affected how people lived. Forgetting this, we find ourselves in a Möbius strip in which our disdain for forced ideology produces its opposite, confirmation of the natural legitimacy of state sovereignty. If we accept that no state is ethnically, culturally, or politically natural, then we must remove ourselves from this cul-de-sac and recognize that all states rely on fictions, some gentle and some fierce, to obscure their invariable incompleteness, their compromises with external interests, and their reliance on coercion to discipline state populations into notional national identities. To dwell too much on the occupation state's fictionality threatens to obscure seeing what was actually going on.

We get closer to the meanings of occupation and collaboration by ignoring official statements that "China and Japan share script and race" or that "England and France have driven our peoples to impoverishment and our finances to exhaustion."[1] Local officials were obliged to perform these ideologies at the behest of their Japanese handlers, who appear to have regarded such declarations of ideological conformity with satisfaction, but these claims were irrelevant to most people's concerns. They were simply gestures that had become part of the repertoire of legitimating political ritual, of no further consequence to anyone on the Chinese side. What mattered in establishing authority in the local setting was not ideology but organization: which local networks were being mobilized, what resources these networks could bring to bear to encourage compliance, and what benefits they could distribute to local people in the forms of running water, electricity, or a functioning fire department. In this way too, the occupation state was much like any other regime coming to power, and its local administrative operations as ordinary as they would be in peacetime. That some people went out of their way to use the opportunities occupation made available to enrich themselves at a severe cost to others is a fact usually too simple to provide a starting place for analysis, given the more complex truths that the history of local collaboration holds.

The dissolution of the SGCs and their replacement by Public Offices in the summer of 1938 was not a straightforward process. The original SGC members were not eager to see their organizations dismantled and their power curtailed, nor were the pacification agents happy to see what they had worked so hard to create removed in favor of arrangements they might not so easily control. But the new central government was not willing to hand off its authority and its access to revenue to whoever happened to have struck a deal with the agents when they arrived on site. Suspicion went both ways. The center was convinced (reasonably enough) that concessions to the localities undermined its power, while the localities were suspicious (just as reasonably) that every central initiative was an attempt to enlarge its grasp at the expense of the local. This put the Japanese agents in a bind. The pacification plan grasped the instrumental logic of relying on locals to bring their localities into the new state, yet it recognized the need to limit local political capacities, lest local power block the viability of that state. The agents had to encourage local collaboration, then block the political ambitions of those who responded to that invitation lest these threaten the sustainability of the occupation state as a Japanese project.

The supersession of the SGCs by regular county administration was written into the SSD plan as early as 18 January 1938, though actual discussions on how to implement the conversion began only in February. The pacification agents were as anxious about this change as the men they handled. Japanese advisors to the Great Way Government, when their opinions were canvassed in early March, doubted the wisdom of disrupting an arrangement that seemed to be working.[2] Agents in the field shared this caution, which may be why the SSD called them all back to Shanghai in May for a three-day reorientation conference. In his report back to his vice-minister, the director of the SSD implied that there was friction between the pacification teams and the local garrisons, and allowed that the department had "to put tighter controls on operations" if pacification work was to improve. He did not specify why the teams required tighter control, but the timing of the reorganization—just as the teams were preparing to convert their self-government committees into county administrations—suggests that the process was not going well. Five days of meetings in Shanghai brought the recalcitrant into line.[3] Through June and July, earlier in some places and later in others, one county after another reemerged under the direction of a centrally appointed magistrate. The self-government phase was over.

Minister of the Interior Chen Qun, whose ministry was in charge of implementing this stage of administrative reconstruction, carried out his own rectification on the Chinese side. In late April, most SGC chairs, roughly forty in all, were ordered to attend three days of meetings in Nanjing.[4] The purpose of the meeting, the SGC chairs were told, was to "strengthen their ties with the Reformed Government"—an indirect way of saying that they now had to report to Chen's ministry. They were presented with a plan to convert their committees into county governments, which would thenceforth be called Public Offices (gongshu), and were made to understand that no other course was open. Sun Yunsheng, head of the Jiading SGC, attended, and Sun Zhao represented the Zhenjiang SGC, but Chongming SGC Huang Zhicheng did not attend, presumably because his administration was only just then being set up.[5] The carrot that went with this stick was money. Nothing of this appears in Chen's official report on the meeting, but the 15,000-yuan gift from the central government in the June ledger of Shanghai's North District United SGC, noted in Chapter 6, suggests the size of the carrot that helped local officials go along with the dissolution order. The SGC chairs were also brought along with the assurance in principle that they would become the new magistrates. This was not a solid promise, as many discovered when they failed to weather the transition.

The ability to hold on to their positions was a matter of concern not just to the SGC chairs but to the pacification agents. As we have seen, the agents often went through great tribulations that spring to get an adequate man in the post. Fearful that this recentralization would jeopardize the arrangements they had so carefully built up, many lobbied for the appointment of local persons as magistrates. This is what Zhenjiang team leader Katō Kōzan did by going in person to the Jiangsu provincial government in Suzhou in May to make sure that his chief collaborator, SGC chair Guo Zhicheng, got the appointment. Discovering what percentage of SGC chairs made the transition is not a simple matter, given the incomplete documentation that survives. The right-hand column of Table 8.1 summarizes what I have been able to determine about the transition from SGC to Public Office in those counties listed in Table 2.1. The evidence shows that the likelihood of continuing in office was about as good as the odds of being replaced.

Participation in an early self-government organ was therefore no guarantee of staying in office. Worse, as the political climate evolved beyond the first year of collaboration, the chances of continuing declined ever further. Indeed, participation at too early a stage was sometimes wielded against early collaborators by their later competitors. The past came, for example, to haunt Chen Xishun. He was the head of a suboffice in the Western District of Shanghai who, as we noted in Chapter 6, was ousted from office by a coalition of "residents." Their method was to tar him with an association with the early peace maintenance phase of pacification. This was when, as their letter phrased it, "hoodlums living here and there rushed forward to take over, wielding power and running an administration under the guise of 'maintenance.'" Chen, they implied, was part of this gang of opportunists who grabbed office in the first PMC in pursuit of their own interests, "with the result that good people vanished without a trace." By the beginning of 1939, this logic was a convenient device to discredit an opponent.

Table 8.1 Self-Government Committees and County/District Public Offices, 1938

Municipality or province	County or district	Date of SGC inauguration	Date of PO inauguration	SCG head becomes magistrate?
Shanghai	South City	1/11	7/12	Yes
	Zhenru	2/21	?	
	Western District 1	3/7	?	
	Western District 2	3/15	?	
Nanjing	Nanjing	1/1	4/24	No
	Jurong	?	8/17	
	Jiangning	?	7/1	
Jiangsu	Baoshan	9/23/37	7/18	Yes
	Jiading	1/21	6/25	No
	Kunshan	?	7/5	
	Taicang	12/29/37	6/25	No
	Qingpu	?	7/1	
	Chuansha	1/19	6/?	
	Nanhui	?	6/10	
	Chongming	4/1	6/7	Yes
	Songjiang	4/1	8/1	
	Jinshan	?	7/5	
	Suzhou	12/7/37	7/1	No
	Changshu	12/23/37	7/1	
	Wuxi	12/4/37	7/?	
	Wujiang	1/5	7/1	Yes
	Jiangyin	?	11/?	
	Zhenjiang	1/10	8/1	Yes
	Yangzhou	12/1/37	8/1	Yes
	Danyang	2/1	9/1	No
	Changzhou	12/29/37	6/25	
	Jintan	?	7/5	
Zhejiang	Jiaxing	1/1	4/?	
	Nanxun	12/?	?	
	Jiashan	3/27	12/11	No
	Hangzhou	3/1	6/10	No
	Huzhou	2/19	?	
Anhui	Wuhu	4/1	12/20	
	Taiping	2/?	?	

Note: SGC = Self-Government Committee; PO = Public (County) Office. Only those places listed in Table 2.1 have been included in this list.

Sources: Inoue, pp. 23–25, 37–39, 42–46, 55, 61, 73, 84, 107, 109, 124–25, 148, 151, 170–73, 180, 182, 200, 248, 266; SMA, Files R1–1–5, R1–1–105, R1–1–152, R1–2–1637; *Jiangsu sheng gongbao xinnian tekan*, pp. 26–27; Xingzhengyuan xuanchuanju, *Ishin seifu no genkō*, pp. 10, 152–54, 526; *Nanjing xinbao*, 11/11/1938, 7/2–4/1939, and 10/2, 7, 9, 11, 25, 30, 31/1939.

Involvement in the early phase of collaboration could now be enough to destroy a collaborator's career, whereas before, it was essential to make it.

Replacement was, however, a luxury that the shortage of willing talent often placed beyond the capacity of the Ministry of the Interior. To fill the vacated posts with officials who would work in the center's interests as well as his own, Minister Chen Qun established a County Magistrates Training Institute in Nanjing, which he kept under close control by naming himself director. The institute was expected to train four hundred local administrators over the next few years.[6] When the institute opened on 15 September, Chen and his ministry were still operating out of Shanghai, but he sent a statement for the opening ceremony in Nanjing, which was printed that day as an unsigned editorial in the *New Nanjing Daily*. Chen begins by praising the commitment shown by the great queller of the Taiping Rebellion, Zeng Guofan, to engage in study despite his onerous military duties. On leave in his native Hunan at the time of the rebellion, Zeng had organized the massive militarization that eventually succeeded in defeating the rebels in 1864. The implication of the references is that the institute's trainees were living in analogous times. Their relationship to the military chaos in the Yangtze Valley in their own time should be as Zeng's was when he brought the region back to peace eight decades earlier. Chen then turns from exemplar to counterexample by criticizing the pattern, established under the Nationalists, of young Chinese heading off to Europe to study philosophy or history, then returning to get government posts. He not only mocks them for having no grasp of practical affairs, but suggests that their separation from the needs of the people was why they sank into corruption when they got to power. The alternative he proposes to the European-trained dilettante is the classical Confucian gentleman, the *junzi,* whose moral education commits him to placing the welfare of the common people above all things.

Six months later, Chen's institute graduated its first class of twenty-nine magistrates and twenty-six vice-magistrates. On this occasion, the graduates were honored by a message from Special Service head Harada Kumakichi, whose agency had since relocated to Nanjing. Alas, no record survives of what he told them. Those in the magistrates class, who ranged in age from twenty-eight to fifty-nine, with a median age of thirty-eight, were all college graduates, including two who had graduated from the universities of Tokyo and Paris. Those in the vice-magistrates class were middle-school graduates ranging in age from twenty-three to forty-nine, with a median age of thirty. Most of this latter group were assigned to jobs in county administrations, as expected. Surprisingly, given the declared purpose of the institute, the graduates of the magistrates' course were all retained to serve in provincial and national offices. Not one went out into the field to do the work for which he was supposedly trained. A shortage of qualified personnel at higher levels, and perhaps Chen's interest in seeing his protégés strategically located at higher levels of his administration, trumped local administrative needs.

As the Japanese army went on to annex more territory to the north and west through 1938 and 1939, the same procedures used to set up county administrations on the Yangtze Delta were repeated north of the river. Self-government committees were set up in each county, and these in turn were later dissolved in favor of county administrations headed by appointments from the center. Most of the large area of Jiangsu province north of the Yangtze was not regularized until 1939, and most of the counties in Anhui province remained under local SGC control until April 1940, when the Interior Ministry of the newly installed Wang Jingwei regime—Chen Qun managed to stay on as minister—ordered all remaining SGCs to dissolve and dispatched magistrates to make sure that the order was carried out.

What any of these magistrates ended up controlling, though, was another matter. Many discovered that the Japanese army may have driven their Nationalist counterparts out of the county seat, but not out of the county, and that they continued to operate alternative regimes from less accessible locations within the county's borders. A Nationalist report in November 1938 asserted that, of the 796 counties affected by the hostilities, only in 59 were magistrates of the National Government unable to exercise their functions.[7] This statistic exaggerates the extent of Nationalist control, though it does indicate that the reach of the central government in Nanjing down to the local level was limited. By way of partial confirmation, the Japanese advisors to the Reformed Government presented an inexactly matching statistic for the other side. By their count, at the end of 1938 the Reformed Government had appointed magistrates to 21 counties in Jiangsu (only one of which lay north of the Yangtze), 12 in Zhejiang, and 10 in Anhui, for a total of 43.[8] The space between 43 and 59 was filled with SGCs and the Japanese garrisons that ensured their safety, which among other things is a reminder that wherever the occupation state reached, it did because the Japanese army made it so. When that reach could not go far beyond the walls of a county seat, as was often the case, one county could end up hosting competing administrations appointed by up to three different states: the occupation state inside the county city, and Communist and Nationalist administrations somewhere out in the hills. Thus Zhenjiang at the start of 1940 had Magistrate Guo Zhicheng representing the occupation in the city, Zhuang Peifang heading a Nationalist county administration in the southwestern hills, and Communist cadre Li Peigen running yet another county government from the county's eastern edge. Together they enacted the fractured state sovereignty into which Japan's occupation had thrown China.

As the little collaborationist regimes that had come into being across the Yangtze Delta went out again, most of the minor figures who came into the story at the beginning fade from documentary sight. A few whom the Special Service recruited, such as Zhenjiang magistrate Guo Zhicheng or Chongming magistrate Huang Zhiqing, managed to stay in office for five or six years, though both would leave politics—or were they pushed?—about two years before the war ended. At that point, their trails go cold. Since the postwar purges have left almost no record of what happened to those who worked for the Japanese, it is possible that their pasts caught up with them then. It is also possible that they managed to make deals with the returning Nationalists that gave them protection against retaliation and then slipped off to Hong Kong or Taiwan when the Republic collapsed.

What then can be said of the Chinese who made themselves active agents of the occupation state? Were the mostly small-time collaborators we have tracked across the Yangtze Delta the lesser evil that many represented themselves as being in the early days of the occupation, when the greater evil was the ongoing social disorder stirred by the unrestrained hand of Japanese soldiers? Arguing this side of the case involves pointing to the work that the SGCs did to provide welfare to those whom war had dislocated and to restore public services such as water and electricity—the latter being so important in urban centers such as Zhenjiang that the manager of the power plant, Guo Zhicheng, became the head of the SGC. The case might also be argued by suggesting that it was better to have local Chinese officials, rather than Japanese colonial officers, administering Chinese. The recurrent theme in the pacification reports about the incompetence and corruption of the men who made it onto the PMCs and SGCs could be cited to argue, on the other hand, that a colonial administrator might have been less disposed than a native one to, as Zhang Yibo colorfully said of

Guo Zhicheng, "suck the marrow out of people's bones and leaving them wailing in the streets."

The ongoing practice of assassination shows that some took a different view and regarded even the appearance of collaborating as a threat to Chinese national sovereignty and an affront to national dignity. One of the tasks of the resistance was to get this message across to other Chinese. Direct assassination was one device, propaganda another. Refusal to collaborate, at the political level at least, was not universal, as we have seen repeatedly, and so propagandists for the Nationalist and Communist resistances kept up a flow of argument against the troubling fact of the occupation: that Japanese were in fact able to find Chinese to help them maintain their presence in China.

Several prominent writers spoke out on this matter. The Communist intellectual Guo Moruo distinguished two types of collaborators: the educated, who simply wanted to get power and wealth for themselves, and the poor and uneducated, whose poverty drove them to collaborate and whose ignorance saved them from even thinking they had to justify what they were doing. Each type resorted to different methods, the one peaceful, the other violent, but both were dangerous because together the educated collaborators and the hoodlums gave the Japanese the two hands they needed, one to soothe and one to strike. Playwright Gu Zhongyi added a third category to Guo's two, and that was the defeatists, who argued that China simply could not win this war and that the sensible course was to accept the situation and do what one could within it. Shanghai novelist Mao Dun took a different approach. Instead of considering what motivated collaborators, he looked at what they did. There were the information gatherers, on whom the Japanese relied for the knowledge they needed as occupiers. There were the saboteurs, who could cause damage in places the Japanese themselves could not reach. And there were the theorists. These he dreaded most of all. They might not cause anyone personal harm, but they could persuade Chinese that a Japanese occupation was in their long-term interests, just as the Japanese propagandists insisted. Sabotage could stiffen resistance; intelligence might bewilder it; but theory would dissolve it.

These arguments are to be found in a booklet Tong Zhenhua rushed into print in Shanghai in October 1937. Writing from the perspective of the Communist Party's United Front, Tong was concerned to challenge the idea, which he feared was gaining ground in some quarters, that a reasonable justification for collaboration might emerge among the educated.

How to Get Rid of Traitors was not an assassin's manual but an extended essay targeting Mao Dun's third category, the theorists. (Tong in fact is careful to argue that collaborators, once exposed, should be not executed but reformed.) Never mind the little collaborators who will do anything for money and have no concept of Japanese imperialism, he argues; they are not the problem. The more important task is to counter certain views popular in Shanghai: that the Japanese were still willing to consider a peaceful resolution to the conflict; that China would benefit by cooperating with Japan; that since arms were decisive, the struggle had to go in Japan's favor; that China's rapid collapse was evidence that resistance was pointless; and that, as Japanese propaganda insisted, Japan was opposed to the Chinese government, not the Chinese people. Beware the traitors in our midst who collect intelligence and perform clandestine tasks, but be even more aware of those who seduce by argument.[9] Here the greater threat was not to be working for the Japanese, but to be saying without qualm or question that it was in everyone's best interests to do so.

Who knows whether these sermons against the evils of collaboration fell on ears other than those pre-tuned to accept their argument? The blunt fact that rises out of the research for this book is that the ranks of those who agreed to collaborate never thinned out. Indeed, as soon as early collaborators were assassinated or dismissed, others were there to take their places. In every location across the Yangtze Delta, local elites of a stature varying from the middling to the marginal came forward in sufficient numbers to staff the new order at its local level. Whether defeatists or opportunists, they made possible the presence of the occupation state. By doing so, their collaboration made a difference. It enabled the Japanese occupation to continue where it had reached, and to extend into the new places the army went on to conquer.

Did their collaboration compromise Chinese sovereignty, as Guo Moruo and Mao Dun insisted? The Japanese pacification program certainly assumed that it did. By setting up and staffing the "self-government" organs in towns and county seats throughout the occupied Yangtze Delta during the winter and spring of 1938, the collaborators provided the building blocks for the Reformed Government, the very existence of which confounded Chiang Kaishek's claim that his National Government ruled China. To all appearances, the cooperation that the members of the SGCs provided to the Japanese contributed to extinguishing the prior regime and bringing the new into being. That indictment stands to the extent that the process of regime building in which they participated ended up producing a regime. However faked and fraudulent the Reformed Government may seem to us, the things it did—from cleaning streets to controlling contraband to executing those its courts condemned as criminals—were the things that all states do. Elites who collaborated at the local level contributed to building that regime, whether they were aware of doing so or not. Merely by serving the new regime, they annulled the legitimacy of the National Government. If their service also suspended Chinese sovereignty in favor of Japanese interests, that abstraction was one they could set aside by appealing to the needs of the moment, or by pointing out that if they did not enter the gap, others would. From either perspective—Chinese state or Japanese empire—their collaboration mattered. Still, if we examine the actual, rather modest doings of the SGCs and Public Offices, their acts could be seen as rather removed from national sovereignty, which was determined elsewhere and through other means, primarily military. Perhaps the occupation did not last long enough for the production of the occupation state at the local level to matter much in terms of contributing to the viability of the national regime the Japanese sponsored in Nanjing. That regime rose and fell on the strength of that sponsorship, not on the rate at which local administrators issued loyal subject certificates or recompiled village tax records.

It is possible to turn this argument around, however, by observing that when local collaborators were successful in meeting local targets, they did so by acting in concert with the Japanese agents, officers, businessmen, and researchers who came to take possession of China for the Japanese empire. The collaborators' work sustained the relationships with Japan on which the occupation depended to function. Collaboration mattered not just in getting administrative tasks accomplished, but in weaving the networks of cooperation on which the Japanese relied to stay in China. Both perspectives are needed in the final analysis.

The situation might have gone in Japan's favor had it been able to provide "an alternative source of wealth and power which, if it could not be excluded, had to be exploited in order to preserve or improve the standing of indigenous elites in the traditional order."[10] This is how Ronald Robinson has described the formula by which the British engaged local elites for their colonial project. Japan's defeat in the Pacific happened too soon after the invasion of China for the seductions of colonial conquest to metastasize among the Chinese elite into a preference for stability over revolution. From this perspective, there was little that a pacification agent could have done to get his potential allies in the local elite on his side and through them engineer the complete transformation of an invaded realm into an occupation state. He could direct his limited military and economic resources to his collaborators in such a way as to bring about the appearance of conformity to whatever ambitious plans were being drawn up in Shanghai or Nanjing, but he could not make available an "alternative source of wealth and power" strong enough to convince most of those who might have become his collaborators to take up the opportunities the Japanese brought and convert them into capital for their own use. This is how Robinson explains why the British, who wanted empire only on the cheap, were able to have it nonetheless. After the initial outlay for military costs, much of which was offloaded onto private operators, British colonialism was created with very little expenditure and only selective subsequent investment. What the empire provided, and what paid for its perpetuation, were exclusive connections to lucrative global trading circuits that provided local benefits but, as much as possible, began and ended in England.

No matter how ambitious the vision of state building under which he operated, the pacification agent did not find himself in the position of the British colonial official a century earlier. In terms of trading opportunities, the Japanese brought less to Chinese elites than what they had enjoyed prior to occupation. Since the occupation was also being done on the cheap, Japan's prime interest was in forcing Chinese businesses into a monopolistic trade regime with itself, not plugging the Chinese economy into larger trading networks than it already tapped. This is what Japan's plan to bring China, Manchuria, and Japan into a unified currency zone was all about, after all.

Given the constraints on "wealth" that collaborators ended up facing, the Special Service had to work the other half of Robinson's dyad, "power." The best offer it could make to collaborators was to open up leadership opportunities that had been closed to them under the National Government. This the Japanese did both at the national level in Nanjing and at the county level across the Yangtze Delta. If the best course, according to Robinson's logic, was "to preserve or improve the standing of indigenous elites," Japan was not successful. Most elites did not regard collaboration as a sensible way of preserving status, so long as there seemed some prospect of the new dispensation failing in the medium term. Those who could afford not to collaborate withheld their political capital in the expectation of being able to trade on it again after the war was over. Some who had enjoyed only modest power under the Nationalists stayed on in the hope of improving their circumstances and amassing political capital that they might invest in other markets once the Japanese were forced to withdraw. Keenest, though, were those who were entirely excluded from power before 1937. They took up the offer of power that Japan made mostly to improve, not preserve, what they had.

For those who threw their lot in with the occupation state, what made the gamble so difficult was their colonial patrons' inability to provide the resources and security needed to make the occupation regime viable. When the pacification team leader in Danyang, the county directly south of Zhenjiang, brought together the chairs of his SGC branch committees to stiffen their resistance in July 1938, the chair of one of the branch committees talked back and pressed the agent for concrete action. He and the other chairs had come forward to collaborate, he said, only to find that the team was not backing them up with substantive support. Why were armed garrisons not stationed in the rural towns? Why were salt offices not set up to deal with salt smuggling, a lucrative business for the guerrillas and a severe loss for local administrations? When would the branch committees receive more funding to cover the cost of their work? Why was there no help to revive primary schools in the rural towns? Could first-aid kits not be provided to branch committees so that they could treat the ill and injured? Why was the team not getting the transportation arteries guerrillas were sabotaging back in repair by organizing the poor into road repair crews, which would also alleviate unemployment? Here were six reasonable, concrete proposals that one Chinese at the bottom of the occupation state believed would improve the viability of local administration. All that the Japanese agent could do was point to the "current situation"—meaning many demands on limited resources—and say that these proposals would be tabled for future discussion.[11] Japan could not afford the costs of occupation.

Local collaborators thus often found themselves having to make do with whatever resources or initiatives were available to them, serving a patron who expected their support but was unable to provide them with any in return. On the other end of the bargain, the agents could only retreat to the comfort of their subjective belief that Japan's historic mission was to bring civilization and enlightenment to the masses of Asia and liberate them from the nationalism, Communism, and colonialism of the white race. For them, too, it was hard going. The burdens they experienced are hinted at by Itō Takeo, who headed the Shanghai office of the Mantetsu when these men were recruited and hosted the reception at the Palace Hotel noted in Chapter 2. In his memoirs, Itō opens his brief discussion of the pacification program with the odd confession that the field agents "were said generally to have done wicked things to the Chinese populace." Not a glimmer of such wickedness can be found in the reports that Itō's own office produced at the time. The personnel transfers noted in Chapter 4 may signal that some agents were not behaving as they should, though the available records suggest incompetence more than misconduct. Perhaps Itō found it convenient to lead with this hearsay so as to distance himself from the imperialist plan of which he was the leading implementer in Shanghai. In the end he rises ambivalently to his agents' defense: "Many of them worked on behalf of the local residents under their charge, negotiated with the military, discharged food supplies, and implemented good government as conscientiously as possible." Again, though, he wants distance from their work, for he closes his comments with this slight: "There were also men who paraded around under the shelter of the might of the military."[12] This abuse may have been true of some ambitious junior staffers who suddenly became the bosses of the counties to which they were sent. Some may well have fallen short of the standards they were expected to uphold. At the same time, though, it is conveniently self-exculpatory for Itō to blame the army for whatever faults the pacification agents committed, and so produce a cloud of innocence around the Mantetsu and himself.

Itō makes one other comment at the end of his quick treatment of pacification work that is worth noting. He observes that the work took a toll on those who did it: "Since there were conscientious staffers who could not bear this pacification work, they left the office one by one and, as a result, not a person from the era of the 'clean-ups' remained." The work of pacification, it seems, proved intolerable to those who had to do it. Here is possibly the most surprising of the unanticipated costs of occupation: that those who volunteered to carry out the pacification program suffered career and even emotional damage for the work they were assigned to do. Finding themselves working with the sort of venal and self-serving elements they disdained ("completely lacking in administrative talent," as one pacification team's work diary characterized the local SGC head, "completely without competence or ability"),[13] the pacification agents watched the ideal regime they dreamed of creating from the bottom disappear into parody.

Eight years of occupation did far more damage to regime legitimacy than this, however. It corroded the reputation of local traditional elites and questioned their viability as a foundation for a modern state. County elites had already been undergoing a transformation during the Republican period, as industrialists and businessmen eager to gain control of the new municipal structures that republicanism introduced edged aside the old gentry. Prasenjit Duara in his study of north China elites before the war has observed the rise of entrepreneurial state brokers at both county and village levels, men who "began to seek office for immediate gain, often at the expense of the community's interests." The invocation of "the community" may be misleading, given that Chinese elites, like elites anywhere, have always pretended to serve Durkheimian communities of solidarity—even when such did not exist. But the new pressures of state building in the Republican period, when the customary rates of extraction were increasing, required competent and responsible political elites to manage the transition to a modernizing state regime. These were rarely forthcoming. The resulting governance arrangement Duara has termed state involution, in which "the formal structures of the state grow simultaneously with informal structures, such as the entrepreneurial state brokers." This reliance on informal structures came at a price, for "although the formal state depends on the informal structures to carry out many of its functions, it is unable to extend its control over them. As the state grows in the involutionary mode, the informal groups become an uncontrollable power in local society, replacing a host of traditional arrangements of local governance."[14]

The Nationalist Party had stronger ties to local political elites in central China than in the north, and was more successful in recruiting them into the modernizing state. But what success it had in yoking elites to state goals collapsed with Japan's invasion. Working from an even more top-down relationship to county and village government, the occupation state had fewer connections with, and less to offer, local leaders. As a result, it drove the involutionary process harder than had the Nationalist regime, relying on improvised mechanisms to supplement, and often entirely replace, formal administration. The PMCs were blunt manifestations of this replacement. In this respect, Duara's observations on north China apply equally well to central: "Although the Japanese regime was able to force through rationalizing measures, the draconian nature of these measures ensured that only entrepreneurial brokers would undertake their implementation."[15] Yet even this does not quite capture what happened under the occupation state, for the entrepreneurial brokers who got involved in politics on the Yangtze Delta were, as one despondent Japanese agent reported, "the supernumerary and the incompetent"[16]—exactly the people with whom the youthful agents did not wish to work, and precisely those whose involvement they could not escape.

The pacification agents regarded state involution as an unfortunate makeshift, a provisional stage to be transcended quickly on the way to reconstructing a new order. The SGCs were to be one phase in a process of replacing the involutionary expedients the army had relied on in the first wave of occupation, and the Public Offices that replaced them were the next. The cases I have examined suggest, though, that the counties where the agents worked never escaped the involutionary pull. The new magistrates may have been superior to the PMC/SGC chairs, but they generally fell below the standards of their Nationalist predecessors. As an American repatriate characterized the people he knew working for the occupation state in 1943, they were "no single class, but opportunists, reactionaries, and those who for one reason or another were in disfavor with the [Chiang] regime."[17] Special Service officers were quite aware of this situation and its liabilities. As one officer assigned to Special Service work in Shandong complained in 1941, "If we simply pick up old leftovers from the Qing dynasty in the areas we have conquered and hand local administration over to county magistrates who are over seventy years old, then I think that we are embarking on a politics that, when compared with the politics of Chiang Kaishek's new system, is fifty years behind the time." The sole hope for making the occupation state viable was to take "a step forward from the Nationalists and engage in a politics based on ideas that express the new spirit of renovation." The Special Service failed in precisely this matter. Standard bearers of Nationalist renovation were not prepared to come forward and collaborate. Those the SSD installed as the leaders of the new order ended up being either the worst of the old elites or the least of the new, without the social and cultural ties that had enabled the old to function or could legitimate the new. The Shandong agent was unequivocal in his judgment of those who wanted to take power. "There was no one you could make a county magistrate, absolutely no one," he declared, in any of the 107 counties in the province. "Administrative power did not follow" military power, as it should if a conquest were to become a state. And yet, "that said, people still came forward in droves and showed not the slightest subtlety about fighting to get positions."[18]

The coercion by which the occupation state prevailed locally, and its weak tendency to ally itself with relatively powerless fractions of the local elite, eroded the authority that the Japanese hoped the occupation state might with time accumulate. This erosion greatly helped the Communist Party to emerge as an alternative authority in the postwar period.[19] The legitimacy and political viability of the old elite may well have been on the way to oblivion in any case, as forces of longer term than foreign military occupation came into play. The occupation certainly sped the process up by delegitimizing the officials and elites who stayed behind, even those who did not collaborate, leaving the returning Nationalists without reliable linkages to local power. The outcome would be the Communist state: sufficiently disciplined to exact conformity to policy all the way down to the bottom of society without needing to borrow the authority of local elites, and sufficiently powerful to replace them once the emergency of civil war gave way to the normalization of political control. In this outcome, collaboration played its part.

Conclusion: Four Ways Truth
Disappears with History

In the opening chapter of this book I asked the reader to expect that the story of China under Japanese occupation, hitherto told as a tale of resistance, would become as well a story of collaboration. As indeed it has. Some Chinese resisted the Japanese army as it pushed across the Yangtze Delta, many more fled, and many more than either of those stayed where they were and made do with the circumstances in which they found themselves. Some allowed themselves to be drawn into active cooperation with the new authorities—not many, perhaps, but enough, and if they quailed, Special Service agents were always able to find others sufficiently cooperative to sustain some measure of administrative control for the next seven and a half years.

I asked as well that the reader be prepared to find the normally discrete categories of collaboration and resistance inadequate for making sense of the choices that people who stayed behind made. I suggested that we are likelier to understand those who worked with the Japanese if we go looking down in the thickets of ambiguity rather than up at either of the familiar trees of collaboration or resistance. I have invoked ambiguity not to doubt the fact that some collaborated and some resisted, but to question the interpretations history has attached to what might once have been the truth.

Let us start at one extreme of collaboration and see how far it is back to the middle position that most people inhabit most of the time. Take helping Japanese officers to identify defeated combatants who have tried to hide among crowds of refugees, as some Chinese did in Nanjing, for example. This certainly seems to qualify as collaboration of the worst sort. The consequences of that act are clear, but are there intentions that stand apart from those consequences, or other consequences that we may fail to anticipate? For instance, if this was done in the hope of limiting the indiscriminate slaughter of civilians, might it not be seen as protecting noncombatants from random attack and forcing the occupier to return to norms ensuring the safety of the occupied? We can reverse the logic for those on the other side of the struggle to protect defeated soldiers. Creating the Nanjing Safety Zone appears to be an unambiguous act of resistance, yet could one not argue, as Communist Party propagandists did in the 1950s, that organizing the population placed the masses of people under greater Japanese scrutiny, thereby exposing combatants to discovery and execution? Were the Germans and Americans on the International Committee, none of whom intended to collaborate and many of whom suffered privately for the extraordinary efforts they made on behalf of the people of Nanjing, guilty then of collaboration? And what do we make of Nanjing's master of ambiguity, Jimmy Wang, supplying food to the refugees and prostitutes to the Japanese? Is feeding refugees an act of resistance or a way of helping the occupier establish control? Is recruiting prostitutes an act of collaborating with the occupier or a way of protecting the majority of women by giving soldiers nonviolent opportunities for sexual activity? And if Jimmy Wang's personal motivation was not to help or hinder the Japanese but to get rich off these unlooked-for opportunities, does that alter our assessment of what he did?

Ambiguity of intention is only half the problem. There is also the ambiguity of unknowable consequences. An act when it is performed may seem to carry the full weight of collaboration or resistance, but when we widen our historical gaze and run the story forward into the messy consequences of that act, contradictions flow back and muddy the picture. Detonating a land mine to blow up a troop truck full of Japanese soldiers, as guerrillas on Chongming Island did in 1940, is an act of resistance, to be sure. But when it results in the massacre of over a hundred villagers in the vicinity, should that retaliation be extraneous in an evaluation of the attack? Is the righteousness of resistance so great that the responsibility for retaliatory violence can be shrugged off as unavoidable collateral damage? Or do the consequences convert this sort of resistance into an act that collaborates with the violent hegemony of occupation, inasmuch as it presented the Japanese army with an excuse to inflict spectacular violence without need of justification or concealment? The "patriotic" interpretation of the Chongming attack—as an act of terrorism that succeeded in tying down troops and exposing the fraudulence of Japanese claims of being in control—is strong enough in most people's minds to push an argument that reverses the significance of events back from their consequences. And yet the gesture traded well over a hundred civilian lives to have its effect.

How we interpret any incident in this or any war depends on what we think we mean by the words "collaboration" and "resistance." To few other historical issues does meaning emerge so far in advance of knowledge of what real people did or intended. My goals in this book have been to provide something to work on besides the judgments that have kept collaboration from becoming the major topic it should be in twentieth-century Chinese history and to ask that these judgments be suspended when we do the work of history. Let me note four of the inhibitive judgments in the historiography of wartime China that could be suspended.

The first judgment is the nationalistic one: that most Chinese for patriotic reasons did not collaborate with the Japanese during the war, and that the few who did were craven, criminal, or corrupt. It is not difficult to understand this way of thinking. Resistance to Japan has been one of China's defining myths. It marks the rise of China as something other than a defeated power. It enables Chinese to escape from the reputation for weakness that a century of difficult international encounters has given them. It allows Chinese to celebrate a national unity of purpose that has not been seen since the brief flurries of the 1911 Revolution or the May Fourth Movement of 1919. Given the weight of national pride that resistance is made to carry, most Chinese naturally find it difficult to digest the evidence of collaboration, except when narrowly defined as a temptation to which only the evil few fell. Postwar cultures elsewhere, however, have had to come to terms with the fact that collaboration went on even as resistance was pursued, and have tried to absorb this contradiction. Chinese have yet to face this challenge. When you speak for the nation, history is always on your side. When you let discourse determine narrative, "truth disappears with history."[1]

A second judgment that interferes with the history of collaboration, often as a consequence of the first, is the political one: that collaboration and resistance were determined not by an external force but by the struggle between internal political factions, one loyal to the nation and the other not. In the history of wartime occupied France, this struggle is referred to as *la guerre franco-française*.[2] This way of explaining collaboration shifts the charge against the Vichy regime and its supporters from colluding with the German outsiders to promoting an indigenous antirepublican and antidemocratic right. The account of the occupation as a civil war accepts that collaboration occurred, but indigenizes the causes and outcomes—in some cases to rescue Vichy with explanation, in others to damn it for its political reaction. One might think of occupied China in similar terms, as a Sino-Chinese war fought out on the backdrop of foreign occupation, the most important consequences of which were entirely internal to China's political future. But the analogy is not salient. At least until 1942, the Vichy regime was a fully French regime that was neither a creation nor entirely a creature of the Germans. True, it pursued a distinctive politics that consciously strove to roll back the policies and ideals of the Third Republic and restore an earlier imagined ethos: resistance was on the left, collaboration on the right. In wartime China, in contrast, both the Nationalists and the Communists operated resistance regimes. Neither capitulated to Japan, and the core of the struggle with Japan was not the struggle between them. They left ultraconservative restorationism to the various collaborationist regimes Japan sponsored in Nanjing and Beijing, none of which was able to establish itself as a viable alternative as a state. The Sino-Japanese war was only weakly a Sino-Chinese war, though the latter blossomed once the former was over. Each regime has subsequently charged the other with spending more energy on *la guerre sino-chinoise* than on the anti-Japanese war, and each has depicted the other's wartime story as a tale of sordid compromise and self-interest, and its own as devoted service to the nation and the people.[3] This rivalry only distracts from seeing anything interesting or important in the study of collaboration.

To these nationalistic and partisan-political judgments embedded in Chinese historiography I would add a third, which has secure footing in the historiography of the war outside China as well as within. This is what I call the humanitarian judgment. This judgment understands war as wasteful and pointless violence, and criticizes collaborators for helping to promote war. The nationalistic and partisan judgments keep the memory of the war alive in order to confirm national identity and reinforce political allegiance. For the humanitarian, however, the war is a memory we have allowed ourselves to forget over the busy decades of wars, revolutions, and genocides from 1945 to the present. These postwar calamities have encouraged many to argue that the signature events of violence of the Second World War cannot be isolated from what followed, that that history did not end in 1945, and that we are still paying a high mortgage on that moral debt. A continuous history of atrocity thus runs in mimic parody alongside the normalizing narratives of modernization, democratization, and rights consciousness that characterize most histories of the modern. Collaborators must take their share of the blame.

The Rape of Nanjing has become one of these signature events. Some have sought to downgrade Nanjing's status as an atrocity by explaining the outbreak of violence as the outcome of battle fatigue or short supplies, among other reasons, though my research indicates that the predations of the soldiers continued the pattern of devastation that Matsui's troops had already inflicted on civilian populations further east. Others have chosen instead to elevate the Rape to the status of another Holocaust, doing so in order to agitate for what they regard as unpaid judicial redress on China's behalf, but as well to publicize the dangers of war. From this perspective, collaboration conspires in atrocity, and no good defense can be raised against the charge.

The powerful impact of the humanitarian judgment on the Vichy regime in France has been to show that, far from shielding the French people, collaboration yielded up Jews to Nazi extermination. Making the connection between the Holocaust and collaboration spurred new research on Vichy in the 1980s, just as the political agitation that grew up around the Rape of Nanjing in the 1990s has created new knowledge and awareness of that event. Yet the convenient connection between atrocity and collaboration is not as secure as it should be to bear the moral weight it is asked to carry.[4] The commission of atrocities is certainly significant to collaboration in raising the stakes for those who consider it expedient, useful, or necessary to work with the occupier; it also affects the viability of collaboration by generating widespread repugnance for the occupier and unwillingness to go along with his plans. But these are the responses that extreme actions elicit at particular moments, not indicators of what the actual conditions of collaboration may oblige in practice, nor what the cost of collaboration may be at other, less violent moments. The humanitarian judgment arises as a natural response to the injustice of war, yet it cannot furnish a history of the people who collaborated, only an opportunity to reimagine the identities we assemble around our judgments of who was right and who was wrong.

Which brings us to the fourth way of judging collaboration in the guise of explaining it, and that is what I will broadly phrase as the moral judgment. Moral condemnation is never far from the other three modes, all of which claim morality as the foundation for the cases they make against collaboration. I have chosen to mark moral judgment as a distinct category of explanation because of its resilience in the face of the deconstructions to which the other three judgments are vulnerable. Nationalism, political partisanship, and humanitarianism can be dismantled as inadequate bases for evaluating collaboration by reducing them to the particular interests they represent, as I have just done. Even so, in the minds of those who stand apart from such claims and interests, the moral dismissal of collaboration stays alive as a value that places steadfastness above capitulation, honor above expediency, loyalty above private advantage. I touched on how we might get behind the judgment of collaboration as innately immoral in Chapter 1. There, working from Teemu Ruskola's analysis of Orientalism's effects on our understanding of Chinese law, I noted that the invocation of the word "collaboration" brings into being a moral subject—and in this case, its opposite as well: a subject who grasps the moral obligation not to collaborate with wartime occupiers. From any national or community perspective, this subjectivity is unexceptional. Producing it is not the historian's role, however; it is the propagandist's. The purpose of propaganda is to set up and validate what Ruskola describes as "normative systems that posit a pre-given moral subject and then elaborate guidelines for proper actions by that subject." History does not fashion moral subjects, nor produce moral knowledge. The historian's task is not to make fault claims against historical actors in the past or against readers in the present. Instead, it is to investigate the norms and conditions that produced moral subjects in the place and time under study. It is useful to ask why some Chinese chose to cooperate with the Japanese, but it may be more important to inquire why cooperation made sense to people at that time.

The value of stepping back from making a judgment on collaboration is not to claim that collaboration was as good or as bad as any other choice being made that winter of 1937–38. It is to realize that each choice had to be made, and that it was made, through a complex calculation of the benefits and losses that individuals thought they could decipher at the time, before the full consequences of their actions could be known. Without question, many of those choices were venal in inspiration and destructive in impact, and the historian is not disqualified from documenting that venality or tracking the damage these choices led to and declaring them to be damaging. I have found it impossible to suspend my personal distaste for some of the characters who appear in this book, and it would be facetious to suggest that the reader should, particularly when the consequences of collaboration were as stark as they were in a place like Nanjing. But the historian is also responsible for documenting all that was not venal and destructive when other motivations came into play and other consequences into view; in other words, to detect ambiguity in what a superficial reading might otherwise dismiss as confirmation of the norms by which a culture, then or now, has constructed its moral subjects.

Most vulnerable to moral judgments at the time were the educated elites, who were expected to serve the Republic and so were held responsible in a way that ordinary people were not. Their obligation to make the correct choice was heightened, though also made easier, by the fact that they could afford to remove themselves from the battlefield as poorer people could not. It was easier for them to find refuge in the international concessions in Shanghai or sit out the war in Sichuan or Yunnan. Their exit left a far less privileged group behind to reconstitute the postconquest economy and rebuild state administration in the face of a rapacious occupation army, a politically divided resistance, and a devastated populace enduring a winter of food and housing shortages. Calculating whether to collaborate involved any mixture of personal salvation from the dangers of war, personal greed for the windfalls of power, or personal revulsion for other contenders for power. To condemn these people under the banner of greed or treason, without looking more closely at actual circumstances, is to reproduce the political terrain on which they were forced to act: to mistake the drama of resistance for the melodrama of supposing that everyone resisted.[5]

Contrary to the usual assumptions, ordinary people seem to have been relatively indifferent to the moral claims of resistance and collaboration. Between Zhang Yibo's call for resistance and the collaborators' call for acquiescence, between those elites who "showed not the slightest subtlety about fighting to get positions" and those who risked their lives to sabotage the occupation state, we find the ordinary people who were active partisans of neither cause. Too far down the social hierarchy to take part in what Henrik Dethlefsen specified as "the continuing exercise of power under the pressure produced by the presence of an occupying power," they went on with their lives, struggling to earn enough to survive, paying the taxes they could not evade, schooling their children in curricula they could not control, living and working within state institutions they were not asked to devise or approve. Robert McClure, a Canadian medical mission-

ary writing from Henan in 1938, declared that the peasants of his acquain-
tance were "used to being conquered" by whichever political faction captured power in the province: "To people accustomed to this method of
government the danger of a Japanese 'capture' was not anything to be
scared of." These people simply got on with their lives. He added that
"one must assume that the Japanese were aware of this condition too."[6] Indeed they were. Mantetsu researchers doing rural surveys in north China
claimed the villagers were as indifferent to the Nationalists as to the Japanese, and by extension to the collaborators as well.[7] All were external powers that had to be accommodated, nothing more. The lesson was a convenient one for Japanese to discover, for it made the occupation state seem
equally plausible as a government of these people, equally good or evil, and
it permitted a cynical manipulation of the tokens of legitimacy and popular representation without having to make an apology for that manipulation.[8]

Zhang Yibo worried that people would be prone to accept the circumstances in which they found themselves, however much they might not like
them. He knew that some were voicing the equal-evil argument, and not
just peasants. Urbanites were particularly susceptible, he felt, and even
likely to rephrase it as an equal-good argument: let any regime stand that
did not oppress them. "Some compatriots in places that have not been
trampled by the enemy don't even think of the enemy as having invaded,
think that it is just another change in regime and we can still go on living
peacefully and taking pleasure in our work, enjoying life as before," he observes. The notion that such capitulation would leave people's lives un-
changed Zhang regarded as a "dream."[9] Zhang wrote in anger, warning that
the costs of submitting to Japan were high. But he wrote too in fear, and
what he feared was time. Time has a capacity to recast the exceptional as
the ordinary, the intrusive as the diurnal, conquest as merely the next regime. It can quietly overpower the claim that submission to military domi-
nation is an illusion and make resistance seem like the illusion. Hindsight
shows us now that time was on the side of the resistance. The resistance
could wait out Japan's hopeless ambition to dominate all of East Asia and
the Pacific. It could wait out as well the slow, seeping losses the Japanese
military was suffering on the continent, confident that Japan's puppets
would eventually fall regardless of who was shuffled forward to be the
leader of the nation. This was not clear at the time, but became so soon
enough.

Time was not on the collaborators' side. The high rate of turnover among committee members indicates that most found working for the occupation state harder going than they anticipated. Some were able to lodge themselves in comfortable bureaucratic niches in the occupation state, and some were able to protect their commercial or family interests by doing so.[10] Many more, unable to master the complexities of wartime politics and unwilling to stay on the invader's side when a more appealing option emerged, withdrew or were forced out. As all the case studies in this volume have shown, collaboration proved to be politically unstable and morally awkward for both sides of the relationship. For the occupier, successes were largely only apparent, costs mounted, and resistance interfered with the installation of a new order of any substance. For the occupied, the costs were also prohibitive, and the complicities and rivalries that collaboration let loose hampered the sort of political process that a regime has to undergo in order to claim legitimacy. Under such conditions, collaboration emerged as the losing option.

However complicated the reasons to collaborate, the actual experience of collaborating was more ambiguous in its effects, and more difficult in its practice, than the myth of heroic resisters and cringing collaborators assumes. Ambiguous does not mean inexplicable, nor does difficult mean that collaboration contributed nothing to the power of the occupying forces. What ambiguous and difficult mean is that we cannot deduce the causes that prompted people to act from the moral claims we impose, nor evaluate their actions solely in relation to consequences the actors could not anticipate. Easing apart historical acts from the assumptions to which nationalist sentiment has bound them, or from the moral presuppositions that have left them to rust, concedes to events an indeterminacy that places them always beyond anticipation. Who could know, at the beginning, that the occupation state would not outlast Japan's defeat by one day, or that four years after that defeat, it would be replaced by a Communist state for which the costs of elite collaboration, with the Japanese, the Nationalists, or even itself, would run even higher?

Notes

Sources

Index

Notes

Abbreviations

ACC   Anglican Church of Canada Archives, Toronto

CNT   China Number Two Historical Archives, Nanjing

HIA   Hoover Institution Archives, Stanford University, Stanford

JDA   Jiading District Archives, Jiading

NAC   National Archives of Canada, Ottawa

SDF   Self-Defense Force (Bōeichō) Archives, Self-Defense Research Institute, Tokyo

SMA   Shanghai Municipal Archives, Shanghai

SMP   Shanghai Municipal Police Special Branch Files, Library of Congress

UCA   United Church of Canada Archives, University of Toronto

1. Considering Collaboration

1. See Gerhard Hirschfeld's introduction to his coedited *Collaboration in France,* p. 2.

2. Dethlefsen, "Denmark and the German Occupation," pp. 198–99.

3. Ruskola, "Legal Orientalism," p. 225.

4. West, *The Meaning of Treason,* p. 102.

5. Ibid., pp. 94, 114.

6. On the myth of resistance in postwar France, see Rousso, *The Vichy Syndrome;* Morris, *Collaboration and Resistance Reviewed;* and Conan and Rousso, *Vichy: An Ever-Present Past.*

7. The letter from the Huangpu West Residents' Association to the Shanghai municipal government (14 January 1939) is archived in SMA, File R18–126.

8. SMA, File R18–689.

9. Katō Kōzan's memoir, "Congshi xuanfu gongzuo zhi huigu" (My reminiscence of doing pacification work), appeared serially in the *New Nanjing Daily* (*Nanjing xinbao*) on 2–3 July 1939.

10. On "collaborationism," see Hoffman, *Decline or Renewal*, p. 27.

11. The phrase "Hitler's willing executioners" is the title of the controversial book in which Daniel Goldhagen argues that moral responsibility for the Holocaust falls not on a limited subset of Germans but on the German people as a whole. "Not economic hardship, not the coercive means of a totalitarian state, not social psychological pressure, not invariable, psychological propensities, but ideas about Jews that were pervasive in Germany, and had been for decades, induced ordinary Germans to kill unarmed, defenseless Jewish men, women, and children by the thousands, systematically and without pity" (p. 9). The complicity of ordinary people in war remains difficult to evaluate.

12. Marrus and Paxton, *Vichy France and the Jews*, p. xii.

13. Zhang, *Zhenjiang lunxian ji*, p. 4.

14. Ibid., p. 44.

15. Brook, "Collaborationist Nationalism in Occupied Wartime China," p. 183.

16. SMA, File R18–689.

17. Zhang, *Zhenjiang lunxian ji*, p. 42.

18. Ibid., p. 26.

19. Ibid., p. 74.

20. Ibid., p. 47.

21. The casualty gender ratio comes from totals compiled by the Nanjing District Court in April 1946, reproduced in Zhongguo di'er lishi dang'anguan, *Qin Hua Rijun Nanjing datusha dang'an*, p. 524. The court revised its total down from 295,525 to 250,800 when it made its submission to the Tokyo tribunal on 4 November 1946; ibid., p. 553.

22. *Nanjing shizheng gaikuang 1938*, p. 15.

23. Diamond, *Women and the Second World War in France*, pp. 16, 75, 96.

24. Hu, *American Goddess at the Rape of Nanking*, pp. 112–14.

25. Li Zhizhong's reminiscence is appended to the 1999 edition of Zhang, *Zhenjiang lunxian ji*, pp. 93–94.

26. Kedward, *Vichy France and Resistance: Culture and Ideology*, p. 5.

27. This early phase has not been without its pioneers, notably Fu, *Resistance, Passivity, and Collaboration*, and Mitter, *The Manchurian Myth*.

2. The Plan

1. Paraphrased in Vespa, *Secret Agent of Japan*, p. 50.

2. Brook, "The Creation of the Reformed Government in Central China, 1938," pp. 86–87.

3. Okada, *Nit-Chū sensō urakata ki*, pp. 109–10.

4. Reprinted in Usui, *Nit-Chū sensō*, p. 145.

5. The Japanese understanding of "Central China" is outlined in Tōa dōbunkai, *Shin Shina gensei yōran*, p. 649; see also p. 337 for the corresponding definition of "North China."

6. Information on the arrival of the first pacification agents is taken from a Mantetsu report of 4 January, which Inoue Hisashi has reproduced in his *Kachū senbu kōsaku shiryō* (Materials on pacification work in central China); it is listed in the bibliography as Inoue #4.

7. Itō, *Life along the South Manchurian Railway*, pp. 3–4.

8. Popular impressions of the Special Service Department as a Japanese Gestapo derive in part from the highly colored reports of the Shanghai Municipal Police, which have influenced scholarly accounts; for example, Frederic Wakeman, *The Shanghai Badlands*, pp. 10ff. The Military Police, in fact, seem to deserve the lurid image given in memoirs such as Hugh Collar's *Captive in Shanghai*. That said, the SSD was often put in close cooperation with the Military Police when security matters arose. In Shanghai's Western District, Wakeman's "Badlands," the two organizations had offices in the same building at 94 Jessfield Road, and so the temptation to see these separate organizations as a unified Japanese operation was strong. As the Shanghai Municipal Police recalled the security situation in 1938, "One Mr. Sakurai was then chief of the [pacification] section. It cooperated closely with the Japanese Military Police from the very outset in tracing the anti-Japanese elements and organizations as well as the property of Chinese officials. In this connection, large numbers of Chinese agents recruited from the loafer class were employed to assist the Japanese in such secret activities"; SMP, File 9114(c): "Report on the Situation in the Western District," 30 January 1939, p. 5. The account is intuitively appealing but impossibly vague.

9. On the pro-Chinese sympathies of officers in the SSD and the Kōain, see Inukai, *Yōshikō wa ima mo nagarete iru*, pp. 125–29.

10. Itō's memoirs have been translated by Joshua Fogel as *Life along the South Manchurian Railway;* his comments on the pacification program appear on pp. 178–79.

11. The figure of 250 employees being involved in pacification comes from Inoue #10, p. 48.

12. Inoue #10, p. 51. *Anju leye* appears in other Japanese planning documents, for example, "Chian shukusei yōkō" (Outline of security and pacification), SDF, Riku Shi mitsu dainikki, File S14–21 (110), #20.

13. Ibid.

14. The initial description of the tasks of the SSD and pacification agents is taken from the North China Area Army's handbook, "Chian shukusei yōkō" (Out-

line of security and pacification), 20 April 1939, archived in SDF, Riku Shi mitsu dainikki, File S14–21 (110), #20.

15. Inoue #2; the description of the teams' work appears on p. 51.

16. Inoue #1.

17. Zhang, *Zhenjiang lunxian ji*, p. 37.

18. Mitter, *The Manchurian Myth*, p. 94; see also Duara, "Transnationalism and the Predicament of Sovereignty." The Special Service did set up the New People's Association (Xinmin hui) in North China, and the Great People's Association (Damin hui) in Central, though it tried to avoid the Manchurian precedent so as not to seem like yet another Japanese concoction.

19. Katō Kōzan describes his early days as a pacification agent in the first part of his "Congshi xuanfu gongzuo zhi huigu," *Nanjing xinbao*, 2 July 1939.

20. Kimura, *Japanese Agent in Tibet*, pp. 2–3, 5, 223.

21. Okada, *Nit-Chū sensō urakata ki*, p. 115.

22. "Gunsenkyō chiiki chian ichi shisshi yōryō (An outline for implementing peace maintenance in the areas occupied by the army), in SDF, Riku Shi mitsu dainikki, File S13–10.

23. Burrin, *The French and the Germans*, p. 1.

24. The phrase comes from the May 1938 report of the British Consulate in Shanghai, "China Summary," 1938, no. 5, para. 26.

25. On earlier peace maintenance committees in Beijing, see Strand, *Rickshaw Beijing*, pp. 203–18; on their use in occupied Manchuria, see Mitter, *The Manchurian Myth*, pp. 80–83.

26. Naka Shina hōmengun shireibu, "Kongo no seiji bōryaku taikō" (Outline of future political strategy), in SDF, Shina: Shina jihen: zenpan 315.

27. Army funding of PMCs is mentioned in a South Manchurian Railway Company publication, *Japanese Spirit in Full Bloom*, p. 27. The setting up of PMCs in Beijing and Tianjin is noted in Tōa dōbunkai, ed., *Shin Shina gensei yōran*, pp. 399–400.

28. SMA, File R1–1–154: "Shisan ri huiyilu"; "Yaoqiu shixiang."

29. The incident arising from language misunderstanding in Gaoqiao is in SMA, File R1–1–103.

30. The term "loyal subject" is used in the founding Ming emperor's preface to the third of his *Grand Proclamations (Dagao)* in 1385. As John Dower observes in *War without Mercy*, p. 212, "ancient texts were ransacked to provide slogans for modern times, suggesting the unsullied survival of tradition and indigenous wisdom."

31. May Watts's letter of September 1939 to L. A. Dixon, archived in ACC, MSCC, Series 3–3, Leonard A. Dixon Files, China—Reference Files, G. S. 75–103, Box 79, File 1.

32. On the Republican understanding of "self-government," see Henriot, *Shanghai 1927–1937*, pp. 35–36. The Japanese also used this term in Manchuria: see Mitter, *The Manchurian Myth*, pp. 109–110.

33. On the relative success of this recruitment process in Manchuria, see Mitter, *The Manchurian Myth*, p. 108. The great difference was that there the Japanese were able to rely on preexisting local agencies and were better positioned to persuade elites to accept some responsibility for maintaining local order.

34. Letter from George Andrew to Canon Gould (20 June 1938), ACC, MSCC, China Files, Box 77.

35. "Naka Shina hōmengun sazen chiiki nai senbu jōkō," in SDF, Riku Shi mitsu dainikki, File 513–4 (113), #119.

36. Reprinted in Usui, ed., *Nit-Chū sensō*, vol. 5, p. 127.

37. The transcript of Mei Siping's trial has been reprinted in Nanjing shi dang'anguan, *Shenxun Wangwei hanjian bilu;* the comment about pacification teams appears on pp. 416–17.

38. NCAA Headquarters, "Kōsaku yōryō," appended to SDF, Riku Shi mitsu dainikki, File S14–87.

39. Inoue #10.

40. On road protection in Zhenjiang, see Inoue #21, p. 181; also *Nanjing xinbao*, 9 July 1939. The SSD set up a Railroad Protection Association in the Western District of Shanghai on 1 February 1939, though the surviving documents give no sense of where the idea came from; SMA, File R18–514.

41. The Pacification Department in Shanghai, for instance, drew up regulations for commodity trading; see Tōa dōbunkai, *Shin Shina gensei yōran*, p. 1231. Local teams enforced these locally by controlling the issuance of shipping permits, especially for grain; see Kōain kachū renrakubu, *Naka Shina jūyō kokuhō shigen shiryō sakubutsu chōsa hōkokusho*, p. 89. Commodity taxes were also something in which pacification teams became involved. To have an SGC collect taxes required not just an SGC but a reliable police force, so when these were not yet functioning, some teams went ahead with tax collection on their own. A team leader in the Western District of Shanghai made taxation his team's top priority when he saw commodities flowing past his office down Suzhou Creek. He published a schedule of transit tax rates on vegetables on 10 January and announced that collection would begin two days later, and that team members would be doing the collecting until such time as the local SGC had a finance bureau up and running; SMA, File R1–1–147.

42. The Nanjing Special Service Agency, for instance, arranged for a theatre company to visit the city in October. Chinese were allowed to attend the performances, but the main purpose was to provide entertainment for the garrison soldiers; *Nanjing xinbao*, 8 October 1938.

43. Mantetsu Shanhai jimusho, *Naka Shina ni okeru nōgyō seisatsu no dōkō*; see pp. 17–18.

3. Appearances / Jiading

1. The Jiading pacification report of April 1938 (Inoue #15) is archived in SDF, Shina: Shina jihen: Shanhai, Nankin, File 22.
2. Kumagai, *Shina kyōchin zatsuwa: Chōkō senbu kiroku,* pp. 3–4.
3. Casualty statistics are taken from an untitled, undated document in JDA, Record Group 104, Index 8, File 165. That document does not indicate how these statistics were collected.
4. Inoue #16, p. 107.
5. Inoue #17, p. 124.
6. The anonymous handwritten SGC report of May 1938, "Taicang xian zizhi weiyuanhui gongzuo baogao" (Work report of the Taicang county self-government committee), is archived in CNT, Record Group 2001(2), File 19.
7. Kumagai, *Shina kyōchin zatsuwa,* p. 7.
8. Ibid., p. 4.
9. Inoue #4, pp. 20–22; Kumagai, *Shina kyōchin zatsuwa,* p. 11.
10. Inoue #15, p. 93; Kumagai, *Shina kyōchin zatsuwa,* p. 9.
11. Kumagai, *Shina kyōchin zatsuwa,* pp. 31–32; Inoue #15, p. 97.
12. Inoue #23, p. 213.
13. Kumagai, *Shina kyōchin zatsuwa,* pp. 19–20.
14. Ibid., p. 58.
15. Ibid., pp. 58–59.
16. Inoue #15, p. 88.
17. The massacre of 1645 is reconstructed in Jerry Dennerline, *The Chia-ting Loyalists.* Dennerline observes that the loyalists were "members of a broad network of literati, whose links with the centers of official power were especially strong and whose links with identifiable local communities were especially weak." Their decision to stage an all-out resistance, he argues, "owed something to their relative freedom from community constraints" (p. 12). Did the principle this observation implies—that the presence of community constraints encouraged collaboration—apply in the 1930s? Or had the shift from rural power to urban and the withering of local ties to national networks rendered this formula inapplicable? Kumagai refers to this event in his *Shina kyōchin zatsuwa,* pp. 89–90.
18. Kumagai, *Shina kyōchin zatsuwa,* pp. 68–71.
19. Inoue #16, p. 111.
20. The December 1938 provincial relief inspection report by Lin Meibo and Qian

Pengyi, dated 26 January 1939, is preserved in CNT, Record Group 2001(2), File 196.

21. On Japanese cotton business dealings, see Sugimura Kōzō, *Shanhai yōran,* pp. 144–45. Cotton prices for Jiading county appear in Mantetsu Shanhai jimusho chōsashitsu, *Naka Shina nōsakubutsu no nōken jijō.*

22. Inoue #15, p. 89.

23. Kumagai, *Shina kyōchin zatsuwa,* p. 59.

24. Ibid., p. 11.

25. Ibid., p. 24.

26. For a summary of guerrilla operations in Jiading, notably Waigang and Loutang, see Yang, *Jiading xianzhi,* pp. 22–23, 669. Xue, ed., *Shanghai jiaoxian kangri wuzhuang douzheng,* pp. 81–94, includes a fuller account, though the editor's relentless effort to discredit anyone associated with the Nationalists diminishes its credibility. The challenges of maintaining organized resistance in the county are reflected in *Shanghai jiaoxian kangri wuzhuang douzheng shiliao,* pp. 38–40, 71–73, 108–12, 128–34.

27. Kumagai, *Shina kyōchin zatsuwa,* p. 37.

28. Inoue #16, p. 113.

29. Xingzhengyuan xuanchuanju, *Weixin zhengfu chengli chuzhou jinian ce,* p. 326.

30. Yang, *Jiading xianzhi,* p. 669.

31. "Jiading xian zhishi Feng Chengqiu xianzheng gaikuang baogao" (Report on county administration by Jiading county magistrate Feng Chengqiu), preserved in CNT, Record Group 2001.

32. Kōain kachū renrakubu, *Katei, Taisō, Chōshū ni okeru juyō nōsakubutsu no kenshū kankō,* p. 30.

33. SMA, File R1–3–1218. The county government in neighboring Baoshan district found itself having to act out the same charade: its report of a public rally held there at the end of March to celebrate the first anniversary of the Reformed Government includes a photograph that shows no adults present other than those in uniform; SMA, File R1–3–808.

34. The roster of district heads and the minutes of the district affairs meeting are preserved in JDA, Record Group 11, Index 1, Files 7 and 9.

35. Mantetsu Shanhai jimusho chōsashitsu, *Shanhai tokubetsushi Katei ku nōson jittai chōsa hōkokusho,* preface.

36. Kumagai, *Shina kyōchin zatsuwa,* p. 94.

4. Costs / Zhenjiang

1. The history of Zhenjiang's early occupation is reconstructed from the pacification team's two reports, one dated April 1938 (Inoue #18) and the other August 1939 (Inoue #21).

2. Zhang, *Zhenjiang lunxian ji*, pp. 8, 14, 12, 27, 24, 27, 65, 30, 23, 43–46.

3. Ibid., p. 38. The 1999 edition footnotes these casualty statistics on p. 84. Yang Fosheng's reminiscence is appended to the same edition, pp. 92–93.

4. Ibid., p. 24. For other accounts of atrocities committed during the takeover of Zhenjiang, see Honda, *The Nanjing Massacre*, pp. 114–19.

5. Ibid., pp. 27, 65.

6. The history of the Zhenjiang Muslim community is summarized in Xu Peihong and Shao Nianbao, *Dantu xianzhi*, p. 836; my thanks to Dru Galdney for further elucidation.

7. American Information Committee, "New Order in East Asia," pp. 12–15. Despite inquiries to several specialists in the history of Christianity, notably Jean-Paul Wiest, I was unable to turn up any documentation on the refugee work at the time of the Japanese takeover by Christians, either the British and American Protestant missions or the Catholic church in Zhenjiang, which was the center of a missionary district within the vicariate apostolic of Nanjing.

8. Inoue #10, p. 50.

9. Zhang, *Zhenjiang lunxian ji*, p. 32.

10. Inoue #10, p. 51.

11. Zhang, *Zhenjiang lunxian ji*, p. 30.

12. Ibid., p. 23.

13. Ibid., pp. 43–44.

14. Xingzhengyuan xuanchuanju, *Ishin seifu no genkō*, p. 159.

15. Zhang, *Zhenjiang lunxian ji*, pp. 45–46.

16. Inoue #5, p. 23. The situation in Songjiang has been reconstructed as well from the Mantetsu's January report on pacification work (Inoue #4, p. 20) and the Songjiang team's report (Inoue #11, p. 55).

17. The weak figure in Songjiang seems to have been the man whom Nakayama replaced, Kawano Masanao, who was transferred to Nanjing and demoted from team leader to team member.

18. Katō, "Congshi xuanfu gongzuo zhi huigu" (Reminiscence of doing pacification work), *Nanjing xinbao* (New Nanjing daily), 2–3 July 1939. A footnote on p. 42 of the 1999 edition of Zhang, *Zhenjiang lunxian ji*, mistakenly identifies a Japanese medical doctor and longtime resident of Zhenjiang, Ōi Hiroshi, as head of the pacification team. Suspected of operating an intelligence network for the Japanese Army in the autumn of 1937, Ōi fled when two of his operatives were exposed and executed. According to this note, he returned to head the pacification team, but he is not mentioned in any team report.

19. Zhang, *Zhenjiang lunxian ji*, pp. 30, 45, 47.

20. Xu and Shao, *Dantu xianzhi*, p. 23.

21. Ibid., pp. 49–50.

22. Inoue #18, p. 141.

23. Coble, *Chinese Capitalists in Japan's New Order,* p. 183. Japanese sources indicate that the financial support the match factory gave to the Zhenjiang administration was more complicated than is suggested by the official biography of the "patriotic capitalist" Liu Hongsheng, the owner of the Great China Match Company, on which Coble relies.

24. Mantetsu Shanhai jimusho chōsashitsu, *Naka Shina nōsakubutsu no nōkō jijō* (1939).

25. For food prices (denominated in yen) in Taicang, see Inoue #16, p. 120; in Danyang, Inoue #17, p. 135; in Zhenjiang, Inoue #6, p. 35.

26. Baumler, "Opium Suppression versus Opium Control."

27. On early Japanese involvement in opium supply to Chuzhou across the Yangtze River, see my "Opium and Collaboration in Central China," pp. 324–25.

28. *Jiangsu sheng gongbao xinnian tekan,* January 1939.

29. *Nanjing xinbao,* 8 December 1938.

30. American Information Committee, "New Order in East Asia," p. 13.

31. Liberman, *Does Conquest Pay?* pp. 110, 115.

32. CNT, Record Group 2001, File 20.

33. Xu and Shao, *Dantu xianzhi,* p. 25; Chen, *Making Revolution,* pp. 84, 96–97.

5. Complicities / Nanjing

1. Gildea, *Marianne in Chains: In Search of the German Occupation, 1940–45,* p. 51.

2. The only surviving official Japanese report from Nanjing is "Nankin tokumu kikan kōsaku gaikyō" (State of work of the Nanjing Special Service Agency; Inoue #19). Among Chinese eyewitness accounts, five are useful: Guo Qi, "Xiandu xuelei lu" (Blood-and-tears record of the fallen capital); Jiang Gongyi, "Xianjing sanyue ji" (Three months in the fallen capital); Li Kelang, "Lunjing wuyue ji" (Five months in the occupied capital); Lin Na's "Xuelei hua Nanjing" (Speaking of Nanjing through blood and tears); and the anonymous "Shishou hou de Nanjing" (Nanjing after it was lost). All are reprinted in Nanjing tushuguan, ed., *Qin Hua Rijun Nanjing datusha shiliao,* pp. 1–155. The principal English-language source is the collection of International Committee documents published in 1939 by Hsü Shuhsi as *Documents on the Nanking Safety Zone,* reproduced in my *Documents on the Rape of Nanking.* China's Ministry of National Defense had Hsü's book translated in 1947 as the Tokyo war crimes trial was proceeding (a copy is in the China Number Two Historical Archives); it has since been retranslated and published. Of the personal records kept by IC members, the most detailed is John Rabe's diary, published as *The Good Man of Nanking: The Diaries of John Rabe.* Quotes from the diary in this chapter may be found, in the order they appear, on pp. 102, 99, 105, 109, and

114. Rabe's letters to Japanese officials appear chronologically in Hsü, *Documents*. Robert Wilson's letters are reprinted in Brook, *Documents on the Rape of Nanking*, pp. 207–54; his description of the collapse of morale at dusk on 12 December appears on p. 209. Records kept by other committee members are reprinted in Zhang Kaiyuan, ed., *Eyewitnesses to Massacre*. The attack on Nanjing has been told in English by Iris Chang in *The Rape of Nanking*, also by Mark Eykholt in chapter 2 of his dissertation, "Living the Limits of Occupation." For a discussion of the historiography surrounding this event, see Eykholt's "Aggression, Victimization, and Chinese Historiography of the Nanjing Massacre." The history of Nanjing during the 1927–1937 decade is reconstructed in Zwia Lipkin, "Keeping Up Appearances."

3. Lipkin, "Keeping Up Appearances," p. 13.

4. Matsui's orders regarding the capture of Nanjing are quoted in Brook, *Documents*, p. 289.

5. Wilson, letter of December 21, in Brook, *Documents*, p. 220.

6. Matsui, "Nankin nyūjō no kangai" (Feelings on entering the city of Nanjing).

7. Okada, *Nit-Chū senṣō urakata ki*, pp. 114–15.

8. Inoue #6, p. 34.

9. Amaya's remark of 5 February appears in Rabe, *The Good Man of Nanking*, p. 178. The exclamation mark belongs to John Rabe, who recorded Amaya's observation.

10. Wilson, letter of 15 December, in Brook, *Documents*, p. 214.

11. Wilson, letter of 19 December, in Brook, *Documents*, p. 217.

12. For a reference to SSA soldiers taking Chinese to execution, see the Kitayama diary, reprinted in Iguchi, *Nankin jihen*, p. 73.

13. For example, Inoue #27, p. 262.

14. Hsü, *Documents*, pp. 14, 19, 22, 23.

15. Wilson, letter of 23 December, in Brook, *Documents*, p. 225.

16. Wang, "Riwei hanjian zhengfu," p. 4.

17. Nanjing shi dang'anguan, *Shenxun Wangwei hanjian bilu*, p. 344. Age and faulty memory made Wen's testimony at his trial often unreliable.

18. Wilson, letter of 21 December, in Brook, *Documents*, pp. 219–20.

19. Wilson, letter of 23 December, in Brook, *Documents*, p. 223.

20. Information on the Nanjing branch of the Red Swastika Society is taken from a printed account of branch activities in 1937–1942, archived in CNT, Record Group 257, File 224.

21. The formation of the Nanjing SGC is examined in Sun Zhaiwei, ed., *Nanjing datusha*, pp. 464–82; also Xia Qiang, "Weihu zuozhang de zizhi weiyuanhui." Additional information on SGC personnel comes from Wang Xiguang, "Riwei hanjian zhengfu"; and Yin Jijun, *1937, Nanjing dajiuhuan*, pp. 174–79, though the latter author indicates no sources for his information.

22. Hsü, *Documents,* p. 38.

23. Fitch's diary, reprinted in Zhang, *Eyewitnesses,* p. 95.

24. Maruyama Susumu's private account of the work of the SSA, "Watakushi no Shōwa shi—Nankin jiken no jissō," appeared serially in a Mantetsu "alumni" publication in 2000. I have particularly relied on part 5, in *Mantetsu wakabakai kaihō,* no. 137 (8 September 2000), pp. 38–44. I am grateful to David Askew for giving me a copy. Maruyama's polemical thrust and occasional factual errors cast some doubt on the veracity of his recollections.

25. I am grateful to Zwia Lipkin for this information.

26. Jiang, "Xianjing sanyue ji," where he is misidentified as Zhan Yongguang. Vautrin's reference to Zhan (she identifies him as Jan Yung-gwang) appears in her diary entry for 1 January 1938, reprinted in Zhang, *Eyewitnesses,* p. 369.

27. Hsü, *Documents,* p. 100.

28. On Xu Chuanyin, see Pritchard and Zaide, eds., *The Tokyo War Crimes Trial,* vol. 2, pp. 2556–61; also Hu, *American Goddess at the Rape of Nanking,* pp. 112–14. The friendship between Tao Xisan and Xu Chuanyin is mentioned by Smythe in Zhang, *Eyewitnesses,* p. 287.

29. The German references to Jimmy Wang appear in "Memorandum of Chancellor P. Scharffenberg, German Embassy, Nanking Office" (13 January 1938), and "Report from the Nanking Office of the German Embassy to the Foreign Ministry" (20 January 1938), both included in Rabe, *The Good Man of Nanking,* pp. 132, 146. For Smythe's and Riggs's comments on Wang, see Zhang, *Eyewitnesses,* pp. 274, 284, 291; also Hsü, *Documents,* p. 99.

30. Wilson, letter of 1 January, in Brook, *Documents,* p. 233.

31. Xingzheng yuan xuanchuanju, *Chūka minkoku ishin seifu gaishi,* p. 370. The frequent misprintings of Chinese names in this book are consistent with Japanese misreadings of Chinese characters (for example, on p. 371, Tao Xisan appears as Tao Xishan, Xu Chuanyin as Xu Chuanying), suggesting that the book was written by Japanese, not just translated into Japanese. The same narrative explains that the SGC was set up for the purpose of controlling the "unexpected terrorist activities" of Nationalist soldiers and Communist agents hiding in the Safety Zone.

32. Rabe, *The Good Man of Nanking,* p. 99. Vautrin was not quite so naïve; she was in fact willing to provide limited cooperation on the matter of prostitution, as noted in Hu, *American Goddess,* p. 101.

33. Regarding Red Swastika burials, see the SSA report: Inoue #19, p. 164. The society's figures appear in an archived Red Swastika document dated 4 April 1938, reprinted in Zhongguo di'er lishi dang'anguan, ed., *Qin Hua Rijun Nanjing datusha dang'an,* p. 436. The Red Swastika figure appears as item 6 in the printed account of branch activities for 1937–1942 archived in CNT, Record Group 257, File 224. Xu Chuanyin's testimony at Tokyo appears in Interna-

tional Military Tribunal for the Far East, *Proceedings*, p. 2,574. Xu insisted that the figure represented civilians only, and that "the number is really too small. The reason is [that] we [were] not allowed to give a true number of the people we buried." For the tribunal's invocation of the data in its judgment, see Brook, *Documents*, p. 261.

34. Fitch's description appears in his diary, which H. J. Timperley reprinted anonymously in *Japanese Terror in China*, p. 43; the same text appears in Zhang, *Eyewitnesses*, p. 98.

35. Iguchi, *Nankin jihen*, pp. 32, 75, 310–11.

36. Hsü, *Documents*, pp. 63, 66.

37. Rabe, *Good Man of Nanking*, p. 109.

38. Bates, "Report of the Nanking International Relief Committee," p. 418.

39. Hsü, *Documents*, p. 67.

40. Sun, *Nanjing datusha*, p. 476.

41. Information on food supply matters comes from Hsü, *Documents*, pp. 83, 91–93, 97, 110–11, 121, 137; Inoue #19, p. 164; Timperley, *Japanese Terror in China*, p. 205; Smythe, diary entry for 9 January 1930, reprinted in Zhang, *Eyewitnesses*, p. 295. Equivalents for units of measure are taken from Bates's "Report of the Nanking International Relief Committee," p. 422. SSD concern over the political effects of foreign food relief is noted in Inoue #10, p. 52.

42. A week after the first rice shop opened, soldiers showed up at the Tianmin Bathhouse, one of two the SGC had reopened for Japanese use (recall that Tao was a bathhouse owner), robbed the employees of their money, and shot three of them, one fatally; Hsü, *Documents*, p. 120.

43. Inoue #19, p. 148.

44. At this point, the operations of the SSA disappear from view. The agency's status as a regional branch of the SSD was confirmed in a mid-May reorganization putting Major Ōnishi in charge, as noted in the 13 May 1938 report of the SSD director to his vice-minister, archived in SDF, Riku Shi mitsu dainikki, File S14–12, no. 136. I have found no record of what Ōnishi did in this capacity.

45. On the renewal of military misconduct at the end of January, see my "Documenting the Rape of Nanking," pp. 8–9.

46. Magee's description of soldiers looking for women: letter of 2 February 1938, reprinted in Zhang, *Eyewitnesses*, p. 193.

47. Steward's description of the devastation appears in a diary entry of 10 December 1938, reprinted in Zhang, *Eyewitnesses*, p. 319.

48. The reopening of the rice trade from Wuhu is noted by Smythe on 21 March 1938, reprinted in Zhang, *Eyewitnesses*, p. 314.

49. Coville's diary is held in HIA, Stanley Hornbeck record group, Joseph C. Grew files, Box 185. The losses of tools, draught animals, and crops, as estimated by

the Reformed Government's Ministry of Enterprise, appear in Tōa dōbunkai, *Shin Shina gensei yōran*, vol. 2, pp. 1217–18.

50. Smythe, *War Damage in the Nanking Area*, pp. 12, 14; Eykholt, "Living the Limits," p. 15.

51. Tōa dōbunkai, ed., *Shin Shina gensei yōran*, vol. 2, pp. 1217–18.

52. Bates, "Report of the Nanking International Relief Committee," reprinted in Zhang, *Eyewitnesses*, pp. 435, 444.

53. On the post-SGC careers of SGC members, see Xingzheng yuan xuanchuanju, *Chūka minkoku ishin seifu gaishi*, pp. 371, 373; Cai and Sun, "Minguo qijian Nanjing shi zhiguan nianbiao," p. 48; Wang, "Riwei hanjian zhengfu," p. 5. The list of heads of organizations appears in *Nanjing shizheng gaikuang 1939*, pp. 84–90.

54. Xu, *Lest We Forget*, p. 118.

55. The Nanjing Red Swastika branch report of 6 September 1942, filed in CNT, Record Group 257, File 224.

56. Regarding Wang's prostitution operations, see Rosen, "Report from the Nanking Office of the German Embassy to the Foreign Ministry" (20 January 1938), in Rabe, *The Good Man of Nanking*, p. 146; Smythe, letter of 8 March 1938, reprinted in Zhang, *Eyewitnesses*, p. 307. Wang's comment to Smythe appears in ibid., p. 307. The official list of "traitors" is held in CNT, Record Group 2001(2), File 189(1).

57. Brook, *Documents*, p. 10.

58. Bates's comment comes from the transcript of the question-and-answer period after a lecture he gave in New York on 25 June 1941, reprinted in Zhang, *Eyewitnesses*, p. 57.

6. Rivalries / Shanghai

1. Although the occupied administration of Shanghai was a creature of the Japanese Army, I found nothing on it in the Archives of the Self-Defense Research Institute or the Foreign Ministry Archives. The Chinese documentation on occupied Shanghai is much better, though not without its difficulties. The Shanghai Municipal Archives (SMA) holds an extraordinarily rich treasury of local documents, quite beyond what is available for any other city in occupied China. But its holdings for the early years are incomplete and scattered, sometimes randomly, through files in different record groups. The problem is not poor archival practice but the dispersed nature of Chinese urban life, especially in Republican-period Shanghai, when the administration of the city was distributed among several municipal councils, numerous commercial associations, and many other public and private agencies and associations. The confu-

sion of authority under the occupation only made this sense of dispersion worse. To this must be added the distaste for the collaborationist municipal administration, which generated indifference to maintaining a strong archival record for the period. Some SMA documents on the Great Way Government are reprinted in Shanghai shi dang'anguan, *Ri-wei Shanghai shi zhengfu*, for example, pp. 1 16, 135 48, 431–43, 791–810.

2. The inaugural declarations of the Great Way Government and the Japanese document of 31 January 1938 are reprinted in *Ri-wei Shanghai shi zhengfu*, pp. 1–11.

3. Legge, *Li Ki*, pp. 364–65.

4. Miyakawa, *Yūbō Shina o kataru*, pp. 98–99.

5. *Xingdao ribao*, 22 November 1939, p. 4; *Shina jihen gahō*, no. 11 (27 January 1938), p. 31.

6. The only obvious Buddhist term using *xi* ("tin") is the collocation *xizhang*, the ceremonial metal staff that a Buddhist abbot carried to symbolize his power to exorcize evil. The characters for *wen* (Xiwen) and *zhang* (*xizhang*) are close enough that a semiliterate reader could easily confuse them. Did Su?

7. The article in the *Eastern Times* caught the attention of the Special Branch of the Shanghai Municipal Police and so was archived in SMP, File D-8636.

8. Tōa dōbunkai, ed., *Shin Shina gensei yōran*, pp. 740–41.

9. SMA, File R1–1–97.

10. The earliest reference to the concept of *gengsheng* that I have noticed comes up in the report of the pacification team sent to Changzhou (Inoue #5, p. 25), which uses the pregnant phrase *zili gengsheng*, "transforming oneself through one's own efforts," which Communist propagandists would later adopt as "self-reliance."

11. The curriculum vitae of secretariat officials are preserved in SMA, File R1–1–60; those of police officials in File R1–1–93.

12. The charter of the Shanghai county PMC is archived in SMA, File R1–1–4; the correspondence of the Gaoqiao PMC in File R1–1–152; the manifesto of the Pudong SGC in File R1–1–152.

13. SMA, File R1–1–154 ("Dadao zhengfu bugao, 8").

14. SMA, Files R1–1–152 and 155.

15. SMA, File R1–1–152 ("Gaoqiao zhen zhenwuhui huize"); File R18–126 ("Shanghai tebieshi shizheng xunling di 532 hao").

16. SMA, File R1–2–1637.

17. The petition on behalf of the coastal fishing population by Wang Zhenjiang and Wu Zhenya and the 4 April letter from the Tanziwan PMC are both preserved in SMA, File R1–1–153.

18. The setting up of a police bureau in 94 Jessfield Road is described in "Report

on the Situation in the Western District" (January 30, 1939), pp. 2–3, in SMP, File 9114(c).

19. Fu Xiaoan's move to close the paramilitary force down is reported in documents from his chief of police dated 31 December 1938 and 28 January 1939 in SMA, File R1–3–169.

20. SMA, File R1–1–152 ("Wei cheng fuchi jucha bao Tangqiao zizhihui zuzhi jingguo").

21. SMA, Files R1–1–4 (Chamber of Commerce) and R1–1–153 (SGC); Zhang Xuezhou's position as town head as of February 1939 is noted in File R1–3–798.

22. "Cheng wei zuzhi Chuansha zizhihui qingqiu," SMA, File R1–1–152; "Chuansha shangmin zizhihui wei baogao shi," CNT, Record Group 2001(2), File 19.

23. Mōgi, *Shanhai shi daidō seifu shisatsu hōkoku*, p. 7.

24. *Ri-wei Shanghai shi zhengfu*, p. 431.

25. Documents on early Great Way attempts to collect taxes are found in SMA, File R1–1–147.

26. Information on the South City has been taken from SMA, Files R1–1–153 ("Cheng wei chengbao shi an"), R1–1–154 ("Shanghai nanshi shangjie lian-hehui tonggao," March 1938), R1–1–157 ("Jin jiang gongli eryue ershiliu ri fu"), R1–2–160 (report of the Social Affairs Bureau, 27 April 1938), and R1–2–1637 (response to municipal order #365).

27. Xingzhengyuan xuanchuanju, *Ishin seifu no genkō*, p. 159.

28. SMA, File R1–2–1284. Ling Jitan and Shen Shijing were the South City's representatives to a national "peace conference," from a document dated 23 November 1938 in File R1–3–492.

29. For example, a Chinese businessman trading wine to retailers in Hongkou, the Japanese zone of the city, was the victim of a failed grenade attack in May 1938. He suspected that he was targeted because his great-uncle was "a clerical assistant in the Japanese Consulate-General"; SMA, File D8351. On Shanghai as a zone of political assassination, see Wakeman, *Shanghai Badlands*, chap. 2.

30. Guo, "Hanjian Fu Xiaoan zhi si."

31. SMA, Files R1–1–2 and R1–1–3.

32. Xingzhengyuan xuanchuanju, *Weixin zhengfu chengli chuzhou jinian ce*, pp. 308–329

33. The levels of compensation were raised by Wang Jingwei's Interior Ministry in 1940; CNT, Record Group 2001, File 20.

34. SMA, File R1–1–153.

35. The letter ("Cheng wei luchen Huxi qu yiwang zhenggou qingxing"), the municipality's response on 25 January, Chen Xishun's position as head of the

Longcao suboffice, his 8 March letter of resignation, and the information concerning his replacement are all contained in SMA, File R18–126.

36. SMA, File R1–1–152. For Li Zidong, see File R18–48; his status as an outsider to the committee-building process is suggested by the absence of his name from the July 1938 list of Western District SGC personnel in File F1–2–1637.

37. Li Zidong's draft preface for the *Great Way Annual* is in SMA, File R18–464.

38. *Ri-wei Shanghai shi zhengfu,* p. 49.

39. The personnel files for suboffices within the Western District are found in SMA, File R18–275.

40. The reference to reliance on "gentry of the local area" appears in the directive of 21 January in SMA, File R1–1–155.

41. The slogans circulated for comment in June 1938 are preserved in File R1–2–504.

7. Resistance / Chongming

1. SMA, File R1–1–152.

2. Li Helu privately printed his "Chongming lunxian ji" soon after the war. A copy has been preserved in the Chongming County Archives and was reprinted in two parts in the fourth and fifth issues of the 1995 volume of *Dang'an yu shixue* (Archives and history), the in-house journal of the Shanghai Municipal Archives.

3. Tang Xuehai and Sun Shaocheng, "Shicha Chongming Jinshan liangxian zaikuang baogao shu" (Report of an inspection of the disaster situation in the two counties of Chongming and Jinshan), in CNT, Record Group 2001(2), File 196. Additional information on conditions on Chongming have been taken from *Nanjing xinbao,* 30 October 1939. Two briefer articles the newspaper published on 6 and 10 July 1939 have also been consulted.

4. Huang Zhiqing, "Yinian lai xingzheng lüeshu ji jinhou zhi qiwang" (Brief account of administration over the past year and hopes for the future), *Shanghai tebieshi zhengfu chuzhou jinian tekan,* pp. 509–10.

5. Inoue #10, p. 48.

6. Li Helu, "Chongming lunxian ji," pt. 1, p. 40.

7. SGC Finance Department work report (31 March–25 May 1938) and SGC People's Livelihood Department work report (1 April–26 May 1938), archived in CNT, Record Group 2001(2), File 19. These are part of a bundle of work reports, regulations, and minutes of SGC Standing Committee meetings compiled at the end of May 1938 and forwarded to the Reformed Government in Nanjing.

8. Li Helu, "Chongming lunxian ji," pt. 1, p. 41.

9. SGC Education Department work report (31 March-26 May 1938), in CNT, Record Group 2001(2), File 19.

10. Li Helu, "Chongming lunxian ji," pt. 1, p. 40.

11. Huang Zhiqing, "Yinian lai xingzheng lüeshu ji jinhou zhi qiwang," p. 509.

12. Li Helu, "Chongming lunxian ji," pt. 1, pp. 42–43.

13. Conflict over the transfer of Chongming to Shanghai is discussed in the 28 November 1938 and 26 March 1939 issues of *Nanjing xinbao*.

14. SGC changwu hui, minutes of 15 April 1938, in CNT, Record Group 2001(2), File 19.

15. SGC changwu hui, minutes of 5 May 1938, in CNT, Record Group 2001(2), File 19.

16. Li Helu, "Chongming lunxian ji," pt. 1, p. 42.

17. SGC changwu hui, minutes of 18 May 1938, in CNT, Record Group 2001(2), File 19.

18. SGC changwu hui, minutes of 25 May 1938, in CNT, Record Group 2001(2), File 19.

19. Chongming zizhihui baojia ke (Neighborhood watch section of the Chongming SGC), "Baojia zhidu zhidao" (Directions for the neighborhood watch system), in CNT, Record Group 2001(2), File 19.

20. Li Helu, "Chongming lunxian ji," pt. 2, p. 36.

21. The two opium retailers appear on the lists archived in SMA, R1–3–127. Fengji opened on Fudong Street in October, and Chengfeng at South Xinqiao in November.

22. Li Helu, "Chongming lunxian ji," pt. 2, p. 37.

23. Ibid.

24. Inoue #16, p. 115.

25. Li Helu, "Chongming lunxian ji," pt. 1, p. 44.

26. Xingzhengyuan xuanchuanju, *Chūka minkoku ishin seifu gaishi*, p. 449.

27. *Nanjing xinbao*, 30 October 1939. A few brief memoirs of resistance are included in Zhonggong Shanghai shiwei dangshi ziliao zhengji weiyuanhui, ed., *Shanghai jiaoxian kangri wuzhuang douzheng shiliao*, pp. 193–95. As so often with this sort of self-celebratory publication, absence of context renders this material almost useless for the non-Communist historian. The picture is somewhat filled out in Xue Zhendong's *Shanghai jiaoxian kangri wuzhuang douzheng*, pp. 94–105, although the writers' boundless enthusiasm for everything the Communist Party ever did interferes with his analysis.

28. Li Helu, "Chongming lunxian ji," pt. 1, p. 40; Zhang Quan et al., *Rijun zai Shanghai de zuixing yu tongzhi*, pp. 267–68.

29. *Ri-wei Shanghai shi zhengfu*, pp. 221–22.

30. Ibid., p. 222.

31. Ibid., pp. 223–24.

32. Li Helu, "Chongming lunxian ji," pt. 1, p. 45.

8. Assembling the Occupation State

1. "China and Japan share script and race" and "England and France have driven our peoples to impoverishment and our finances to exhaustion" have been taken from the manifesto of the Greater Shanghai Youth Corps, quoted in Chapter 1 (note 16).

2. Hesitation among advisors to the Great Way Government regarding the revival of the county system is noted in the summary of Ōtani Tamotsu's views in SMA, File R1–1–151.

3. SSD director's report of 13 May 1938, archived in SDF, Riku Shi mitsu dainikki, File S14–12, no. 136.

4. Zhongguo tongxinshe, "Ishin seifu shu kikan no gyōsei kikō," pp. 28–29. Chen Qun's report on this meeting ("Neizhengbu gongzuo gaikuang") has been preserved, though misfiled, in CNT, Record Group 2001, File 20.

5. Xingzhengyuan xuanchuanju, *Ishin seifu no genkō*, p. 159.

6. *Neizheng bu xianzheng xunliansuo yilan*, pp. 97–107.

7. The November 1938 report on Nationalist county magistrates is summarized in the British Consulate's "China Summary," 1938, no. 11.

8. Xingzhengyuan xuanchuanju, *Ishin seifu no genkō*, pp. 152–54. As of the beginning of November, only eight magistrates had been appointed to counties in Zhejiang, according to an article in *Nanjing xinbao*, 1 November 1938.

9. Tong Zhenhua, *Zenyang qingchu hanjian*, pp. 8–9, 12–17, 25–26.

10. Ronald Robinson, "Non-European Foundations of European Imperialism," p. 121.

11. Inoue #27, pp. 260–61; the team leader was Morozumi Shōichi.

12. Itō Takeo, *Life along the South Manchurian Railway*, p. 179.

13. Inoue #17, p. 126.

14. Prasenjit Duara, *Culture, Power, and the State*, pp. 159, 193, 74.

15. Ibid., p., 253.

16. The phrase "the supernumerary and the incompetent" *(mui munō)* comes from the first report of the Danyang pacification team (Inoue #17), p. 126.

17. Office of War Information, "Analysis of Gripsholm Questionnaires: Far Eastern Propaganda Objectives and Techniques." p. 96.

18. Watanabe, "Senryōchi tōji (chian shukusei) ni kansuru Watanabe taisa kyōgen shokiroku," 3a–b, 11a.

19. On Communist mobilizational strategies in localities affected by the war, see Chen Yung-fa, *Making Revolution*, especially ch. 8 on local elites. As he points out, the Communist Party developed a united-front strategy that succeeded in

undermining the authority of the old rural elites without relying on an anti-Japanese ideology. The Communists did not so much fill a vacuum created by Japan as displace elites who did not see how the occupation had eroded their position.

Conclusion

1. Michael Ondaatje, *Running in the Family*, p. 53.
2. Henry Rousso, *The Vichy Syndrome*, pp. 6–8.
3. For an exception to this simplistic way of interpreting the war in Communist historiography, see Huang Meizhen and Yang Hanqing, "Nationalist China's Negotiating Position During the Stalemate, 1938–1945."
4. Attempts to analogize the Rape of Nanjing to the Holocaust are examined critically in Joshua Fogel, *The Nanjing Massacre in History and Historiography*; see especially the Foreword by Charles Maier and the chapter by Daqing Yang.
5. Rana Mitter has critiqued the effect of resistancialism on assessments of the Japanese occupation of Manchuria, which he characterizes as a place where imperialism was "relatively more collaborative" than on the Yangtze Delta. The level of violence was lower and the state structures that pre-existed the Japanese arrival weaker. Elite willingness to work under the new dispensation looks more like a bargain with colonial masters than capitulation to an invader. The strident new nationalism of the early 1930s which excoriated Japanese imperialism "did not recognize any ground between nationalist discourse and treachery." Such polarization was out of touch with the reality of living in Manchuria and "failed to convince many of those actually under occupation, who saw shades of gray in the reality of the occupation that the constructed image did not allow"; *The Manchurian Myth*, p. 226.
6. Robert McClure's comment appears in an undated letter in UCA, Finding Aid 186, Box 8, File 141. McClure's movements behind Japanese lines induced the Japanese army in April 1938 to offer a reward for his capture; see Munroe Scott, *McClure: The China Years*, p. 214.
7. *Chūgoku nōson kankō chōsa*, vol. 1, pp. 101–102.
8. Some Japanese intellectuals looked similarly to the long history of China's recurrent occupation by Inner Asian conquerors as a device for aligning Japan's occupation with the tradition of the conquest dynasty. This seems to be the lone and lonely purpose of the massive 457-page mimeographed book, stamped "secret," in the library of Stanford University, volume 2 of *Senryōchi tōchi oyobi sengo kensetsu shi* (A history of ruling occupied territory and post-war reconstruction). Edited by an entity called the Total War Institute (Sōryokusen kenkyūjo), the book is a long description of the history of foreign occupations of China since the Liao dynasty, with brief attempts to analyze the

secrets of the successes and failures of the Khitans, Jurchens, Mongols, and Manchus. Its thematic drift is that foreign occupation works when the occupier takes a conciliatory attitude toward the occupied and adopts Chinese methods of rule once the occupation is consolidated. Was this a lesson in the need to consolidate, or the need to conciliate (or just an idle intellectual exercise)?

9. Zhang Yibo, *Zhenjiang lunxian ji*, p. 37.
10. This is one of Parks Coble's conclusions to his study of commercial collaboration, *Chinese Capitalists in Japan's New Order*, p. 211.

Sources

"When the wartime generation is gone," Sarah Farmer has observed in her book *Martyred Village: Commemorating the 1944 Massacre at Oradour-sur-Glane*, "historians of the Second World War will be left with four major sources: official records, personal testimonies, physical traces of the events of the war, and the reworking of these events in history, fiction and film" (p. 212). The historian of China has roughly the same set of materials from which to write the history of the Japanese occupation, now that those who actually experienced the war are passing. The physical traces of the war on the Chinese landscape have largely disappeared with the huge political and economic transformations of the second half of the twentieth century. In a few places they have been artificially preserved to illustrate nationalist narratives about the past, but this largely drains them of any but anecdotal value to the historian of the war (though not the historian of memory), and I have made almost no use of them in writing this book. Far more valuable for reconstructing the history of China in 1937–38 are the official records and personal testimonies that have survived, each of which helps to tell a different part of the story. Official records have tended to outsurvive personal accounts. The striking exception is Nanjing, where the presence of some two dozen foreigners and an intense public interest in knowing what happened when the Japanese army took over that city have turned up many personal testimonies in English, German, Chinese, and Japanese.

The official records from the Japanese side most useful for this study are the classified reports of pacification work in Central China, preserved in the military archives of the Self-Defense Research Institute in Tokyo. They were compiled in the Shanghai office of the South Manchurian Railway Company on the basis of work diaries and monthly reports that pacification teams in the field sent back to Shanghai. These reports, along with several planning documents from the North China office, have been reprinted by Inoue Hisashi in his documentary collection entitled *Kachū senbu kōsaku shiryō* (Materials on pacification work in Central

China). They are referred in these notes by the number assigned in that collection (for example, Inoue #1); full information for each of the twenty-seven documents in the collection is given in the bibliography.

Given the distaste with which Chinese regard the wartime regimes, few compilations of official documents from the collaborators' side have been published. The major exception is *Ri-wei Shanghai shi zhengfu* (Shanghai municipal government under the Japanese and puppets), which the Shanghai Municipal Archives edited from documents in its collection. Otherwise, official Chinese materials are available only as archives, principally in the China Number Two Historical Archives in Nanjing and the Shanghai Municipal Archives. The other useful official source from the Chinese side, although it was produced under Japanese supervision, is the one newspaper published in Nanjing during this early period, the *New Nanjing Daily (Nanjing xinbao)*. A full run of this newspaper is preserved in the Tōyō Bunko in Tokyo.

Both Chinese and Japanese have left personal testimonies of their experiences of the occupation. On the Chinese side, I found the most valuable to be Zhang Yibo's account of occupied Zhenjiang *(Zhenjiang lunxian ji)* and Li Helu's of Chongming *(Chongming lunxian ji)*. On the Japanese side, the most useful have been Kumagai Yasushi's memoir of his career as a pacification agent in Jiading and Bengbu *(Shina kyōchin zatsuwa: Chōkō senbu kiroku)*, published in 1943, and Katō Kōzan's much briefer memoir of working in Zhenjiang ("Congshi xuanfu gongzuo zhi huigu"), which appeared in two parts in the *New Nanjing Daily* on 2–3 July 1939.

The Japanese occupation of Central China has not generated anything approaching the extraordinary volume of histories, novels, and films that commemorate the Second World War in Europe. Nanjing is, once again, the exception, although the intensity of the struggle of commemoration and counter-commemoration surrounding the Rape of Nanjing means that these productions tend to interfere with understanding what happened as much as they inform. But then, the same observation could apply to the literature on the Second World War in Europe. The pasts we choose to remember when we write about the war are the pasts we find troubling, pasts that commemoration in any genre can only further disturb. This book is no different.

American Information Committee. "New Order in East Asia: Conditions in Nine Chinese Cities after from Eight to Nineteen Months of Japanese Occupation." Shanghai: American Information Committee, 1939.

Barrett, David, and Larry Shyu, eds. *Chinese Collaboration with Japan, 1932–45: The Limits of Accommodation.* Stanford: Stanford University Press, 2001.

Bates, M. Searle. "Report of the Nanking International Relief Committee, November, 1937 to April, 1939." Reprinted in *Eyewitnesses to Massacre,* ed. Zhang Kaiyuan, pp. 413–45. Armonk, NY: M. E. Sharpe, 2001.

Baumler, Alan. "Opium Suppression versus Opium Control: The Origins of the 1935 Six-Year Plan to Eliminate Opium and Drugs." In *Opium Regimes: Britain, China, and Japan, 1839–1952,* ed. Timothy Brook and Bob Tadashi Wakabayashi, pp. 270–91. Berkeley: University of California Press, 2000.

British Consulate General (Shanghai). "China Summary." 1938–1941. Copy in NAC Record Group 6045, File 40c.

Brook, Timothy. "Chinese Collaboration during the Rape of Nanking." In *The Nanking Atrocity: Complicating the Picture,* ed. Bob Tadashi Wakabayashi, forthcoming.

———. "Collaborationist Nationalism in Occupied Wartime China." In *Nation Work: Asian Elites and National Identities,* coedited with Andre Schmid, pp. 159–90. Ann Arbor: University of Michigan Press, 2000.

———. "The Creation of the Reformed Government in Central China, 1938." In *Chinese Collaboration with Japan, 1932–45: The Limits of Accommodation,* ed. David Barrett and Larry Shyu, pp. 79–101. Stanford: Stanford University Press, 2001.

———. "Documenting the Rape of Nanking." Introduction to Brook, ed., *Documents on the Rape of Nanking,* pp. 1–29. Ann Arbor: University of Michigan Press, 1999.

———. "The Great Way Government of Shanghai." In *Shanghai under Japanese Occupation,* ed. Christian Henriot and Wen-hsin Yeh. New York: Cambridge University Press, 2004.

———. "Opium and Collaboration in Central China, 1938–40." In *Opium Regimes: Britain, China, and Japan, 1839–1952,* coedited with Bob Tadashi Wakabayashi, pp. 323–43. Berkeley: University of California Press, 2000.

———. "The Pacification of Jiading." In *Scars of War: The Impact of Warfare on Modern China,* ed. Diana Lary and Stephen MacKinnon, pp. 50–74. Vancouver: University of British Columbia Press, 2001.

———. "Toward Independence: Christianity in China under Japanese Occupation, 1937–1945." In *Christianity and China: From the Eighteenth Century to the Present,* ed. Daniel Bays, pp. 317–37. Stanford: Stanford University Press, 1996.

Brook, Timothy, ed. *Documents on the Rape of Nanking.* Ann Arbor: University of Michigan Press, 1999.

Brook, Timothy, and Bob Tadashi Wakabayashi, eds. *Opium Regimes: China, Britain, and Japan, 1839–1952.* Berkeley: University of California Press, 2000.

Burrin, Philippe. *France under the Germans: Collaboration and Compromise.* New York: New Press, 1996.

Cai Hongyuan and Sun Biyou. "Minguo qijian Nanjing shi zhiguan nianbiao" (Chronology of Nanjing municipal officials during the Republican period). *Nanjing shizhi* 1983, no. 1, pp. 47–48.

Chang, Iris. *The Rape of Nanking.* New York: Basic Books, 1997.

Chen, Yung-fa. *Making Revolution: The Communist Movement in Eastern and Central China, 1937–1945*. Berkeley: University of California Press, 1986.

Chūgoku nōson kankō chōsa (Studies of customs in Chinese villages). 1952. Reprint, 4 vols. Tokyo: Iwanami shoten, 1981.

Coble, Parks. *Chinese Capitalists in Japan's New Order: The Occupied Lower Yangtzi, 1937–1945*. Berkeley: University of California Press, 2003.

Collar, Hugh. *Captive in Shanghai*. Hong Kong: Oxford University Press, 1990.

Conan, Éric, and Henry Rousso. *Vichy: An Ever-Present Past,* trans. Nathan Bracher. Hanover, NH: University Press of New England, 1998.

Damin hui boyin yanjiang ji (Lectures broadcast by the Great People's Association), no. 5. Nanjing, 1939.

Dennerline, Jerry. *The Chia-ting Loyalists: Confucian Leadership and Social Change in Seventeenth-Century China*. New Haven: Yale University Press, 1981.

Dethlefsen, Henrik. "Denmark and the German Occupation: Cooperation, Negotiation, or Collaboration?" *Scandanavian Journal of History* 15:3 (1990): 193–206.

Diamond, Hanna. *Women and the Second World War in France, 1939–1948: Choices and Constraints*. Harlow: Longman, 1999.

Dower, John. *War without Mercy: Race and Power in the Pacific War*. London: Faber and Faber, 1986.

Duara, Prasenjit. *Culture, Power, and the State: Rural North China, 1900–1942*. Stanford: Stanford University Press, 1988.

———. "Transnationalism and the Predicament of Sovereignty: China, 1900–1945." *American Historical Review* 102:4 (October 1997): 1030–51.

Eykholt, Mark. "Aggression, Victimization, and Chinese Historiography of the Nanjing Massacre." In *The Nanjing Massacre in History and Historiography,* ed. Joshua A. Fogel, pp. 11–69. Berkeley: University of California Press, 2000.

———. "Living the Limits of Occupation in Nanjing, China, 1937–1945." Ph.D. diss., University of California at San Diego, 1998.

———. "Resistance to Opium as a Social Evil in Wartime China." In *Opium Regimes: China, Britain, and Japan, 1839–1952,* ed. Timothy Brook and Bob Tadashi Wakabayashi, pp. 360–79. Berkeley: University of California Press, 2000.

Farmer, Sarah. *Martyred Village: Commemorating the 1944 Massacre at Oradour-sur-Glane*. Berkeley: University of California Press, 1999.

Fogel, Joshua A., ed. *The Nanjing Massacre in History and Historiography*. Berkeley: University of California Press, 2000.

Fu, Poshek. *Resistance, Passivity, and Collaboration: Intellectual Choices in Occupied Shanghai, 1937–1945*. Stanford: Stanford University Press, 1993.

Gildea, Robert. *Marianne in Chains: In Search of the German Occupation, 1940–45*. London: Pan Macmillan, 2003.

Goldhagen, Daniel Jonah. *Hitler's Willing Executioners: Ordinary Germans and the Holocaust.* New York: Alfred Knopf, 1998.

Guo Qi. "Xiandu xuelei lu" (Blood-and-tears record of the fallen capital). Reprinted in *Qin Hua Rijun Nanjing datusha shiliao* (Historical materials on the invading Japanese Army's massacre in Nanjing), ed. Nanjing tushuguan (Nanjing library), pp. 1–59. Nanjing: Jiangsu guji chubanshe, 1985.

Guo Xu. "Hanjian Fu Xiaoan zhi si" (The death of traitor Fu Xiaoan). Reprinted in *Ershi shiji shanghai wenshi ziliao wenku* (Treasury of historical documents on twentieth-century Shanghai), vol. 2, pp. 51–54. Shanghai: Shanghai shudian, 1999.

Henriot, Christian. *Shanghai, 1927–1937: Municipal Power, Locality, and Modernization,* trans. Noël Castelino. Stanford: Stanford University Press, 1993.

Hirschfeld, Gerhard, and Patrick Marsh, eds. *Collaboration in France: Politics and Culture during the Nazi Occupation, 1940–44.* Oxford: Berg, 1989.

Hoffman, Stanley. *Decline or Renewal: France since the 1930s.* New York: Viking, 1974.

Honda, Katsuichi. *The Nanjing Massacre: A Japanese Journalist Confronts Japan's National Shame,* ed. Frank Gibney, trans. Karen Sandness. Armonk: M. E. Sharpe, 1999.

Hsü Shuhsi, ed. *Documents on the Nanking Safety Zone.* Shanghai: Kelly and Walsh, 1939. Photoreproduced in *Documents on the Rape of Nanking,* ed. Timothy Brook. Ann Arbor: University of Michigan Press, 1999.

Hu, Hua-ling. *American Goddess at the Rape of Nanking: The Courage of Minnie Vautrin.* Carbondale: Southern Illinois University Press, 2000.

Huang Meizhen and Yang Hanqing. "Nationalist China's Negotiating Position during the Stalemate, 1938–1945." In *Chinese Collaboration with Japan, 1932–45: The Limits of Accommodation,* ed. David Barrett and Larry Shyu, pp. 56–76. Stanford: Stanford University Press, 2001.

Iguchi Kazuki et al., eds. *Nankin jihen: Kyōto shidan kankei shiryō shū* (The Nanjing incident: a collection of materials concerning the Kyoto divisions). Tokyo: Aoki shoten, 1989.

Inoue Hisashi, ed. *Kachū senbu kōsaku shiryō* (Materials on pacification work in central China). Tokyo: Fuji shuppan, 1989. This documentary collection includes:

1. "Jūichigatsu senbu kōsaku kika" (November plan for pacification work). Mantetsu Hoku Shina jimukyoku, 1 November 1937.
2. "Daisankai senbuhan renraku kaigi gijiroku" (Minutes of the third pacification team liaison meeting), 8 November 1937. Mantetsu Hoku Shina jimukyoku, 25 November 1937.
3. "Daiyonkai senbuhan renraku kaigi gijiroku" (Minutes of the fourth pa-

cification team liaison meeting), 8 December 1937. Mantetsu Hoku Shina jimukyoku, 14 February 1938.

4. "Mantetsu haken Naka Shina senbu kōsaku jōkyō hōkoku" (Report on the situation of pacification teams sent to Central China by the South Manchurian Railway Company), 30 December 1937. Mantetsu Shanhai jimusho, 4 January 1938.

5. "Naka Shina hōmen senbu kōsaku jōkyō" (The situation of pacification teams in the Central China area), 30 December 1937. Mantetsu Shanhai jimusho, 12 February 1938.

6. "Naka Shina senryō chiiki ni okeru nanmin no jōkyō narabi busshi no jōkyō" (The situation of refugees and resources in the occupied region of Central China). Mantetsu Shanhai jimusho, 12 February 1938.

7. "Naka Shina senryō chiiki nai fukkimin narabi nanmin shūjō ni kansuru sho kōsaku" (Various work concerning returnees and refugee accommodation within the occupied region of Central China), 4 February 1938. Mantetsu Shanhai jimusho, 21 February 1938.

8. "Naka Shina senryō chiku nai jichi iinkai setsuritsu jijō" (The situation regarding the founding of self-government committees in the occupied region of Central China), 4 February 1938. Mantetsu Shanhai jimusho, 21 February 1938.

9. "Naka Shina senbukō kōsei yōzu" (Sketch map of the formation of the pacification network in Central China). Mantetsu Shanhai jimusho, 21 February 1938.

10. "Naka Shina senryō chiiki ni okeru senbu kōsaku gaiyō" (Summary of pacification work in the occupied region of Central China). Mantetsu Shanhai jimusho, 3 March 1938.

11. "Shōkō senbuhan kōsaku gaikyō" (State of work of the Songjiang pacification team). Mantetsu Shanhai jimusho, April 1938.

12. "Kazan senbuhan kōsaku gaikyō" (State of work of the Jiashan pacification team). Mantetsu Shanhai jimusho, April 1938.

13. "Kakō senbuhan kōsaku gaikyō" (State of work of the Jiaxing pacification team). Mantetsu Shanhai jimusho, April 1938.

14. "Kōshū senbuhan kōsaku gaikyō" (State of work of the Hangzhou pacification team). Mantetsu Shanhai jimusho, 20 April 1938.

15. "Katei senbuhan kōsaku gaikyō" (State of work of the Jiading pacification team). Mantetsu Shanhai jimusho, April 1938.

16. "Taisō senbuhan kōsaku gaikyō" (State of work of the Taicang pacification team). Mantetsu Shanhai jimusho, April 1938.

17. "Tanyō senbuhan kōsaku gaikyō" (State of work of the Danyang pacification team). Mantetsu Shanhai jimusho, April 1938.

18. "Chinkō han kōsaku gaikyō" (State of work of the Zhenjiang team). Mantetsu Shanhai jimusho, April 1938.

19. "Nankin tokumu kikan kōsaku gaikyō" (State of work of the Nanjing Special Service Agency). Mantetsu Shanhai jimusho, April 1938.
20. "Buko senbuhan kōsaku gaikyō" (State of work of the Wuhu pacification team). Mantetsu Shanhai jimusho, April 1938.
21. "Senbu kōsaku gaikyō: Chinkō han, kan 2" (State of pacification work: Zhenjiang team, volume 2). Mantetsu Shanhai jimusho, August 1939.
22. "Senbu kōsaku gaikyō: Shōkō han, kan 2" (State of pacification work: Songjiang team, volume 2). Mantetsu Shanhai jimusho, November 1939.
23. "Senbu kōsaku gaikyō: Taisō han, kan 2" (State of pacification work: Taicang team, volume 2). Mantetsu Shanhai jimusho, November 1939.
24. "Senbu kōsaku gaikyō: Kōshū tokumu kikan, kan 2" (State of pacification work: Hangzhou Special Service Agency, volume 2). Mantetsu Shanhai jimusho, March 1940.
25. "Senbu kōsaku gaikyō: Kasan han, kan 2" (State of pacification work: Jiashan team, volume 2). Mantetsu Shanhai jimusho, April 1940.
26. "Senbu kōsaku gaikyō: Yōshū han, kan 2" (State of pacification work: Yangzhou team, volume 2). Mantetsu Shanhai jimusho, April 1940.
27. "Senbu kōsaku gaikyō: Tanyō han, kan 2" (State of pacification work: Danyang team, volume 2). Mantetsu Shanhai jimusho, 30 April 1940.

Inukai Takeru. *Yōshikō wa ima mo nagarete iru* (The Yangtze River is flowing still). Tokyo: Bungei shunjū, 1960.
Itō Takeo. *Life along the South Manchurian Railway: The Memoirs of Itō Takeo*, trans. Joshua A. Fogel. Armonk, NY: M. E. Sharpe, 1988.
Ji Junsheng. "Zhenjiang diqu lunxian qianhou" (Events that occurred during the occupation of the Zhenjiang region). In Zhang Yibo, *Zhenjiang lunxian ji* (A record of Zhenjiang under occupation), pp. 80–87. Beijing: Renmin chubanshe, 1999.
Ji Lu. "Riwei shiqi Bengbu kuilei zhengfuquan gengdie qingkuang" (The situation with regard to shifts in puppet politics in Bengbu during the Japanese/collaboration period). *Wenshi ziliao xuanji* (Bengbu), no. 6 (1985): 96–100.
Jiang Gongyi. "Xianjing sanyue ji" (Three months in the fallen capital). Reprinted in *Qin Hua Rijun Nanjing datusha shiliao* (Historical materials on the invading Japanese Army's massacre in Nanjing), ed. Nanjing tushuguan (Nanjing library), pp. 60–100. Nanjing: Jiangsu guji chubanshe, 1985.
Jiangsu sheng gongbao xinnian tekan (Jiangsu provincial gazette: special New Year's issue). Nanjing, 1939. Copy in the Stanford University Library.
Jiangsu wenshi ziliao bianjibu (Editorial office for materials on culture and history for Jiangsu province), ed. *Changshu zhanggu* (Historical notes on Changshu). Nanjing: Jiangsu wenshi ziliao, 1992.
Kaikōsha, ed. *Nankin senshi* (History of the war in Nanjing). 2nd ed. Tokyo: Kaikōsha, 1993.

Katō Kōzan. "Congshi xuanfu gongzuo zhi huigu" (Reminiscence of doing pacification work). 2 parts. *Nanjing xinbao* (New Nanjing daily), 2–3 July 1939.

Kedward, Roderick, and Roger Austin, eds. *Vichy France and Resistance: Culture and Ideology.* London: Croom Helm, 1985.

Kimura Hisao. *Japanese Agent in Tibet: My Ten Years of Travel in Disguise.* London: Scrindia, 1990.

Kōain kachū renrakubu (Central China liaison office of the Asia Development Board). *Naka Shina jūyō kokuhō shigen shiryō sakubutsu chōsa hōkokusho* (Report on an investigation into grain crops as an important national defense resource in Central China). Shanghai, March 1940. Copy in the Stanford University Library.

———. *Katei, Taisō, Chōshū ni okeru juyō nōsakubutsu no kenshū kankō* (Cultivation practices for major agricultural crops in Jiading, Taicang, and Changshu). Shanghai: Kōain, December 1939. Copy in Tōyō bunka kenkyūjo, Tokyo University.

Kumagai Yasushi. *Shina kyōchin zatsuwa: Chōkō senbu kiroku* (Observations on village China: memoirs of pacification along the Yangzi River). 1943.

Lary, Diana, and Stephen MacKinnon, eds. *Scars of War: The Impact of Warfare on Modern China.* Vancouver: University of British Columbia Press, 2001.

Legge, James, trans. *Li Ki.* The Sacred Books of the East, ed. Max Müller, vol. 27. 1885.

Li Helu. "Chongming lunxian ji" (A record of Chongming under occupation). Reprinted in 2 parts in *Dang'an yu shixue,* ed. Shanghai shi dang'anguan (Shanghai Municipal Archives), 1995, no. 4, pp. 39–45; no. 5, pp. 34–38.

Li Kelang. "Lunjing wuyue ji" (Five months in the occupied capital). Reprinted in *Qin Hua Rijun Nanjing datusha shiliao,* ed. Nanjing tushuguan (Nanjing library), pp. 101–18. Nanjing: Jiangsu guji chubanshe, 1985.

Liberman, Peter. *Does Conquest Pay? The Exploitation of Occupied Industrial Societies.* Princeton: Princeton University Press, 1996.

Lin Na. "Xuelei hua Nanjing" (Speaking of Nanjing through blood and tears). 1938. Reprinted in *Qin Hua Rijun Nanjing datusha shiliao,* ed. Nanjing tushuguan (Nanjing library), pp. 141–47. Nanjing: Jiangsu guji chubanshe, 1985.

Lipkin, Zwia. "Keeping Up Appearances: The Nanjing Municipal Government and the City's Elements Déclassés, 1927–1937." Ph.D. diss., Stanford University, 2001.

Mantetsu Shanhai jimusho (Shanghai Office of the South Manchurian Railway Company). *Naka Shina ni okeru nōgyō seisatsu no dōkō* (Trends in agricultural policies in Central China). Shanghai: South Manchurian Railway Company, October 1939. Copy in the Stanford University Library.

Mantetsu Shanhai jimusho chōsashitsu (Survey group of the Shanghai Office of the South Manchurian Railway Company). *Kōsōshō Chōshūken nōson jittai chōsa hōkokusho* (Report of the survey of conditions in rural Changshu county, Jiangsu province). Shanhai Mantetsu chōsa shiryō, no. 34. Shanghai: South Manchurian Railway Company, 1939.

———. *Naka Shina nōsakubutsu no nōkō jijō* (Conditions for the cultivation of agricultural commodities in Central China). Shanghai: South Manchurian Railway Company, 1939. Copy in Stanford University Library.

———. *Shanhai tokubetsushi Katei ku no jittai chōsa hōkokusho* (Research report on the rural situation in Jiading district of Shanghai special municipality). Shanghai: South Manchurian Railway Company, 1939.

Marrus, Michael, and Robert Paxton. *Vichy France and the Jews.* New York: Basic Books, 1983. Reprint, Stanford: Stanford University Press, 1997.

Maruyama Susumu. "Watakushi no Shōwa shi—Nankin jiken no jissō" (My history of the Showa era: a true picture of the Nanjing Incident). 6 parts. *Mantetsu wakabakai kaihō,* nos. 133–138 (5 August–1 October 2000).

Matsui Iwane. "Nankin nyūjō no kangai" (My feelings on entering the city of Nanjing). *Shina jiken ichinen shi* (History of the first year of the China Incident), special issue of *Hanashi* (Discussions), July 1938, pp. 234–37.

Mitter, Rana. *The Manchurian Myth: Nationalism, Resistance, and Collaboration in Modern China.* Berkeley: University of California Press, 2000.

Miyakawa Sōtoku. *Yūbō Shina o kataru* (Speaking about our friend-country China). Tokyo: Genshōdō, 1938. Copy in Tōyō bunka kenkyūjo, University of Tokyo.

Mōgi Kikuo. *Shanhai shi daidō seifu shisaku hōkoku* (On-the-spot report on the Great Way Government of Shanghai municipality). Tokyo: Kinzensha, 1938. Copy in the Stanford University Library.

Morris, Alan. *Collaboration and Resistance Reviewed: Writers and the Mode Rétro in Post-Gaullist France.* New York: Berg, 1992.

Naka Shina hōmengun shireibu (Headquarters of the Central China Area Army). "Kongo no seiji bōryaku taikō" (Outline of future political strategy), 4 December 1937. SDF, Shina: Shina jihen: zenpan 315.

Nanjing shi dang'anguan (Nanjing municipal archives), ed. *Shenxun Wangwei hanjian bilu* (Transcripts of the trials of the Wang Jingwei puppet traitors). 2 vols. Nanjing: Jiangsu guji chubanshe, 1992.

Nanjing shizheng gaikuang 1938 (The Nanjing municipal government handbook, 1938). Nanjing: Yichunge, 1939. Copy in the Stanford University Library.

Nanjing shizheng gaikuang 1939 (The Nanjing municipal government handbook, 1939). Nanjing: Xinghua, 1940. Copy in the Stanford University Library.

Nanjing tushuguan (Nanjing library), ed. *Qin Hua Rijun Nanjing datusha shiliao* (Historical materials on the Nanjing massacre by the invading Japanese army). Nanjing: Jiangsu guji chubanshe, 1985.

Nanjing xinbao (New Nanjing daily). Nanjing, 1938–45.

Neizheng bu xianzheng xunliansuo yilan (Ministry of the Interior's County Magistrate Training Institute at a glance). Nanjing: Neizhengbu, 1940. Copy in the Stanford University Library.

Office of War Information, Bureau of Overseas Intelligence. "Analysis of Gripsholm Questionnaires: Far Eastern Propaganda Objectives and Techniques." Washington, February 1944. Copy in NAC, File 2864-C-40C.

Okada Yūji. *Nit-Chū sensō urakata ki* (An inside account of the Japan-China war). Tokyo: Tōyō keizai shimbunsha, 1974.

Ondaatje, Michael. *Running in the Family.* Toronto: McClelland and Stewart, 1982.

Pritchard, R. John, and Sonia Zaide, eds. *The Tokyo War Crimes Trial.* Reprint, 22 vols. New York: Garland Publishing, 1981.

Rabe, John. *The Good Man of Nanking: The Diaries of John Rabe,* ed. Erwin Wickert, trans. John Woods. New York: Knopf, 1998.

Robinson, Ronald. "Non-European Foundations of European Imperialism: Sketch for a Theory of Collaboration." In *Studies in the Theory of Imperialism,* ed. Roger Owen and Bob Sutcliffe, pp. 117–42. London: Longman, 1972.

Rousso, Henry. *The Vichy Syndrome: History and Memory in France since 1944,* trans. Arthur Goldhammer. Cambridge, Mass.: Harvard University Press, 1991.

Ruskola, Teemu. "Legal Orientalism." *Michigan Law Review* 101:1 (October 2002): 179–234.

Scott, Munroe. *McClure: The China Years.* Toronto: Canec, 1977.

Shanghai jiaoxian kangri wuzhuang douzheng shiliao (Materials on the history of the armed struggle against Japan in the suburban counties of Shanghai). Shanghai: Shanghai shehui kexueyuan chubanshe, 1986.

Shanghai shi dang'anguan (Shanghai municipal archives), ed. *Ri-wei Shanghai shi zhengfu* (Shanghai municipal government under the Japanese and puppets). Shanghai: Dang'an chubanshe, 1986.

Shanghai tebieshi zhengfu chuzhou jinian tekan (Special commemorative volume on the first anniversary of the Shanghai Special Municipality). Shanghai, 1940.

Shina jihen gahō (China incident pictorial). Tokyo, 1937–38.

"Shishou hou de Nanjing" (Nanjing after it was lost). 1938. Reprinted in *Qin Hua Rijun Nanjing datusha shiliao* (Historical materials on the Nanjing massacre by the invading Japanese army), ed. Nanjing tushuguan (Nanjing Library), pp. 148–55. Nanjing: Jiangsu guji chubanshe, 1985.

Smythe, Lewis S. C. *War Damage in the Nanking Area, December, 1937 to March, 1938: Urban and Rural Surveys.* Shanghai: Mercury Press, 1938.

Sōryokusen kenkyūjo (Total war research institute), ed. *Senryōchi tōchi oyobi sengo kensetsu shi* (A history of ruling occupied territory and postwar reconstruction), volume 2. Mimeograph, 1942. Copy in the Stanford University Library.

South Manchurian Railway Company, Information and Publicity Department. *Japanese Spirit in Full Bloom: A Collection of Episodes*. South Manchurian Railway Company, 1937.

Strand, David. *Rickshaw Beijing: City People and Politics in the 1920s*. Berkeley: University of California Press, 1989.

Subei xingzheng juanyuan gongshu minzhengke (Civil affairs bureau of the administrative personnel office for northern Jiangsu), ed. *Subei gexian zhi gaikuang* (Conditions in each county of northern Jiangsu). 1939. Copy in the Stanford University Library.

Sugimura Kōzō, ed. *Shanhai yōran* (Overview of Shanghai). Shanghai: Shanhai Nihon shōkō kaigisho, 1939.

Sun Zhaiwei, ed. *Nanjing datusha* (The Nanjing massacre). Beijing: Beijing chubanshe, 1997.

Timperley, H. J. *Japanese Terror in China*. New York: Modern Age Books, 1938.

Tōa dōbunkai (East Asian Common Culture Association), ed. *Shin Shina gensei yōran* (Overview of current conditions in New China). Tokyo: Tōa dōbunkai, 1938.

————, ed. *Shin Shina gensei yōran* (Overview of current conditions in New China), vol. 2. Tokyo: Tōa dōbunkai, 1940.

Tong Zhenhua. *Zenyang qingchu hanjian* (How to get rid of traitors). Shanghai: Shenghuo shudian, 1937. Copy in the Stanford University Library.

Usui Katsumi, ed. *Nit-Chū sensō* (The Sino-Japanese war), vol. 5. Gendaishi shiryō (Materials on modern history), vol. 13. Tokyo: Misuzu shobō, 1966.

Vespa, Amleto. *Secret Agent of Japan*. Introductory note by H. J. Timperley. Boston: Little, Brown, 1938. Reprint, Garden City, NY: Garden City Publishing, 1941.

Wakeman, Frederic, Jr. *The Shanghai Badlands: Wartime Terrorism and Urban Crime, 1937–1941*. Cambridge: Cambridge University Press, 1996.

Wang Xiguang. "Riwei hanjian zhengfu: Nanjing zizhi weiyuanhui" (A Japanese puppet traitor government: the Nanjing Self-Government Committee). *Nanjing shizhi* (Nanjing history magazine), 1987, no. 4, pp. 4–6.

Watanabe. "Senryōchi tōji (chian shukusei) ni kansuru Watanabe taisa kyōgen shokiroku" (Transcript of a lecture by Colonel Watanabe concerning the control of occupied territory [peace preservation and liquidation]) (7 May 1941). Handwritten xylograph in Tōyō bunka kenkyūjo, Tokyo University.

West, Rebecca. *The Meaning of Treason*. 1949, 1965, 1982. Reprint, London: Phoenix Press, 2000.

Xia Qiang. "Weihu zuozhang de zizhi weiyuanhui" (The self-government committee doing its master's bidding). *Nanjing shizhi*, 1989, no. 5.

Xingzhengyuan xuanchuanju (Propaganda bureau, Executive yuan). *Chūka minkoku ishin seifu gaishi* (A general history of the Reformed Government of the Chinese nation). Nanjing: Weixin zhengfu, 1940.

——. *Ishin seifu no genkō: seiritsu isshūnen kinen* (Current situation of the Reformed Government: commemoration of the first anniversary of its founding). Shanghai: Kimura insatsujō, 1939.

——. *Weixin zhengfu chengli chuzhou jinian ce* (Commemorative volume for the first anniversary of the founding of the Reformed Government). Shanghai: Kimura insatsujō, 1939.

Xu Peihong and Shao Nianbao, ed. *Dantu xianzhi* (Gazetteer of Dantu county). Nanjing: Jiangsu kexue jishu chubanshe, 1993.

Xu Zhigeng. *Lest We Forget: Nanjing Massacre, 1937,* trans. Zhang Tingquan and Lin Wusun. Beijing: Panda Books, 1995.

Xue Zhendong, ed. *Shanghai jiaoxian kangri wuzhuang douzheng* (The armed struggle against Japan in the suburban counties of Shanghai). Shanghai: Shanghai renmin chubanshe, 2001.

Yang Yubai, ed. *Jiading xianzhi* (Gazetteer of Jiading county). Shanghai: Shanghai renmin chubanshe, 1992.

Yin Jijun. *1937, Nanjing dajiuhuan: xifang renshi he guoji anquanqu* (1937, the great rescue of Nanjing: Westerners and the International Safety Zone). Shanghai: Wenhui chubanshe, 1997.

Zhang Kaiyuan, ed. *Eyewitnesses to Massacre: American Missionaries Bear Witness to Japanese Atrocities in Nanjing.* Armonk, NY: M. E. Sharpe, 2001.

Zhang Quan, Zhuang Zhiling, and Chen Zhengqing. *Rijun zai Shanghai de zuixing yu tongzhi* (The Japanese army's criminal activities and control in Shanghai). Shanghai: Shanghai renmin chubanshe, 2000.

Zhang Yibo. *Zhenjiang lunxian ji* (A record of Zhenjiang under occupation). 1938. Reprint, Beijing: Renmin chubanshe, 1999.

Zhonggong Shanghai shiwei dangshi ziliao zhengji weiyuanhui (Party history materials collection committee of the Shanghai municipal committee of the Central Committee), ed. *Shanghai jiaoxian kangri wuzhuang douzheng shiliao* (Historical materials on the armed struggle against Japan in the suburban counties of Shanghai). Shanghai: Shanghai shehui kexueyuan chubanshe, 1986.

Zhongguo di'er lishi dang'anguan (China Number Two Historical Archives), ed. *Qin Hua Rijun Nanjing datusha dang'an* (Documents on the invading Japanese Army's massacre in Nanjing). Nanjing: Jiangsu guji chubanshe, 1987.

Zhongguo tongxinshe diaochabu (Investigation department of the China News Agency). "Ishin seifu sho kikan no gyōsei kikō" (Administrative structure of the various organs of the Reformed Government). Shanghai: Zhongguo tongxinshe, 1938. Copy in Tōyō bunka kenkyūjo, Tokyo University.

Index

Adoption, 88–89
Aerial bombardment, 25, 67–68, 75, 77
Allison, John, 148
Amaya Naojirō, 92, 132, 260n9
Anhui province, 88, 208, 216, 227, 229
Anju leye ("living in peace and taking pleasure in one's work"), 38, 40, 247, 253n12
Archives, 8, 14, 15, 18, 26, 31, 39, 49, 51, 55, 65, 86, 170, 173, 180–181, 192, 263n1, 266n2, 271–272
Asahi shinbun, 144
Asaka, Prince, 130
Asia Development Board (Kōain), 36, 44, 86, 223
Assassination, 76, 82, 85, 87, 107–108, 155, 166, 184–185, 188, 197, 208, 214, 231, 265n29
Atrocities, 2–3, 17–18, 23–25, 93–95, 127, 132–133, 141–142, 218, 244, 258n4

Banks, 56, 91, 130
Baojia. See Neighborhood watch system
Baoshan, 41–42, 59, 69, 75, 169, 176, 178, 209, 227, 257n33
Bates, M. Searle, 135, 138, 140, 154, 158
Beijing, 2, 33, 35, 39–40, 47, 168–169, 243
Bengbu, 60, 65, 88–89, 272
Bicycles, 82, 205
Boats, 51, 78, 91, 112, 180, 186, 199, 202, 205, 211
British colonialism, 233–234
Buddhist associations, 156, 214

Burial of corpses, 47, 55, 67, 79, 87, 93–94, 126, 136, 141–142. *See also* Red Swastika Society
Burrin, Philippe, 46
Business firms, 110–116

Camera pacification, 69, 88
Casualties: civilian, 24, 67, 94, 126, 141–142, 200, 218, 252n21; military, 92
Central China, 34, 38, 253n5; contrasted with North China, 55, 58, 237
Central China Area Army (CCAA, Naka Shina hōmengun), 27, 33–35, 41, 43, 54, 62, 126–127, 132, 150, 168
Central District (Shanghai), 160, 169, 176
Chamber of Commerce, 109, 111, 162, 172, 179, 182, 188, 220
Chen Gongbo, 188
Chen Qun, 225, 228–229, 268n4
Chen Rong, 136
Chen Yun, 184
Chen Zemin, 209
Chiang Kaishek, 12, 33, 38, 41, 127, 198, 222, 232, 238, 259
Children: control of, 57; orphans, 210; use of labor, 98; use in propaganda of, 16, 25–26, 86; wartime experience of, 25, 96, 201, 215
China Mutual Aid Association, 166
Chizhi College, 165
Chongming Island, 18, 27–28, 30, 169, 198–220, 225, 227, 230, 241, 272
Chuansha, 59, 169, 177–178, 180–181, 209, 227

Classic of Rites, The, 174
Collaboration: ambiguities of, 4–5, 11, 30–
    31, 90–91, 102, 157–160, 240–242, 248;
    appearances of, 9, 28, 62–63, 86–88;
    based on personal ties with Japan, 3–4,
    136–138, 165–168, 172; Chinese terms
    for, 9–10, 12; comparative, 10–12, 158,
    244; complicities with, 29, 125–126, 131–
    132, 138–139, 141, 146–147, 157–158;
    costs of, 28–29, 90–91, 108–123, 154, 184,
    198, 232–233, 241, 246; definition of, 1–
    2, 9–13, 63, 159, 222, 240, 242; ideology
    of, 231–232; as mode of relationship to
    state authority, 12, 172, 216, 222, 224,
    233–234; moral subject produced by, 4–
    7, 245; personal dimensions of, 88–89;
    politics of, 197, 222, 226, 239; rivalries
    within, 29, 159–161, 173–178, 188–196;
    sources for the study of, 14–19, 64–65,
    108–109, 130–131, 147–148, 271–272. *See
    also* Historiography of collaboration;
    Ideology
Collaborationism, 10–12
Colonialism, 234. *See also* British
    colonialism; Japan, as colonial power
Commodity circulation, 109–112
Communism, Japanese opposition to, 40,
    44, 56–57, 132, 144, 174, 194, 235
Communist Party, 14, 21, 108, 157, 212,
    214–216, 230–231, 239, 241, 243, 248
Concordia League (Xiehe hui), 41, 114,
    254n18
Confucianism, 192, 194, 205, 213
Cooperatives, 57, 70, 82
"Co-prosperity," 8, 65, 105, 110
Corvée labor, 77, 98–99
Cotton, 78, 202, 210–211; mills, 113, 178,
    202, 218
County governments, formation of, 52, 54–
    55, 63, 73, 85–86, 105, 221, 224–228. *See
    also* Public Office
Coville, Cabot, 152

Danyang, 15–16, 54, 59, 67, 92, 103, 106,
    113, 227, 235
Denmark, as a comparative case of
    collaboration, 1, 11
Dethlefsen, Henrik, 1–2, 9, 11, 246
Diamond, Hanna, 24–25
Dower, John, 83

Duara, Prasenjit, 237
Durkheim, Émile, 237

East Asian Anti-Communist League, 172
Eastern Times, 166
Elites, alleged Western tendencies of, 54, 83.
    See also Local elites
EuroAmerica, as Japan's anti-imperialist
    object, 38, 40, 97, 132, 133
Eykholt, Mark, 260n2

Factories, 112–116; 202. *See also* Cotton,
    mills
Farmer, Sarah, 271
Feiwo zulei ("not of the same kin-category
    as us"), 21
Feng Chengqiu, 86
Feuds, 216–217
Fires, 94–95, 135, 150, 152
Fitch, George, 137, 142
Food supply, 97–98, 108, 115–120, 140, 144,
    147–152, 157
France, as a comparative case of
    collaboration, 1–2, 5, 10–11, 24–25, 30–
    31, 195, 224, 242, 244
French Concession (Shanghai), 160, 182
Fu Xiaoan, 179, 193, 218–219
Fujian province, 165–166, 170
Fukuda Tokuyasu, 145, 147
Fukui Kiyoshi, 136

Gao Guanwu, 154–156, 208
Gaoqiao, 50, 174–176
Gender: effect of invasion on, 23–24, 93,
    199; ratio of survival, 24, 70
Gildea, Robert, 125
Goldhagen, Daniel, 252n11
Grand Canal, 91, 109, 172
Great People's Association (Damin hui), 9,
    114–115, 155, 254n18
Great Way Government, 78, 162–165, 169–
    188, 193–196; ideology of, 165–166, 168,
    174, 192–194
Gu Zhongyi, 231
Guerrillas, 18, 81, 84–85, 107, 199, 211–212,
    214–219, 235, 241
Guilds, 111–112
Guo Moruo, 231
Guo Zhicheng, 100–106, 114–122
Guomindang. *See* Nationalist Party

Hangzhou, 60, 227
Hanjian ("traitor to the Han Chinese"), 10, 13
Harada Kumakichi, 37, 39, 150, 228
Henan province, 52, 54, 216, 247
Hidaka Shinrokurō, 148
Historiography of collaboration, 30–31, 240–248, 259n2; Chinese, 7, 14, 31, 147, 157–158, 241–244; postcolonial, 15, 243–245
Hitler, Adolf, 1–2, 10
Hong Kong, 230; and Britain, 222; newspapers in, 230
Hoodlums (liumang), 189–190, 226, 231, 253n8
Housing, 67–68, 150
Hsü Shu-hsi, 259n2
Hu Hammin, 165
Hu Qifa, 137
Huang Yuexuan, 137, 156
Huang Zhiqing, 200–201, 207, 215, 217–220
Huangpu West Residents' Association, 8–9, 189

Ideology, 20–21, 23, 38, 83, 223–224; as barrier to understanding collaboration, 7, 240–248. See also Collaboration, ideology of; Great Way Government, ideology of
Inland waterways, 78, 185–186
Inoue Hisashi, 271
International Committee for the Nanking Safety Zone, 128–135, 138–140, 144–151, 155–157
International Military Tribunal for the Far East (Tokyo), 129, 139, 141
Interpreters, 101, 103, 137–138, 210
Involution, 237–238
Itō Takeo, 37, 61, 236

Japan: as colonial power, 40, 45, 65, 69, 233; decision to occupy China, 33; embassy in Nanjing, 133–134, 136–137, 142, 144, 148; euphemized as "friend-country" (youbang) or "friend-army" (youjun), 8, 200, 208, 217–219; goals in East Asia, 32
Japan-China Buddhist League, 156
Jiading, 27, 63–88, 91, 99, 169, 206, 225, 227
Jiang Jieshi. See Chiang Kaishek
Jiaxing, 61, 227

Kalgan, 44
Katō Kōzan, 10, 16, 18, 43–44, 103–121, 226, 272
Kawano Masanao, 129, 258n17
Kedward, Roderick, 30–31
Kimura Hisao, 44–45
Kitaoka Takeo, 190–192
Kojima Tomō, 129
Korea, 32, 123
Kumagai Yasushi, 16–17, 28, 41, 64–89, 104, 272
Kunshan, 42, 81, 227
Kurami Sadakichi, 201, 205

Language: instruction, 85, 206; as source of misunderstanding, 50
Legitimacy, 49, 125, 132, 146, 148, 162, 164, 169, 194, 223, 233, 237, 239, 247–248
Li Gengsheng, 170–171
Li Helu, 18, 28, 199–201, 203–205, 207–208, 210, 215–216, 272
Li Zhizhong, 25
Liang Hongzhi, 223
Liberman, Peter, 122–123
Liu Zhaoqing, 3, 101–102, 104
Local elites, 4, 7, 47–49, 54, 140, 246; difficulty of controlling, 80–83; as grassroots of occupation state, 46–48, 269n5; removal from power of, 86–87, 155–156, 221; role in collaboration, 73–76, 224, 230–239
Looting: by Chinese, 70–71, 150, 152; by Japanese, 90, 92–93, 137, 148–151, 199
Lou Xiaoxi, 136–137
Loyal Subject Certificates (Liangmin zheng), 47, 51, 56, 70, 88, 117, 204, 218, 233
Lu Mengxiong, 208
Lytton Commission, 32

Ma Chaojun, 4
Ma Xihou, 137
Mabuchi Seigō, 129, 132
Magee, John, 17, 135, 151
Manchuria, 2, 32–34, 41, 123, 170, 222, 234, 269n5; contrasted with Central China, 61
Mantetsu. See South Manchurian Railway Company
Mao Dun, 231–232
Marrus, Michael, 11

Maruyama Susumu, 16, 129, 137, 141, 149
Matsui Iwane, 7, 13, 33, 127, 129, 139, 149, 244
Matsuoka Tsutomu, 129, 132, 150–151
McClure, Robert, 246
Medical services, 72–73, 104–105
Mci Siping, 55
Memoirs, as historical sources, 16–17, 45, 161, 236, 267n27
Memory, 6–7, 25, 75, 125, 243, 260n17, 271
Military-civilian conflicts, 50, 77
Military Police (Kempeitai), 36, 39, 58, 66, 97, 107, 138, 143–144, 174, 178–179, 192, 203, 210, 212, 253n8
Militia, 54, 57–58, 107, 203, 212–216. *See also* Self-Defense Corps; Youth Corps
Mission civilitrice, 15, 23
Missionaries, 121; as observers, 17, 52, 54, 246; as relief workers, 96–128, 258n7
Mitter, Rana, 269n5
Modernity, as claimed attribute of occupation state, 71, 94, 213, 237, 244
Muslims, 96, 137, 156
Mussolini, Benito, 165

Nakayama Yojirō, 97, 99–100, 103, 129
Nanhui, 180, 209, 227
Nanjing, 2, 27, 45, 60, 92, 98, 125–158, 168–169, 172, 207, 220–222, 227, 229, 233, 241, 259n2
Nanyang Tobacco Company, 172
National Government (Guomin zhengfu), 4, 12, 34, 36, 38, 62, 118, 127, 198, 229, 232–234
Nationalism: 123, 132, 235, 269n5; collaboration and, 242, 245
Nationalist Party (Guomindang), 33–34, 38, 71–73, 92, 136–138, 142, 154, 165–167, 172, 178, 180, 184–185, 190, 198–199, 208, 222, 228–231, 235, 237, 243; Japanese opposition to, 44, 85, 107, 140, 144, 163, 194
Native-place associations, 218–219
Neighborhood watch system *(baojia),* 56, 77, 82, 84, 106, 155, 203–204, 210, 212–214, 217
"New China," 7–8, 83, 200
New Chongming Daily (Chongming xinbao), 206–207
New Nanjing Daily (Nanjing xinbao), 104–

105, 119–120, 122–123, 155, 200–201, 208, 228, 272
"New Order in East Asia" *(Tōa xin seisho),* 2, 121
New Zhenjiang Daily (Zhenjiang xinbao), 113
Nikkei Company, 202
Nishimura Tenzō, 164–165, 167–168, 174, 183, 188, 192
Nora, Pierre, 125
North China Area Army (NCAA, Kita Shina hōmengun), 33, 35, 46, 55–58, 168

Occupation: challenges of, 62–63; collaboration and, 224; conditions of, 46–47; definition of, 221–222; funding of, 90–91; instability of, 186; tasks of, 33–34; politics of, 159–160
Occupation state, 12–13, 45, 158, 184, 190, 193–196, 198, 207–208, 216, 221–225, 229–230, 232–235, 237–239, 246–248; funding of, 82–84, 87, 188, 212
Okada Yūji, 16, 45, 130
Opium, 36, 71–72, 118–119, 121, 172, 213–214

Pacification, 30, 34–35, 45–46, 62–63, 67–73; in North China, 39–41; rural, 105–107, 123–124
Pacification agents, 15–17, 23, 35–46, 97–101, 103–104, 129, 164, 167–168, 182, 219, 221, 224–226, 234, 236, 238, 272
Pacification Department (Tokumu bu) of the Mantetsu Shanghai Office, 35, 43, 60, 70, 80, 160, 255n41
Pacification Team (Senbu han), 15, 39–47, 58–61, 69–71, 76–79, 87–88, 99, 164, 178, 180, 183, 201, 203–208, 212, 216–217, 225, 235–236, 271, 255n41
Paxton, Robert, 11
Peace: as concept, 22; as codeword for Japanese hegemony, 163
Peace Maintenance Committee (PMC, Zhian weichihui), 47–54, 69, 73–76, 79, 131, 185–186, 221, 226; bypassed, 99–100, 135; rogue, 80
Peddlers, 110
Pétain, Philippe, 1–2, 10
Philanthropy, 120, 136

Police, 54, 73, 90, 138, 154, 172, 176, 178–183, 194, 202, 211–213, 255n41; Chinese policemen, 50–51, 79, 85, 91, 106, 118, 134–135, 144, 169–170, 191; trained in Japan, 3, 101, 138
Population figures, 67, 70, 91, 106–107, 110, 201
Poverty, as a consequence of occupation, 121–122, 154, 202–203
Printing, 112–113
Propaganda, 245; Chinese, 13, 38, 231; Japanese, 3, 8, 20, 47, 57, 126, 164, 167, 205–206, 223, 232
Prostitution, 99, 141, 143, 150, 157–158, 199, 241
Public Office (Gongshu), 184, 186, 191, 224–227, 233, 238
Public utilities, 57–58, 97, 103, 112, 121, 134–135, 230
Pudong, 160, 162, 169, 171, 173–175, 179–182
"Puppet" (kuilei), 13, 34, 63, 122, 137, 150, 247, 272

Qingdao, 208
Qingpu, 42, 81, 227

Rabe, John, 128, 131–132, 134, 140–141, 145–147
Race, as mobilizational ideology, 3, 20–22, 132, 224, 235
Railways, 57–58, 67, 91
Rape, 23–24, 93, 143, 151, 158, 189, 199
"Rape of Nanjing," 2, 17, 95, 128, 142, 272; as Holocaust, 244, 269n4
Red Cross, 94, 134
Red Swastika Society, 94, 126, 136, 138–142, 156
Reformed Government (Weixin zhengfu), 36, 111, 114, 118–119, 154–155, 166, 185–186, 201, 208–209, 221, 223, 225, 229, 232–233
Refugees, 39, 56–57, 93, 96–98, 144–146, 150–151, 178, 182, 216, 240–241
Religion, 168, 213–214
Ren Yuandao, 154
Resistance: 29–31, 75, 106–109, 195–198, 214–220, 231–232, 235, 240, 242–243, 247, 267n27; as a cost of occupation, 122–123, 246, 248

Résistancialisme, 6
Riggs, Charlie, 139, 147
Robinson, Ronald, 233–234
Rosen, Georg, 140
Ruskola, Teemu, 4, 245

Sakata Shigeki, 129, 132–135
Salt, 107, 117, 172, 235
Satō Tsukito, 129
Schools, 85, 88, 94, 186, 203, 206
Security, as condition for collaboration, 80–88, 106, 109–110, 116, 122–123, 185, 202, 211–212, 217, 220, 235
Self-Defense Corps, 51, 107, 212
Self-Government Committee (SGC, Zizhi weiyuanhui), 40–41, 52–54, 136–137, 173–177, 232–233; dissolution of, 54–55, 105, 177, 207, 221, 224–228; finances of, 82, 117–119, 150, 186–188, 210; inauguration of, 101, 139, 142–144; Beixinjing SGC, 191; Caojin SGC, 193; Chongming SGC, 200–211, 225; Danyang SGC, 54; Hongqiao SGC, 193; Jiading SGC, 73–87, 225; Nanjing SGC, 142–157, 261n31; North District United SGC, 186–188, 226; Pudong SGC, 175; Songjiang SGC, 54; South City SGC, 177, 182–184, 190, 193; Taicang SGC, 54, 72; Tangqiao SGC, 179, 186; Wusong SGC, 181; Zhenjiang SGC, 97, 100–102, 225; Zhoupu SGC, 180
"Self-reliance," 106
Shanghai, 27, 29, 33, 41, 160–196; as flight alternative, 76, 83, 91, 111, 202; Japan's 1932 attack on, 67, 75–76; Municipal Commission, 177, 188; suburbs, 49–50, 173–177; trade with, 109. See also Central District; French Concession; Great Way Government; South City; Western District; Zhabei
Shanghai county (Beiqiao), 169, 174
Shanghai Municipal Police, 172, 189, 253n8
Smythe, Lewis, 14, 134, 136, 139–140, 147, 150, 152–153, 157
Soldiers: Chinese 123–124, 126, 133–135, 138, 144, 199, 211, 241; Japanese, 92–93, 133, 147–148, 150–152, 171, 179, 199, 211, 216, 218, 230, 241, 244, 262n42
Songjiang, 41, 103, 118, 129, 186, 227

South City (Nanshi), 173, 176–177, 181–184, 186, 190, 193, 227
South Manchurian Railway Company (Mantetsu), 15, 34–35, 39, 43–45, 60, 66, 97, 104, 129, 130, 160–161, 201, 236, 247, 271
Sovereignty, 12, 27, 132, 220, 222–223, 231–232
Special Service Agency (Tokumu kikan), 40, 43, 58–60, 129–130, 133–136, 142–146, 219, 255n42
Special Service agents. See Pacification agents
Special Service Department (Tokumu bu) of the CCAA, 33, 35–37, 43, 45, 129, 150, 160, 206, 222, 253n8
State building, 52–53, 63, 71, 221, 232–233, 237
Steward, Albert, 151–153
Su Xiwen, 3, 14, 23, 162–168, 175–177, 179–181, 183–185, 188, 198
Sun Shurong, 137–138, 145, 149, 156
Sun Yunsheng, 69–70, 74, 81–82, 84, 86, 225
Suzhou, 41, 60, 105, 111, 120, 130, 209, 226–227

Taicang, 61, 67–68, 72, 75–76, 83, 85, 115, 206, 216, 227
Taiwan, 32, 123, 222, 230
Takada Mitsusaburō, 15–16
Tamaki Hajime, 72, 85
Tanaka Sueo, 137
Tao Juesan, 138, 155
Tao Xisan, 3, 14, 136–138, 144, 149, 154–157, 261n31
Taxation, 82, 106, 117–119, 152, 204–205, 210–211; ferry tax, 181; fish tax, 178. See also Transit tax
Teahouses, 71, 81–82, 110
Times, The (Shibao), 184
Tobacco, 109, 172
Tong Zhenhua, 231
Tongwen ("people of the same script"), 20
Transit tax, 118–119, 255n41
Transportation infrastructure, 57, 78, 90, 110
"Two concepts of the Japanese," 105

Vautrin, Minnie, 24, 138–141, 157
Vichy regime. See France
Victimization, as a narrative of occupation, 6, 125, 244

Wang Chengdian (Jimmy), 14–15, 138–141, 147–149, 155–158, 188, 241
Wang Chunsheng, 137–138, 144, 156–157
Wang Jingwei, 155, 229
Wang Zhongtiao, 138
Wen Zongyao, 135–155
West, Rebecca, 4–5
Western District, 160, 177–179, 181, 189–191, 193, 226–227, 253n8, 255n41
Wheat, 107, 115–117, 120, 202
Wilson, Robert, 127, 133, 135, 139–140
Women, wartime experience of, 23–25, 139, 141, 158, 199, 201, 210, 219, 241. See also Rape
Wuhan, 60, 112
Wuhu, 60, 151, 227
Wusong, 169, 181
Wuxi, 41, 59, 227

Xiaguan, 136, 148, 151
Xu Chuanyin, 138–139, 141–142, 147, 261n31

Yamazaki Kaikō, 16, 23
Yangzhou, 98, 109, 116–117, 227
Youth Corps, 9, 21, 56, 115

Zeng Guofan, 228
Zhabei, 44, 160, 169, 177–178, 181
Zhan Rongguang, 138, 156, 261n26
Zhang Nanwu, 138
Zhang Yibo, 17–22, 24, 28, 40, 90–95, 98–99, 101–105, 107, 112, 121, 230, 246–247, 272
Zhao Gongjin, 137–138, 149, 155
Zhao Weishu, 137–138
Zhejiang province, 43, 170, 227, 229
Zhenjiang, 17–19, 24–25, 27, 29, 42–43, 91–124, 129, 172, 186, 206, 225–227, 230, 272
Zhenru, 61, 160, 227
Zhou Yongqiao, 113–114
Zhu Yuzhen, 169, 176, 182, 185